Sarah Winnemucca of the Northern Paiutes

Sarah Winnemucca

OF THE NORTHERN PAIUTES

BY
GAE WHITNEY CANFIELD

University of
Oklahoma Press
Norman and London

Library of Congress Cataloging in Publication Data

Canfield, Gae Whitney, 1931-
Sarah Winnemucca of the Northern Paiutes.

Bibliography: p. 291.
Includes index.
1. Hopkins, Sarah Winnemucca, 1844?-1891. 2. Paiute Indians—History. 3. Paiute Indians—Biography. I. Title.
E99.P2H722 1983 970.004'97 [B] 82-40448
ISBN: 0-8061-2090-8

 Manufactured in the U.S.A. First edition, 1983. First paperback printing, 1988.

3 4 5 6 7 8 9 10 11 12

To my family

Bob, Lynn, Noel, and my mother,
Fern Whitney, who gave me
a love of history

Contents

Illustrations

Maps

Preface

Sarah Winnemucca was a self-educated Northern Paiute Indian who, in the short span of her life, sparred with Indian agents, local politicians, and the United States government to try to improve the living conditions and the education of her people. She enlisted many influential citizens in her cause, partly through her autobiography, *Life Among the Piutes: Their Wrongs and Claims,* published in 1883, which was one of the first works of literature by an American Indian. She also made many spirited stage appearances in San Francisco and on the East Coast.

The Northern Paiutes are a desert-plateau people native to western Nevada, southeastern Oregon, and a strip of northeastern California east of the Sierra Nevada. In the 1860s, after the discovery of gold and silver in the Sierra, they found themselves in the path of white progress. The small, roaming Northern Paiute bands had two choices: they could seek friendship with the whites in hopes of becoming assimilated into the new order, or they could move north to hidden areas where there was still unspoiled land not yet desired by the emigrants.

Captain Truckee, Sarah Winnemucca's grandfather, chose the path of friendship. Because of his expansive nature and great curiosity, he continued his efforts to be friendly even when rebuffed by early explorers. On occasion he would remind his people of an ancient Paiute tale that prophesied the return of long-lost white brothers of the Paiutes, the reconciliation of the white and dark-skinned peoples, and lasting peace. This tale was later used by Sarah when she tried to influence the white world, as an admonition to the newcomers that the Paiutes had always expected great things of their white brothers.

Chief Winnemucca, Sarah's father, did not share Captain Truckee's innate trust of the emigrants. He had heard too many stories of outrage and murder. The Paiutes were well aware, for example, of the cannibalism in the Donner party near Truckee Lake in the winter of 1846-47. As a result Winnemucca guided his followers away from the Humboldt River emigrant trail. The white men had a penchant for burning Paiute villages and destroying food supplies. Many of them simply wanted to "get themselves an Injun."

Sarah Winnemucca was torn between those two philosophies. Her sympathy with her father's point of view contended with her own need to make an honest living within the white man's economy (which she sometimes did at the expense of her own people, as when she worked as a scout and interpreter for the United States Army). It was at great sacrifice that she made a decisive choice in favor of her people.

After reading Sarah's autobiography, I was intrigued by her personality and the sense of purpose emanating from her story. I wished for a larger understanding of her place in history. I soon found that I had to learn about the Northern Paiutes, her people. After considerable anthropological reading and several visits to the history collections of the Inter-Tribal Council of the Shoshoni, Washo, and Paiute peoples, at Pyramid Lake and Reno, Nevada, I began to develop some background. One particular book, Margaret W. Wheat's *Survival Arts of the Primitive Paiutes,* was of inestimable value in informing me of the old ways of the Northern Paiutes, because of its excellent photographs and explanations of house building; basketry; the making of rabbitskin blankets, duck decoys, arrowheads, and tule boats; and the harvesting and preparation of foods.

The Bancroft Library of the University of California, Berkeley, was a haven for several years. There I started putting together the pieces of Sarah Winnemucca's puzzle from old newspapers, the National Archives microfilm records of the United States Bureau of Indian Affairs, and the published personal accounts by people who were important in Sarah's life—from Indian agents to army generals. The stage-costumed Indian woman became a person of flesh and blood. Although Sarah was slightly on the plump side with features not as refined as those of her younger sister, Elma, she still caught the attention of the public. She was a strong woman determined to succeed for her cause while essentially alone in a man's world. She had to fight for her own integrity as well as for a good life for her people.

Not all the pieces of the puzzle of Sarah Winnemucca have been found, and perhaps some are lost forever, but I hope that the voice of aboriginal America, the voice of another age that is gone may be heard in the pages that follow. Any words attributed to Sarah are quoted from her autobiography or another source indicated in the notes. I found her autobiographical account to be largely confirmed by other historical records except for inconsistencies in dates and the spelling of proper names.

Much that has been written about Sarah Winnemucca is not based on research from authentic documents, but is only a working of the same mistakes. This book brings together a useful bibliography for future writers, who can perhaps reveal more layers of her personality. I suspect, however, that, as time moves on from Sarah Winnemucca's lifespan, it will be more difficult to discover the truth. I hope that this book defines her rightful place in history and demonstrates the importance of the problems in assimilation that still face American Indians.

My special thanks to the Inter-Tribal Council, Reno-Sparks, Nevada, and to Winona Holmes, their historian, for permission to use their historical collection. I extend my appreciation to Carolyn Schooley, who introduced me to *Life Among the Piutes: Their Wrongs and Claims* in 1965, and to Elinor Richey for sharing her material on Sarah. Essential information on Sarah's later years came from Sam Eagle, historian of West Yellowstone, Montana, and Mrs. R. W. Talbot of Henry's Lake, Idaho. Also of service were James Abajian, archivist for the Archdiocese of San Francisco; Sister Mary Dominica McNamee, historian of College of Notre Dame, Belmont, California; Mrs. Donna Rob Spainhower of West Yellowstone, Montana; and the Oliver Historical Museum of Canyon City, Oregon. I thank Ella Thorpe Ellis, Celeste MacLeod, Betty Howell and Gail Landis for their helpful suggestions after reading the manuscript. My appreciation too for Carmilla Duran, Robert Emory Johnson, Dana Johnson, Joy Whitney Scott,

John Howell, and Joanne Richert for their contributions. I have been fortunate in having the outstanding support and assistance of my editor, Sarah Morrison. Most of all, I thank my husband, Robert Lane Canfield, for his continued enthusiasm throughout this enterprise and his help with photography and map reproduction.

It was a delight slowly to turn the microfilm reels, straining my eyes over page after page of dim letters and elaborate calligraphy, and suddenly come across another clue or a letter in Sarah's crimped handwriting. I hope that some of that excitement is conveyed in this biography and that readers will catch such a glimpse of Sarah Winnemucca, too.

GAE WHITNEY CANFIELD

Berkeley, California

Sarah Winnemucca of the Northern Paiutes

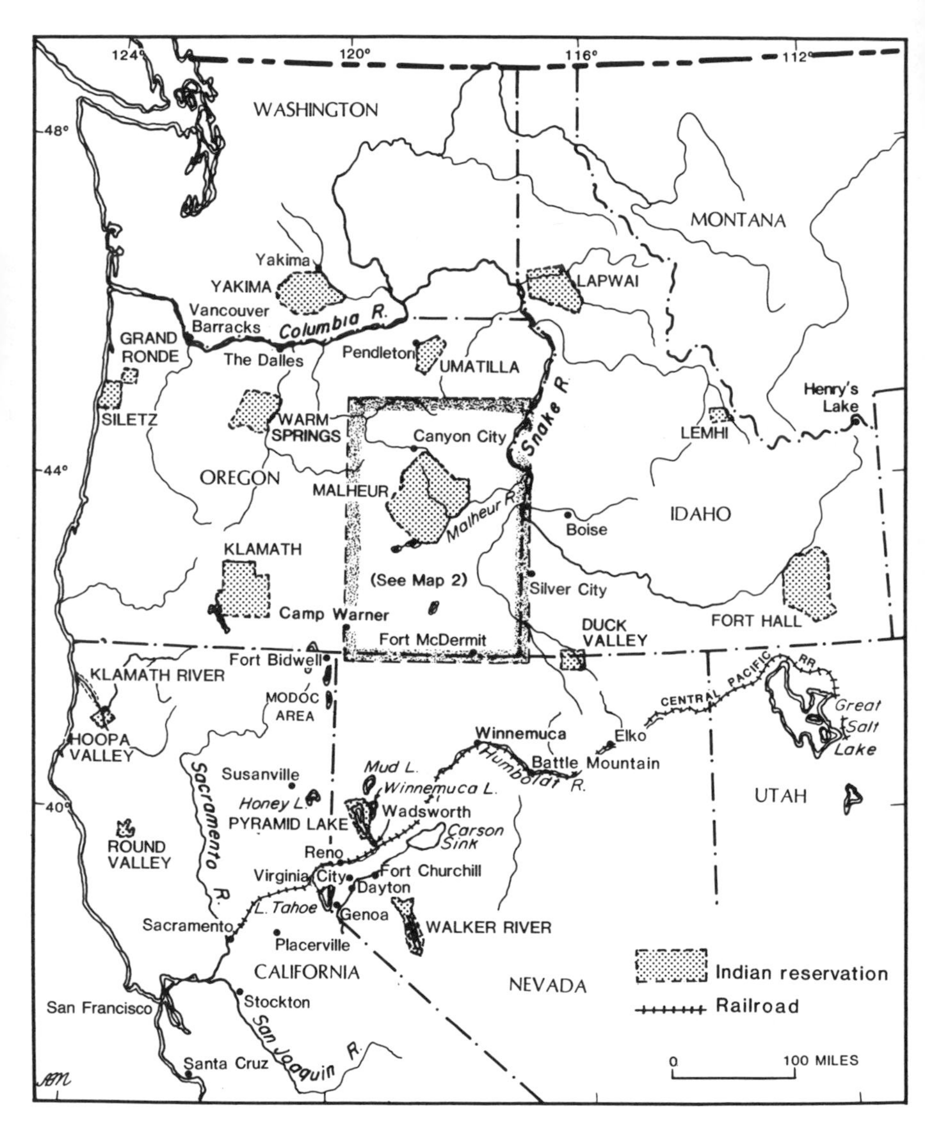

Map 1. *The Area of Sarah Winnemucca's Activity.* (Map 2 is on page 95.)

1
Early Years

Before the invasions of the white man in the mid-nineteenth century, Sarah Winnemucca's people, the Northern Paiute Indians, freely roamed the high deserts of the Great Basin of what is now western Nevada, northeastern California, and southern Oregon. Having no notion of themselves as a formal political unit,[1] they called themselves simply the Numa, or "People." In anthropological terms they were not a tribe, though history has accorded them tribal status. With the Bannock Indians on the east they constituted a Shoshonean dialectic group in the Uto-Aztecan Indian language family. Like most other Native American peoples they were unaware of the names that were bestowed on them by the first whites. In early accounts their name was spelled in a variety of ways, such as Piute, Pi-Utah, and Paviotso, and they were known as the Snake Indians in parts of Oregon. They were not related to the Southern Paiutes, whose language was very different.

Sarah was born about 1844, the fourth child and second daughter of the older Chief Winnemucca (who was called Old Winnemucca to distinguish him from a nephew of the same name).[2] Winnemucca's name meant "the giver" or "one who looks after the Numa."[3] As an antelope shaman he oversaw the communal antelope hunts. At other times he led his band as they wandered in their searches for food. Even at an early age Sarah helped elevate her father so that he was regarded as the "Big Chief of the Paiutes." She recognized an opportunity in the white emigrants' desire to deal with a few leaders who could parley and answer for the Numa.

Winnemucca was not a war leader in the sense that the Plains Indian chiefs were, since the Paiutes possessed few horses and had no raiding tradition. Although there were occasional altercations, and there was fighting on a small scale, survival under hard living conditions was the Paiutes' prime object of attention. Bands shared food sources with other bands and, in times of abundance, even with neighboring tribes, including the Shoshonis on the east and the various California tribes on the west.

Sarah's Paiute name was Thocmetony, or Shell Flower. She was born in the vicinity of Humboldt Lake in present-day Nevada. Her mother, Tuboitonie,[4] like all other native women living in the Great Basin, spent much of her time gathering wild seeds, roots, and herbs and grinding and preparing them as food. It was a strenuous life; the women were accustomed to traveling miles each day to the sources of the foods as they came in season.

Single families might wander for days without seeing other Numa, but when food was in abundance, there were large gatherings. Bands would get together for games, gossip, and courtship when the leaders decided on a collective rabbit or mud-hen hunt and during the traditional pine-nut collecting in the fall. As antelope shaman Old Winnemucca first discovered the location of a herd in a dream. Then he would lead his band in a ritual preparing them to lure the animals (which appeared to be in a hypnotic state) into a brush corral, where they could be easily killed.

Sarah's maternal grandfather was Captain Truckee, for whom the Truckee River in California and Nevada is named. He had been a guide to early emigrants crossing the Great Basin. There is evidence that he acted as guide for the Stevens-Townsend-Murphy[5] party of 1844 and also for Captain Joseph Aram in 1846.[6] When Sarah was a baby, Truckee was away in California with General John C. Frémont's army and fought in the Bear Flag Rebellion against continued Mexican control of California.

Sarah Winnemucca spent her childhood in a time of great disruption in the life of the Numa. The activities of eastern emigrants on the sage plains of the desert were abruptly changing the conservative aboriginal existence based on a balance with nature. The Numa had either to move away from the roving cattle of the settlers, which decimated the grass seed and brought diphtheria and typhus to the alkaline waters of the Humboldt river, or adapt to the white man's ways, learn from him, and, unfortunately, accept him as master.

Sarah developed an early fear of white men, which was reinforced by the death of a favorite uncle, who was shot while fishing on the Humboldt.[7] At the time, emigrants had recently erected tents in the Humboldt meadows. Members of the band demanded revenge on them, but Captain Truckee reminded his followers that the same emigrants had given sacks of flour to the Numa and had welcomed Truckee and Winnemucca. They were not the transgressors who had killed Truckee's son.

As an adult Sarah remembered her father describing these early emigrants, the first white men whom Winnemucca had encountered close at hand. He called them "owls," because of their unfamiliar beards and light-colored eyes. Young Sarah connected this description of her father's with the Cannibal Owl,[8] a Paiute boogeyman who, in a well-known tale, carried away crying, misbehaving children, pounded them into a tender pulp, and ate them with relish.

Sarah's fear of the emigrants was increased by another traumatic experience. Once, when the cry had gone out that the whites were coming, Tuboitonie and a woman companion could not keep up with the other members of the band and carry the burden of their two young ones. Consequently they buried Sarah and her cousin in the sand, and the two children were left through the heat of the day, their heads protected from the sun by sagebrush. Sarah imagined that at any moment the "cannibal owls" would spring upon them. In the darkness of night Tuboitonie returned to rescue her, but the experience was an indelible memory for Sarah.[9]

For their part, the emigrants, observing the Paiutes in their insubstantial grass shelters and minimal clothing, thought of them as primitive "diggers." The word "digger" was used in a derogatory way to refer to the natives of the Great Basin and California, because the Indian women often dug with sticks for bulbs and roots. Also the whites were put off by the Paiutes' willingness to eat roasted crickets and grasshoppers and ground squirrels and other small desert rodents. The emigrants failed to appreciate the natives' ability to use all of their resources to avoid starvation in a sparse land. Existence required a keen observation of nature and remembrance from season to season when and where to find the natural harvests that were available.

Sarah's early childhood, while largely happy, was often intruded upon by the presence of her maternal grandfather, Captain Truckee, who frightened her with his strange ways and talk of "white brothers." Chief Truckee would return from trips to California with amazing stories of the abundance of food and horses there and the great towns and houses built by the white man, some of which floated on water.[10] The men who accompanied him to California returned with guns and ammunition and demonstrated their prowess with them by shooting mud hens. When the Paiute bands came together at harvest times, there was much talk of the experiences of the Numa who had gone to California. What they described was almost beyond the comprehension of those who had continued to lead the traditional life.

Captain Truckee had learned many English words. He proudly displayed what he called his "rag friend," a letter of introduction from General Frémont commending the Paiute leader for his active part in the war against Mexico.[11] Whenever Truckee presented it, emigrants were liberal with handshakes and gifts. The men of the Numa were tempted when Truckee explained that horses would be given to those who chose to return with him to California to work for white ranchers. Horses would greatly increase the food-gathering capabilities of the bands.

It was probably in the spring of 1850 when, contrary to Winnemucca's wishes, Truckee took his daughter Tuboitonie and her five children in a group of about thirty Paiutes on another journey to California.[12] Winnemucca remained behind with his second wife and her family. Six-year-old Sarah was placed on a horse behind her brother Tom, and Truckee's small band started from the Humboldt Sink toward the Carson River. There were many miles of emigrant tracks to follow, tracks strewn with broken wagons decaying in the sand and sun. Truckee used his rag friend to great advantage among the white travelers, and the Paiutes were treated to sacks of flour, shirts for the men, and dress goods for the women, some of whom still wore the traditional skirt of tule fiber that left them bare above the waist.

In the eyes of her grandfather Sarah behaved badly during her first encounter with the "cannibal owls," for she hid under her blanket and cried. Truckee took Sarah's new baby sister, Elma, from Tuboitonie's back and showed her to an emigrant woman. The woman offered them a powdery substance that Tom and Natchez tried and liked. Sarah finally had the courage to taste the sugar and found it sweet like the Paiutes' own *pe-har-be,*[13] which was taken from a cane growing along the Humboldt River.[14]

At Mormon Station, a settlement on the Carson River that later became Genoa in present-day Nevada, Sarah saw for the first time the manner of living of the whites. When the Paiutes crossed the Sierra into California, the newcomers were awe-struck with the thriving town of Stockton, on the San Joaquin River. Sarah saw brick buildings three stories high and the busy steamboat traffic between San Francisco and the gold fields.[15] Her grandfather had been right: the whites did build houses that made noises and moved up the river.

At six years old Sarah was at a sensitive age to assimilate such drastic change. She cried incessantly, calling her grandfather a bad man to have brought the family among the whites, and begged to return home. Finally she fell ill. Tuboitonie thought that Sarah had been poisoned by a gift of food, but her illness proved to be only a severe case of poison oak. An emigrant woman, who had just lost a child of her own, helped nurse Sarah back to health. With the care and kindness of this woman Sarah found a new trust in the white race. She was, however, terribly disappointed when she could not keep the lovely dresses that the grieving woman had given her, which had belonged to her own daughter. Captain Truckee insisted that the gifts be burned, for it was the Paiute custom that all possessions of the dead, including clothing, must be destroyed.

From their camp near Stockton the Paiutes moved up the San Joaquin River to the ferry crossing owned by Hiram Scott and Jacob Bonsall, who hired the men as vaqueros on their large ranch. Sarah's brothers, Tom and Natchez, worked on the Bonsall ferry.[16] It was an opportunity to learn English and become acquainted with white ways. The women worked in the ranch kitchen, where Sarah was attracted to the bright dishes in the

The Stockton, California, waterfront in the 1850s. Stockton was the first large white settlement that Sarah Winnemucca knew. (Courtesy of Bancroft Library, University of California, Berkeley.)

cupboards. Most of all she loved the red plush chairs around the dining table. She sat on them whenever she could, twisting in her seat to gaze at the tapestry pictures on the backs.

Sarah's older sister, Mary, would never forget the treatment that she received from some of the cowboys at the ranch. She continued to despise white men for the rest of her life. Tuboitonie desperately tried to protect Mary from their attentions. Finally Hiram Scott came to their aid by assigning the women a room in the ranch house. The other Numa remained in the Indian camp. Truckee was not aware of the situation, for he was tending cattle and horses in a camp miles from the home ranch.[17] Tuboitonie had reason to be concerned. In California, Indian women were commonly seized and forced to serve as servants and concubines. Some were cast aside after a time, while others became common-law wives. Legal marriage between whites and Indians was prohibited in both California and Nevada.

At the end of the work season the Numa brought in the stock that they had herded. The ranchers killed several beefs for the

Paiutes, and the Indians celebrated with a thanksgiving dance. If any horses had been missing, there could have been serious consequences for Truckee. Not long before, Jacob Bonsall had led twelve Americans in hanging five Mexicans for horse stealing, despite their protestations that they were not guilty. There had been no jury trial, and the bodies were simply left hanging.[18]

When the band returned to their homeland with their newly acquired horses, at the head of the Carson River they met some of their own people who had recently come from the Humboldt River region. They told a chilling story of the death of many of the Numa on the Humboldt. They were convinced that the emigrants had poisoned the waters of the river. Sarah learned with relief that her father and his band were safe. They had stayed in the mountains away from the river.[19]

The Numa mourned, cutting off their hair and brushing their faces and bodies with ashes. Truckee sent a message to Winnemucca, and his band hurried on their journey to Mormon Station, where they would eventually meet Winnemucca. There had been much activity in this settlement since their previous stop. Now there was a sawmill and a gristmill, and men were out in the plowed fields planting wheat and corn. Great logs had been cut and laid on the ground for fences between the fields.[20]

Hundreds of prospective gold miners were following the trail to California. They stopped at the Reese store in Mormon Station only long enough to buy provisions for the trip over the Sierra. A strong stockade had been built around the log store, but it was an unnecessary precaution. The Washos, the Indians who lived in that country, were peaceful. Though they occasionally drove off horses and cattle, this was really an uneven trade, since so much of their land was now possessed by the newcomers.[21]

Many days later Winnemucca came from the desert regions with a large band of his people. Their crying and wailing could be heard from afar. The two groups fell into each other's arms. Everyone was in mourning because whole families had died of typhus. Tuboitonie found that she had lost two sisters, their husbands, and all her nephews and nieces except for one niece. The Paiutes thought that the whites must have poisoned the Humboldt River. Truckee talked to his people for a long time, and they listened quietly as he defended the whites, saying:

"Oh, my dear children, do not think so badly of our white fathers, for if they had poisoned the river, why, . . . they too would have died when they drank of the water. . . . It must be some fearful disease or sickness unknown to us, and therefore, my dear children, don't blame our brothers."[22]

After his speechmaking Truckee went into Mormon Station with his rag friend. He procured sacks of flour for the hungry people, and Winnemucca received a new blanket and a shirt. Thus Truckee's interpretation of the situation prevailed, and the Numa moved on down the Carson River. On its green margins they found emigrants felling trees and building cabins. There were way stations and whiskey shops where wayfarers traded their run-down stock for fresh animals and supplies. Eventually the miners would invade the eastern foothills of the Sierra when gold was found on the Great Basin side. There was only a small quantity of the precious metal, but enough to keep a few men working. They established a settlement, which was christened Johntown, in Gold Canyon, one of the Paiutes' traditional pine-nut-gathering areas.[23]

While Truckee did not hesitate to bring his people in close proximity to the white miners during his band's annual pine-nut pilgrimage, Winnnemucca chose to take his people farther north, where there was less emigrant activity. The Winnemucca band pursued their wandering life on Smoke Creek in the vicinity of Honey Lake, in a remote area of northeastern California.[24] The country was high-plateau sage desert, but large game animals were still available. The Indians found grazing for their increasing herds of ponies along the banks of the rivers and lakes.

When Truckee made more trips into California with those of his people who wished to follow, Sarah and her brothers accompanied him. Some of their relatives had married Spaniards in the Santa Cruz area, and Sarah thus learned to speak Spanish before she was ten years old.[25] Truckee and his band were attracted to the Santa Cruz Mountains because there was much wild game there and space to wander freely as they had previously in the Great Basin.

The personable Truckee made friends at the old Santa Clara Mission. His friend Captain Aram, whom Truckee had guided across the Sierra in 1846, had fought near the mission ruins during the Mexican War. Now the Sisters of Notre Dame de

Namur were starting a school near the mission. Truckee found them friendly and willing to instruct him regarding their religious beliefs. Most of the Paiute men found jobs as ranch hands or agricultural workers, but Natchez and Tom continued to work for Scott and Bonsall on the San Joaquin River ferry.[26]

In 1873, Sarah told an interviewer that she owed a great deal to a Mrs. Roach, of Stockton, who adopted her, but we do not know how old Sarah was when that occurred.[27] She worked for several white families and was probably given her Christian name during this period. Then, in 1857, she and her younger sister, Elma, moved again to the eastern side of the Sierra to live in the household of Major William M. Ormsby in former Mormon Station, which was now a bustling town known as Genoa.[28] Ormsby's store was located on the main street and was also a stage stop for the Carson Valley Express, for which the major was an agent. Sarah and Elma worked at household chores and helped serve passengers. Sarah was now thirteen years old and, like most of the Paiute children who were adopted by settlers, was expected to earn her keep. Besides doing housework, the two girls were companions to Lizzie Ormsby, the only child of Major and Mrs. Ormsby. Lizzie was four years younger than Sarah. Although Major Ormsby did not share the religion of his Mormon neighbors, Genoa was a close-knit community, and Sarah grew to know the citizens well. When she wrote her autobiography twenty-five years later, she remembered the settlers' names (though she misspelled some of them) and where they lived.[29]

The Paiute sisters were separated from their family, but many other Paiutes lived in the Carson River valley, where they had proved most adaptable to white ways. The men were employed as herdsmen and laborers, and the women as cooks and household help. Generally they acquired some English and dressed as whites.[30] It was at this time that English became Sarah's major language, and she picked up the rudiments of reading and writing.

While Sarah was living with the Ormsbys, a tragic incident occurred that colored her view of white justice. The Washo Indian tribe was accused of killing two traders, James Williams and John McMarlin, who owned a store in Chinatown, now Dayton, Nevada (Sarah spelled their names MacWilliams and McMullen).[31] Both men were on their way to California in charge of separate packtrains when they were attacked. The white community demanded

Lizzie Ormsby at age thirteen. Sarah Winnemucca and her sister Elma were companions of Miss Ormsby while living in Genoa, Nevada, in 1857. (Courtesy of Mrs. Eleanor Johansen.)

that the guilty persons be found and prosecuted immediately. The bodies of the dead men were brought into Genoa, and the Washo arrows were removed and saved for evidence.[32]

Chiefs of the Paiute tribe were asked to come and identify the arrows. Sarah's brother Natchez was now a young man. He came to Genoa with his cousin, Young Winnemucca, who was respected by the whites as an important leader. The Paiutes identified the arrows as Washo to Major Ormsby's satisfaction, and he sent for Captain Jim, a leader of that tribe. Captain Jim admitted that the arrows were Washo but said that all of his people had been harvesting pine nuts and that they were innocent of the killing of the two white men. Major Ormsby said that Captain Jim must bring in the guilty parties or his tribe would find themselves at war. His threat was backed by the Paiutes, who regarded the deceased McMarlin as a loyal friend.[33]

In a few days three Washo men were brought in by Captain Jim. They were accompanied by their wives and mothers, who pleaded for their release, saying that they were innocent. Nevertheless, the three were taken into custody and held overnight. On the next day thirty men with arms came to take the prisoners to California for trial, but the Washos were so terrified that they broke and ran. The militia shot them down, and all three died of their wounds.

Sarah and Elma saw the bloodshed and ran crying to Mrs. Ormsby. Sarah said, "I believe those Washo women who say their men are innocent."

Mrs. Ormsby replied: "How could the Washo arrows be there if they are innocent? Their chief himself has brought them. Besides, my husband knows what he is doing."

One of the mourning women cried to Natchez and Young Winnemucca: "Oh, may the Good Spirit send the same curse upon you! You may all live to see the day when you will suffer at the hands of your white brothers, as you call them."[34]

The Washo bodies were burned, as was the tribal custom. Meanwhile the Washo chief confessed to Natchez that he had known that the men were innocent: "It is true what the women say—it is I who have killed them. Their blood is on my hands. I know their spirits will haunt me, and give me bad luck while I live."[35]

Elma was inconsolable for days after this event. Sarah explains that two white men later were found with the money that had been stolen from McMarlin and Williams. They admitted that they had used the Washo arrows to make it appear that the Indians had murdered the two packers.[36]

The episode seemed to mark the beginning of new misunderstandings and loss of faith in the tenuous relationship between the newly established white settlers in the Great Basin and their darker-skinned neighbors.

2

The Pyramid Lake War

In 1857, Sarah and Lizzie Ormsby were old enough to go from Genoa to the occasional square dances at Johntown, accompanied by Major and Mrs. Ormsby. There were not many women in the Utah Territory at this time, and even little Elma was sometimes brought in to round out a foursome and dance to the fiddle.[1] The Johntown gold miners knew Sarah as a Paiute girl with long raven hair and flashing eyes. They thought of her as a bit haughty and proud, which, of course, made her all the more attractive to them.

Major Ormsby was becoming a leading figure in the Carson River valley. He bought out John McMarlin's store downriver in Chinatown (later Dayton, Nevada)[2] and was made the chief judge of a murder case.[3] Meanwhile he continued to act as the agent for the stage company. Living with the Ormsbys acquainted Sarah with many important local people. Among them was a young man named Frederick Dodge, who was the first United States Indian agent to work exclusively in the western part of the Utah Territory. He set up his office in Genoa. Sarah was undoubtedly pleased to hear that he had distributed hickory shirts, overalls, and tobacco to many of her kinsmen.

In recent years Old Winnemucca had watched emigrants appropriate land and settle on his hunting grounds in the Honey Lake

Genoa, Nevada, in 1870. In this community, originally called Mormon Station, Major William Ormsby acted as the agent for the Carson Valley Express. A steep trail near the town led over the mountain to Lake Bigler (later renamed Lake Tahoe) in the Washo Indian country. (Courtesy of Nevada Historical Society, Reno.)

valley in northeastern California. Although the intrusions were unwelcome, the old leader found some loyal friends among the whites. One was old Peter Lassen, who had lived amiably with the Indians along Deer Creek farther west in California. Lassen often prospected and hunted near Honey Lake. Another was Warren Wasson, who had established a ranch in Long Valley, California, and had spent a good amount of his time working for the welfare of the Paiutes who roved in his area. He knew their language and was of significant help to Agent Dodge in gathering the various bands for a council rendezvous with their new agent.

At the rendezvous Dodge talked with the chiefs, estimated the numbers of the bands, and established himself as a representative of their interests.[4] In making his reports on the Indians, he wrote: "As near as I can ascertain at present, the Piute nation numbers some 6000 souls. I have seen and given presents to 3735. . . . Wun-a-Muc-a (The Giver) is the head chief of the nation. He generally stays on Smoke Creek: near Honey Lake. His family and small band that stays with him number 155." Dodge named twelve bands that he had visited. They included the band of Wa-he, or Fox (a brother of Old Winnemucca) at the big bend of the Carson River, numbering 130; San-Joaquin's band in the Carson valley, numbering 170; and Young Winnemucca's band along the shores of lower Mud Lake, numbering 300.[5]

As has been noted, there had been no head chief of the Paiutes up to this time. Since the settlers now felt a need to communicate with a responsible tribal representative, it is probable that Sarah, when she talked to Dodge in Genoa, gave him the impression that her father held the honors. She continued to support the notion of Old Winnemucca's predominance from this time on.[6] That is not to say that he did not deserve the status that was awarded him. He was well-known to the many Paiute bands and was a respected leader.

While Agent Dodge was with the Paiutes, he made a point of looking over the high plateaus of the Great Basin to determine what lands should most appropriately be set aside for future Paiute reservations. It was clear that the tribe's roaming way of life was necessarily changing. He found much of the best land already taken by settlers.

A third man who had a close acquaintance with Chief Winnemucca was Captain William Weatherlow. He praised the Paiutes because they did not beg for food or clothing, or steal, but brought furs and game to the homesteaders of Honey Lake in exchange for the articles that they wanted.[7] The Honey Lake settlers made an agreement with Winnemucca that, if Indians committed any depredations, the settlers would go to the chief to complain instead of taking revenge on the Indians. Similarly, if the Indians were molested by the whites, or their horses or cattle were stolen, the chief would come to the settlers for redress. The agreement was faithfully observed on both sides.

Major Ormsby's business affairs had so progressed that he took an interest in starting a new town in the Eagle River valley, called Carson City. In the growing little town he built himself a two-story adobe building that was both his hotel and residence, and in 1858 the Ormsby family moved there. The major had a hunch that settling closer to Chinatown and the gold fields would be to his advantage. He continued in the general-merchandising and hotel businesses.[8]

When Frederick Dodge frequented Carson City, he stayed either at the St. Nicholas Hotel or Major Ormsby's establishment. Dodge was an emotional, opinionated young man. He irritated the Mormons because of his outspoken criticism of the dominance of that religious group in the affairs of the Utah Territory. There was little doubt, however, that he had the interest of "his" Indian charges at heart. He spent $5,000 of his own money to purchase four mules, an ambulance, harness, packsaddles, presents for the Indians, provisions, and pay for employees. He expected to be reimbursed by his superior in Salt Lake City,[9] but Superintendent Jacob Forney did not respond to Dodge's requests for payment. After months of waiting and many requests Dodge made a trip to the seat of Mormonism and indignantly forced his way into the superintendent's private quarters to demand the money. Forney gave him a draft on a Saint Louis bank for the disputed amount, but it bounced. The frustrated Dodge still lacked the money that had been legally budgeted for his use. He took affidavits from citizens that Forney had made promises to the Indians to give them cattle and grain that Dodge could not possibly provide because of lack of funds.[10]

When Winnemucca's friend Peter Lassen was murdered while on a prospecting trip in the spring of 1859, some settlers suspected the Indians. Others remembered the warm friendship between the chief and Lassen. Although the Paiutes remained friendly, the question remained unresolved. As for Agent Dodge, he suspected the Mormons, whom he blamed for most Indian troubles.

Dodge foresaw that there would be another influx of whites to occupy more land when a new emigrant road was completed across the Great Basin. The road's destination was Genoa. Captain James H. Simpson, the road superintendent, spent an agreeable evening at the Ormsbys' in Carson City, where, for the first time since he had left Camp Floyd (west of Utah Lake), he encountered the society of ladies.[11] When he rode into Genoa on the following day, the citizens gave his company a thirteen-gun salute and ran up the American flag.

Then, in late June, 1859, the excitement of the discovery of the new Washoe silver mines stirred the country. Hundreds of miners left unpromising diggings in California and hurried on horseback, on foot, or with teams of horses or pack mules to lay claims in the Washoe district, which was just over the border in present-day Nevada. The black rocks that the gold miners around Johntown and Gold Hill had been throwing away for months as worthless debris were now recognized to be solid silver.[12] The Carson valley had been a bustling area before, but now it was a beehive. Towns expanded, new businesses opened, and, perhaps most important of all, there was talk of wresting the western part of Utah away from Mormon control and establishing a new territory.

In late September five wagons from the new mines at Virginia City passed through Carson City. They were en route to California loaded with silver ore. All along the main street people cheered and hollered after the procession. It would create even more excitement when it crossed the Sierra into California with the loads of sudden wealth.[13] At this time, however, Sarah and Elma were suddenly requested by Chief Winnemucca to return to him. Their father was concerned about the increased emigrant activity and sent Natchez to accompany them.[14]

Agent Dodge pleaded once more with the commissioner of Indian affairs in Washington, A. B. Greenwood: "Yesterday's overland mail brought me advices from Carson Valley that there was a general stampede of persons from California to the mining localities within my agency which devolves in me an additional reason for appealing to your kind consideration on behalf of my

Indians." He requested that land be set aside for the Pyramid Lake and Walker River reservations and sent accompanying maps to show the boundaries. He remarked:

These are isolated spots, embracing large fisheries, surrounded by mountains and deserts, and will have the advantage of being their home from choice.

The Indians of my agency linger about the graves of their ancestors—"but the game is gone," and now, the steady tread of the white man is upon them. The green valleys too, once spotted with game are not theirs now.[15]

A traveler who met Sarah at this time wrote of her:

Near the sink of the Humboldt river a strange but interesting woman visited our camp. She was a full blood Piute Indian woman, highly intelligent and educated and talked the English language fluently. She ate breakfast with me and became so interested in our conversation that she offered to travel with me, across the desert to Carson Valley. Her name was Sarah Winnemucca, the only daughter of Chief Winnemucca, the great chief of the Piute Nations. There is a station on the Union Pacific Railroad named Winnemucca in honor of her father. He was the head to whom all sub-ordinate chiefs reported when anything was wrong all the way from the Humboldt river to the sink of the Owens river, four hundred miles south.[16]

Sarah had impressed this newcomer too with the importance of her father's role in tribal affairs. It is doubtful that he had much influence south of the Humboldt, since he and his band usually moved north from that river, going as far as central Oregon. Sarah's conversation with the traveler might have included information about Agent Dodge and the growing tensions between the settlers and the Paiutes.

The winter of 1859 was the worst that the Indians could remember. Large numbers of Washos died in Truckee valley. The whites helped build fires for them and offered food, but the starving Indians refused to eat. They thought that the bread was poisoned and that the whites had brought the severe weather upon them.[17] In January, while the fierce storms were still raging, there was talk of an "Indian outrage" near Honey Lake. A young man, named Dexter E. Demming, had been murdered, and his horses and property stolen. The settlers at Honey Lake demanded that Captain Weatherlow lead a company of men after the offenders, whom they were convinced had been Smoke Creek Paiutes.

The captain reasoned with the settlers that those Indians had always been friendly and had kept the Honey Lake treaty, but the tracks in the snow from the scene of the murder proved to be Paiute. A party came back and reported that the murderers were from the Smoke Creek band, who had drawn away from Winnemucca's control and recognized Smoke Creek Sam as their leader. An agreement was reached that Weatherlow should have a talk with Winnemucca, inform him of the murder, and demand that the guilty parties be given up. When the captain arrived at Pyramid Lake, he was accompanied by a representative of Provisional Governor Isaac Roop. The two men found themselves suddenly surrounded by Paiutes, who were well armed and mounted. The Indians took them prisoner and refused to let them interview Winnemucca.

Weatherlow recognized the men as Smoke Creek Paiutes. He parleyed with them, finally agreeing to return to Honey Lake. He and his companion set off in the direction of the white settlement, but they later took cover in a dense fog and changed their course again to Pyramid Lake. There they found Young Winnemucca, who invited them in to his *nobee*, or *karnee*, the rounded hut of woven rushes or cattails that was the traditional Paiute dwelling. Since Young Winnemucca had spread a blanket for them to sit upon, and had always been cooperative, Weatherlow was surprised to find that the chief would not agree to return to Honey Lake valley to settle their differences, nor would he admit that Paiutes had committed the murder. Weatherlow added, "We then asked him to appoint some future time for visiting us; he replied that he would not come at all, but that the people of Honey Lake must pay to his people $16,000 for their land."[18]

Weatherlow believed that the request for payment for the land did not originate with the Paiute leader, but that some white man had put the notion in Young Winnemucca's head. He concluded, "My belief was, from the manner and actions of Winnemucca that we were going to have trouble with the Pah-utes—he did not say in so many words that he was preparing for war, but from my knowledge of Indian character and from the excited and unusual manner of the warriors I was convinced that they contemplated mischief." The captain gave warning to the cattlemen in the vicinity of Pyramid Lake, who begged the Honey Lake settlers not to "demonstrate" against the Indians until they could remove their stock when the snows had melted in the spring.[19]

In late February, Old Winnemucca came with an interpreter into Virginia City, which is about fifty miles southeast of Honey Lake. He made bitter complaints to the citizens. Curious miners crowded around him on a saloon porch while he told them that the cattlemen at Pyramid Lake had threatened his men and taken his ponies. He said Agent Dodge had promised that the herders would pay for the use of the land, but now they would not because they claimed that the Paiutes had stolen some of their cattle: "They say they will bring down white men from this town and kill all the Indians at Pyramid Lake."[20] The citizens told him that nobody from Virginia City was going out to fight Indians, but Winnemucca was not satisfied with their assurances. In a few days the people of Virginia City noted that most of the Paiutes who lived on the outskirts of town had left, but they thought little of it because the Indians usually returned to Pyramid Lake for the spring fishing season.

Sarah must have been fully aware at this time of her people's disenchantment with the white invasion. Many bands came into Pyramid Lake in the early spring, even the Paiutes' distant relatives, the Bannocks of Idaho, whose appearance was more like that of Plains Indians because of their beaded leather clothing and long, braided hair. The abundance of cutthroat trout, called *hoopagaih*, meant that there was food for all. All the bands had their own camps, which were sometimes separated by miles of sagebrush, but the leaders met, and there was much talk.

Young Winnemucca's high qualities of leadership were generally recognized,[21] for he was a powerful man of intelligence and dignity. He spoke strongly for continued peace with the whites. He reminded the other leaders that Major Dodge had promised them a reservation and believed that they should turn to tilling the soil. Old Winnemucca also wanted peace, but he wished to continue the traditional hunting and gathering; he knew of land that could sustain his band where no white man had settled. His words were not favorably received by the majority, who were tired of being driven from their accustomed hunting areas.

The deliberations in council went on for many days, as the people continued to linger, waiting for something to be decided. Young Winnemucca was adamant for peace, and, when he saw that he was not winning, he fell in a coma and lay as though

Young Winnemucca, also called Numaga, a cousin of Sarah's and a respected leader of the Paiutes at Pyramid Lake. (Courtesy of Nevada Historical Society.)

dead.[22] Shamans did this, because it was thought that while in such a trance they could leave their bodies to call upon the dead or the Great Spirit.[23] When Young Winnemucca again stood before the council, there was new interest in what he had to say. His temperate words were lost, however, when a rider dashed up with solemn news.

Two young Paiute girls had been found in the Williamses' cellar at Williams Station, a whiskey shop on the Carson River that also provided provisions and water. Their parents had thought them drowned or lost, but now they were found, and, though still alive, they had been abused by the Williams brothers. A party of warriors, headed by Captain Sou, had burned the station and killed the two Williamses and a traveler with them. Thus an act had been committed that was an excuse for conflict, and the feelings of the Paiutes were inflamed for battle. When Young Winnemucca heard of the revenge that the Numa had taken on the Carson River, he knew that it would be only a matter of time before the whites descended upon the Paiutes. He became war chief and prepared his people for battle.[24]

Rumors circulated in the white settlements that besides the horror at Williams Station other settlers along the Carson River had been attacked and there was a general uprising of the Paiutes. Each town got up a company of volunteers to chastise the Indians, while riders raced through the countryside to warn isolated settlers of the danger. In Carson City on May 9 a company was organized of thirty mounted men, who were under the command of Major Ormsby. Genoa, Silver City, and Virginia City also formed motley companies, who were armed with firearms of all kinds and ages. The white men moved toward Williams Station with little plan and no central command, though it seems that in the end Major Ormsby accepted leadership through default.[25]

When they followed the Truckee River to the Paiute stronghold at Pyramid Lake, the volunteers found that their initially pleasurable Indian hunt turned into a nightmare. As they pursued them, the Paiutes would fade away behind sagebrush and rocks, only to reappear and move away again. Ormsby suspected an ambush and posted guards at a narrow spot on the trail that was blocked by high cliffs on the right and the Truckee River on the left. As the wary volunteers moved down the trail to a meadow that was surrounded on two sides by cottonwood trees and brush, the Indians attacked. Paiute horsemen charged from behind a line of trees, while other warriors opened fire from rocks and low vegetation on the hillside above. The volunteers found themselves in a well-conceived trap, with no way out but to go back the narrow trail along the Truckee River.

Many volunteers and their terrified, rearing horses lost their lives in the first minutes of the battle. A general white retreat followed. At the place where the trail narrowed, most of the men who had been in charge of covering their comrades fled for their lives, though a few stood their ground and died for their bravery.[26] The volunteers who reached the plateau were pursued for miles, and those whose horses gave out found death awaiting them. Major Ormsby was shot in the mouth and both arms. Attempting to ride a wounded mule, he climbed the trail to the plateau, but, when he saw that there was no hope, he turned to face his death. In her autobiography Sarah claims:

> My brother [Natchez] had tried to save Major Ormsbey's life. He met him in the fight, and as he was ahead of the other Indians, Major Ormsbey threw down his arms, and implored him not to kill him. There was not a moment to be lost. My brother said,—"Drop down as if dead when I shoot, and I will fire over you," but in the hurry and agitation he still stood pleading, and was killed by another man's shot.[27]

Only the darkness of night saved many. In the next few days those who had hidden or outrun the Paiutes straggled back to the settlements. The news of the high number of casualties, which totaled close to eighty, plus the discipline of the Indians amazed and frightened the settlers. Expecting the worst, they sent to California for reinforcements and barricaded themselves in the strongest buildings in the towns. The residents of western Utah were panic-stricken. Some decided that California was a more promising place to reside and headed back over the Sierra. Four regular companies of United States troops were brought from San Francisco and Benicia to chastise the Paiutes.[28]

On June 1 over five hundred volunteers plus the regulars joined forces and began a second march to Pyramid Lake. When they reached the point where the trail dropped to the wide meadow, scouts observed three hundred mounted warriors approaching and more Indians following on foot. After a furious battle the whites had to admire the tactics of the Paiutes: The

Major William Ormsby, the leader of an attack by settlers on the Northern Paiutes. He died along with more than eighty other whites in the Pyramid Lake War. (Courtesy of Nevada Historical Society.)

women and children had escaped behind the lines while the warriors kept the enemy occupied. A few days later, when they reached the main Paiute encampment, the soldiers found the village deserted.[29]

Meanwhile, Captain Weatherlow and his thirty-five Honey Lake volunteers had waited in a three-day sleet storm for the Indians to come through a pass on the northern end of the lake. They gave up just one day too soon.[30] A few white scouts pursued the retreating Indians as they moved toward the northern deserts, but, when one of their number was killed, they lost heart, and they returned to the settlements.

Before the year 1860 was over, the United States government had reacted to the battle of Pyramid Lake by building a fort on the Carson River, called Fort Churchill. It was meant to be a bulwark of defense against the Paiutes. The mutual trust of the days of Peter Lassen was no more. Yet Captain Weatherlow was convinced that, if Chief Winnemucca had been visited by Major Dodge with full power to make a treaty to create a reservation, the bloody massacre would never have occurred.[31] The Honey Lakers, now stranded in an isolated community far from the new fort on the Carson, were fortunate that Colonel Frederick Lander and his men were building a United States wagon road in the vicinity. Lander arranged a meeting with Young Winnemucca, and, though he could not treat with him in an official capacity, he offered to write about their conversations to Washington, D.C.[32]

Young Winnemucca greatly impressed Lander with his desire for peace and his understanding of the Paiutes' critical situation. The young chief complained that he was accused of killing Pete Lassen, who had been one of the best men he had ever known, and with whom he had slept in the same blanket. His people had shown the whites much kindness when the whites had nothing, but now there was no corresponding help from the whites. He spoke repeatedly of the promises that the whites had made and broken. The young chief was especially upset by the example of the California Indians, who had been put on reserved lands and promised food by the whites, only to find themselves starving. When they stole some cattle, the whites retaliated by murdering them all: men, women and children. Lander had no good rejoinder to Young Winnemucca's accusations, for he also knew of the massacre of reservation Indians in northern California. He reported to U.S. Commissioner Greenwood: "I told the Chief that his tribe was more like the whites than the Daggers [*sic*]. That much of the Pah-Ute territory, especially the mountain-sheep and antelope ranges, the whites would never covet, that their lakes were full of fish which the whites did not want."[33] Young Winnemucca was not persuaded. The good white man who was to teach him had never been sent, and a reservation had not been provided for his people.

Terms were negotiated for an armistice that was to last until the next summer when the grass was dry. The young chief sent for Old Winnemucca, who was on the Oregon border, and promised that the old leader would arrive in two weeks. He explained that Old Winnemucca had always been averse to war and would await Major Dodge's arrival at the Big Meadows on the Humboldt River.[34] Dodge had been in the East at the outbreak of the war. When he returned, Lander sent an urgent letter to him, asking him to treat with both Winnemuccas. Warren Wasson, who had been employed as a guide and scout for the army, arranged a meeting, which was held at Pyramid Lake. A peace settlement was finally negotiated.[35]

Agent Dodge was so delighted by Wasson's influence with the Indians that he engaged him in the Indian Service and left him in charge of his agency while he returned to Washington (where he was later recruited into the Civil War and killed). Dodge left behind him many white critics who felt he was too easy on the Indians and had an ulterior purpose in setting up the reservations: "It is known that he is on amicable terms with the Pah-Utes, and it is surmised that he wishes them to resist prospectors in the neighborhood of Pyramid Lake, where, it is said, he knows there is a rich mineral deposit—hoping, that when the Indians should get rid of all prospectors, he could get a large slice himself."[36] Warren Wasson refuted Dodge's critics, stating in a written report to the Office of Indian Affairs, "I may as well state from actual personal knowledge of Mr. Dodge, I know he was scrupulously honest and zealous in the discharge of his duties, but unacquainted with Indian character, and, therefore, unfit for the position of Indian agent."[37]

3
Growing Up Proud

It seems probable that Sarah Winnemucca was able to find a refuge during and after the Pyramid Lake War. She did not describe the hostilities in her autobiography as if she had actually experienced them with the "'squaws and papooses' who were hungry and tired of living in the rocks" whom Young Winnemucca reported at the close of the war.

In October, 1860, five months after the hostilities had ended,[1] Captain Truckee became ill with a serious infection in his hand caused, some sources say, by a tarantula bite. He and his band had been harvesting pine nuts in the Palmyra Mountains near Como, south of Dayton, Nevada. The miners nearby tried to alleviate his suffering with poultices and disinfectants, but Truckee's wives knew that he was dying. In her account of the death Sarah relates that signal fires were placed on the mountains to call in the Paiutes. As his granddaughter she was at Truckee's side, along with other members of the family.[2] She was about sixteen years old.

Captain Truckee asked one of his white friends, a Mr. Snyder, to come to him. Sarah quotes him as saying to Snyder:

There . . . are my sons' children, and the two little girls I want you to take to California, to Mr. Bonsal and Mr. Scott. They will send them to school to "the sisters," at San José. Tell them this is my last request to them. I shall soon die. I shall never see them in person; they have promised to teach my two little girls when they become large enough.[3]

Then Truckee spoke to Winnemucca: "He told him what he must do, as he was to be head chief of the Piute nation. He cautioned him to be a good father, as he had always been, and, after talking awhile, he broke down. We all cried."[4]

After a day and two nights Truckee's death was imminent. "He opened his eyes in his usual bright and beautiful way," Sarah recorded. After admonitions to all present he said, "Don't throw away my white rag friend; place it on my breast when you bury me." Then after a few more words, he died. Sarah described her feelings as follows:

I could not speak. I felt the world growing cold; everything seemed dark. The great light had gone out. I had father, mother, brothers, and sisters; it seemed I would rather lose all of them than my poor grandpa. I was only a simple child, yet I knew what a great man he was. I mean great in principle. I knew how necessary it was for our good that he should live.[5]

Truckee had always cautioned his people to be honest and never to take articles from the miners in the mountains that were around the new reservations even if they left them on the ground. The miners might return for them and think the Numa had stolen them.[6]

Sarah's tribute to her grandfather, written with genuine affection, emphasized his importance as a calming influence and as a leader who was well regarded by both races. In reality, however, Truckee had no authority to bestow the high chieftainship of the Paiute nation upon his son-in-law. Sarah was doing some wishful thinking in this regard. In the years to come Old Winnemucca would be a well-known chief to white society, but this was partly because of Sarah's insistence that he was such a personage.

In *Life Among the Piutes,* Sarah described her time at the San Jose convent school as brief:

In the spring of 1860, my sister and I were taken to San José, California. Brother Natchez and five other men went with us. On our arrival we were placed in the "Sisters' School" by Mr. Bonsal and Mr. Scott. We were only there a little while, say three weeks, when complaints were made to the sisters by wealthy parents about Indians being in school with their children. The sisters then wrote to our friends to come and take us away, and so they did,—at least, Mr. Scott did. He kept us a week, and sent word to brother Natchez to come for us, but no one could come, and he sent word for Mr. Scott to put us on the stage and send us back. We arrived at home all right.[7]

Inconsistently, in an 1873 interview Sarah said, "I was sent to the Convent of Notre Dame in San Jose in 1861 where I remained nearly three years."[8] In 1879 she related that she was educated by the Sisters of Charity at Saint Mary's in San Jose in 1858, 1859, and 1860,[9] though there were no Sisters of Charity and there was no Saint Mary's Church in San Jose in those years. It is hard to account for the discrepancies, since Sarah could well remember names and dates on other occasions.

The Academy of Notre Dame had been established by the Sisters of Notre Dame de Namur in San Jose in 1851.[10] It was a prestigious school for daughters of the wealthy, where girls were taught languages, science, literature and handiwork. Although the school possessed beautiful gardens and buildings and a fine music and drama department, all of that cultivation had grown from austere and primitive beginnings. In 1851 the sisters had been thankful to receive a bear haunch to supplement the cabbages from their garden.[11] Unfortunately, when Sarah and Elma arrived in 1860, the case of two Indian girls attempting to enter the academy presented problems. There are no records of the two Winnemucca sisters at the academy, though it is possible that they were at least admitted. It is likely that the Paiute girls were dismissed from the school after a short stay because of parents' complaints—as Sarah explained. The upper echelon of San Francisco society would have been offended by their presence, Indian princesses or no.[12] Both girls must have been deeply hurt by the affair. The Catholic sisters surely would have tried to disguise the insult, but it would have been apparent to Sarah that the equality and brotherly love that her dear grandfather had sought was not accessible to his granddaughters.

It is probable that Sarah claimed that she had attended the school for a longer period because she thought that it would strengthen her in white society. In fact, however, it is a credit to her individualism and character that she became culturally assimilated and educated by her own determination and persistence. The shame was not on her side in this affair.

Settlers in the Nevada Territory had generally been kind to

Academy of Notre Dame in San Jose, California, in the 1880s. (Courtesy of Bancroft Library, University of California.)

Sarah. She had lived with the Ormsbys and other white families, and, although her appearance and culture were different from theirs, that had been accepted. Many Paiute children had been adopted into settlers' homes, and, though it is true that they worked hard, so did everyone who was building the new towns, cultivating the soil for the first time, digging ditches for water, or searching for the riches of the mines. In Virginia City people had stared at Sarah, but she had known that that was because she was attractive and there were not many women in the populace. She was ambitious and had always had a sense of her own worth. That was not destroyed by the rejection from the sisters' school.

At about the time when the Winnemucca sisters returned to the Great Basin, President Abraham Lincoln appointed James W. Nye to be the first governor for the new Nevada Territory. When Nye visited Pyramid Lake Reservation on official business he was pleased with the war chief, Young Winnemucca: "I found him a most intelligent and appreciative man, one who reasons well and talks like a prudent, reflecting leader."[13] The governor found that white settlers had established themselves along the Truckee River on the most valuable reservation land. He ordered them off as soon as they could bring in their crops, but surely he must have known as well as the Paiutes that the settlers were there to stay unless dragged off by military force.

A pageant was prepared in honor of the arrival of the new territorial official, and Old Winnemucca, who always reveled in pomp and circumstance, made himself conspicuous in the proceedings. The *Carson City Silver Age* described the occasion as follows:

The visit is represented as being highly successful in every particular, and extremely gratifying to the old chieftain. Winnemucca, it seems, had been apprised of their approach, and with 150 of his picked warriors, "dressed from top to toe," met the Governor and party 20 miles this side of the Lake, and escorted them to his camp, where they were entertained in the most superb style known to the Pi-Utes. Captain Price and his soldiers were also partakers in the hospitalities of the tribe, and encamped at the lake during the sojourn of the Governor and suite. The Indians were greatly impressed with the importance of a visit from so many of our distinguished men, and used every means to render their stay agreeable, and the ceremonies that came off upon the separation are described as very appropriate and imposing. When the time approached for our men to depart, Winnemucca assembled his tribe, and compliments were freely exchanged, all of which wound up with a grand dance, soldiers, Indians and everybody else taking part. When the Governor and suite left, they were highly pleased with the manner in which they were entertained by the Indians and it is generally supposed that Old Winnemucca was much elated and considered himself about that time a leetle greater man than Governor Nye. This, we presume, will settle affairs in that quarter for at least six months and perhaps a year.[14]

Despite the attentive niceties of this ceremonial occasion the plight of the Numa continued to deteriorate. The general attitude of the whites toward the Indians was to "keep them on the reservations and let them take care of themselves," but various efforts were already underway to decrease the size of their reserve. The new Paiute agent, Jacob T. Lockhart, expressed the fear that the territorial legislature's grant of a franchise for a toll road across the southern end of the Pyramid Lake Reservation would introduce hotels and whiskey shops to a population that had not yet been greatly harmed by the evils of white society. The *Carson City Silver Age* quoted him as saying that the toll road was a beginning attempt to get the reservation abolished.[15]

Paiutes who wished to pursue their traditional roaming existence off the reservation were considered to be showing "unrest." The bands had to be careful about their movements. Changing campgrounds or kindling large fires at night caused wary settlers to believe that the Indians were getting ready for an uprising. The cavalry from Fort Churchill with Captain Almond B. Wells in charge moved through the country, reminding the Numa of their presence. Young Winnemucca spoke to the citizens of Como,[16] a community in the vicinity of Captain Truckee's grave, protesting the destruction of the pine-nut trees. He said that they were welcome to fallen or dead timber, but he would not permit the cutting of the living trees, which provided food for his people. The trees were cut down anyway.

In the spring of 1863 new gold and silver mines opened in southern Idaho. Agent John C. Burche, who lived in the Big Meadows on the Humboldt requested that Old Winnemucca go to the Bannock chief Pas-sé-quah in Idaho and ask that prospectors from California receive safe passage as they moved through his land. Winnemucca agreed to the proposal, and his son Natchez accompanied the old man to act as interpreter. Sometime later Burche received a telegram:

We are here one hundred miles from Star City and all is peace and quiet. I have been to see the Bannock Chief, Paseco; and all is right. If the whites wish to prospect through the country there is no danger from the Piutes or Bannocks; for there is an agreement with those tribes to that effect, and I am going north for the purpose of seeing that there is a perfect understanding with all the surrounding tribes.

The Young War Chief is within one day's ride of this place, and I am going to see him in a few days. He is not out on the Salt Lake Road fighting as was reported. . . .

Yours respectfully,
Winnemuc, Indian Chief
Per Natchez, Interpreter[17]

Old Winnemucca received a Spanish sombrero, a red silk sash, and a few blankets for his efforts as roving ambassador. Agent Burche on the Humboldt understood that the Indians needed food, not pretty dainties for their leaders. He wrote Governor Nye that, if he could not distribute supplies to the hungry Paiutes, whose traditional foods were disappearing, he could not guarantee future peace.[18]

Meanwhile Sarah and her father, confronted with the same facts, helped develop a plan that, they were determined, would save the Numa.

4

On Stage

It seems paradoxical that Old Winnemucca, who had shunned white society and searched for new hunting grounds in which to keep the traditional Paiute way of life, was the same person who enjoyed leading the ceremonies at Pyramid Lake at the time of Governor Nye's first visit. But there was pomp and circumstance in his nature, which Sarah understood. She once said, "The Indian is like my white brother, Emperor Norton: he likes epaulets."[1]

In 1864, Virginia City, Nevada, was a burgeoning town of 15,000 built atop the fabulous wealth of the Comstock mines. The city was completely overrunning the Johntown that Sarah had known when she went square dancing with the Ormsbys in her youth. Residents were familiar with the Paiutes, whose *nobees* were erected on the eastern fringes of the town, their frames covered with blankets, sacking, and sagebrush. When it was announced that Chief Winnemucca and his two pretty daughters were to appear on stage in a local theater, they were a major attraction. The performances were held at Sutcliff's Music Hall, where Max Walter, the manager, gave his seasoned advice to the inexperienced performers.[2] Jim Miller, a resident of the city, also took an interest in the proceedings. Sarah, with her quick ear for language probably helped with the dialogue.

Before performances Winnemucca appeared in the streets of Virginia City mounted upon a pony and surrounded by a cavalcade of his followers. He was described "as one used to authority and command, though the wrinkles in his full, heavy face showed the mark of age." On his head he wore a crown of feathers and on his shoulders brass epaulets. Two of his followers held a crescent above his head that was bound with red, white, and blue stripes. Elma sat behind him on his horse, and Sarah rode abreast on another pony.[3]

Before the first performance the old man addressed a large crowd who had assembled in front of the International Hotel to see them. Sarah interpreted for him in very good English, saying that her father and his tribe were friends of the white man. Winnemucca told how overtures had been made to him by the tribes on the plains to join them in their war against the whites. He had refused to do so. Though he and his tribe were poor, they would not fight against the palefaces. After his talk, hats were passed through the crowd, and a sum of money collected and given to him. The procession then turned and rode down B Street, as Winnemucca waved his hand to the people on the boardwalks, who were craning their necks for a better look at the Indians.[4]

A reporter interviewed Sarah later. She told him that the chiefs of some hostile tribes had endeavored to enlist Winnemucca in their cause, but that her father had said there was fighting enough in the country (the American Civil War) without the Indians adding to it, and he had refused. Sarah also reported that the hostile chiefs had told him to go to his friends the whites, because, if he or any of his tribe crossed a certain boundary line, they would kill them. "WINNEMUCCA WARNS THE WHITES AGAINST THE APPROACH OF THE HOSTILES,"[5] read the newspaper headlines.

The Bannocks were probably "the plains tribe" that had offered to join with the Paiutes in battle against the whites, despite the treaty that Burche had made with Pas-sé-quah. The agent recognized that the Bannocks were much more aggressive than the Paiutes or Shoshonis and that they were rich in ponies and weapons. Winnemucca tried to use this information to the advantage of the Paiutes by representing his tribe as the allies of the whites. Captain Truckee had followed a similar course, teaching his people to sing "The Star Spangled Banner" and to salute the flag. Nevertheless, when Sarah praised her father as a chief loyal

Virginia City, Nevada, a few years after Sarah Winnemucca's stage debut in 1864. Maguire's Opera House is in the background. (Courtesy of Nevada Historical Society.)

to the whites' interests, her advocacy, exaggerated or not, was met with indifference.

After their stage experience in Virginia City the performers moved on to San Francisco. Miller still backed the Paiutes' enterprise. On October 22 a San Franciscan might have noticed this unusual item in the amusement section of the *Daily Alta California*:

METROPOLITAN THEATRE

Unique Attraction
For Saturday Afternoon and Evening, Oct. 22
The Citizens of San Francisco are respectfully informed that:

Winnemucca
The Chief of the Piutes
Accompanied by his
Two daughters and eight braves
Now on their way to Washington, will at the request of numerous
citizens appear in a series of
Tableaux Vivants
Illustrative of Indian Life
A Descriptive Lecture and Appropriate Music
will accompany this romantic entertainment

Prices of Admission
Orchestra and Dress Circle $1.00
Parquette 50 cts. Gallery 25 cts.[6]

"Romantic entertainment" was a good description of what followed on the stage in the Metropolitan, which was the most popular theater in San Francisco. The program bore little relationship to the true life of the Paiutes, but it did fulfill the public's notion of a good stage show, such as they might expect from an Indian troupe.

Before the performance Winnemucca, Sarah, Elma, and six warriors rode in open carriages through the crowds near the theater on Montgomery Street.[7] The warriors were painted with ochre and vermilion, and all of the party wore buckskins and bright-colored feather headdresses that the *San Francisco Daily Alta California* claimed resembled enormous mops more than anything else. The latter description makes it appear that the men wore California rather than Plains Indian headdresses.

On the next morning reporters had a heyday reviewing the entertainment. They made slurring remarks about Indians in general and these Paiutes in particular, ridiculing their costumes and their names on the program:

> The Royal Family were introduced to the audience by a gentleman in black . . . as Winnemucca, Chief of the Piutes, and his two daughters. Royal Family bowed. The audience returned a rapturous greeting. Warriors to the right and left of us also presented. The eight arose from their seats as one man, made a mechanical, half-military salute, half-Oriental salaam, and subsided. The gentleman in black then read a lecture on Piutes "and any other Indians," which sounded in its delivery like a school boy's production and spoke of pale faces, red men, tented plains, warriors with a hundred wounds, etc.

Metropolitan Theatre, circa 1865, the location of Sarah's first performances in San Francisco. (Courtesy of California Historical Society, San Francisco.)

It was intended, however, to be highly eulogistic of the Great Chief. . . . The lecture finally came to an end, and after an intermission . . . the tableau vivante, with the accompaniment of forest scenery and Greek fire, were introduced in the following order: "The Indian Camp," "The Message of War," "The War Council," "The War Dance," "The Capture of a Bannock Spy," "Scalping the Prisoner," "Grand Scalp Dance," "Scalping of an Emmigrant Girl by a Bannock Scout," "The Wounded Warrior," "The Coyote Dance," and a series of five tableaux's representing Pocahontas saving the life of Captain John Smith. One of the "Flowers" acted the part of the famous Indian Maiden, and old Winnemucca the hard-hearted old parent, Powhatan. A white man in the costume of an "honest miner" did the John Smith. . . . Some of the tableaux were very good, the Indians seeming to possess the power to maintain an inanimate position as if carved of bronze. . . . Of the dances the Coyote was the best and was decidedly the favorite with the youngsters, especially when the "Flower" . . . got a back fall by pulling too hard on the tail of the Coyote.

The crowning feature of this unique entertainment was the address in the Pi-Ute dialect, by Winnemucca, and interpreted by one of his daughters. The old fellow came forward to the front of the stage, supported by the two daughters, Shell and Lattice, and with a self-possession and assurance that would do honor to a Copperhead stump speaker, spoke as follows:

> Rub-a-dub, dub! Ho-daddy, hi-daddy; wo-hup, gee-haw
> Fetch water, fetch water, Manayunk!

That's about as near as we could catch the words as they fell, and they were taken up and rendered by the Shell, in very good English thus:

"My father says he is very glad to see you. He has heard a great deal about San Francisco, and wanted very much to see it; so he has come to see it for himself!"

His part of the speech being loudly applauded by the appreciative audience, the old fellow became inspired and rattled off at such a telegraphic rate that we couldn't come up with him at all. Not so with Shell Flower: she had been there and knew just what to say, and it came to us in her sweet English voice to this effect, "My father says he is glad to see so many of you here, and he hopes there will be a great many more tonight when he hopes to accomodate you—I mean please you better." The curtain fell amidst the most rapturous applause from the ladies, and the Pi-Ute war whoop from the boys. The aboriginal entertainment was over. People like novelty, let them have it. Opera and minstrelsy will pall after a season or two, and if we do go now and then to see an aboriginal entertainment or a Chinese theatrical troupe, whose business is it? we would like to know.[8]

A woman, who had been a settler on the Carson River in 1853 and knew the Winnemuccas well, wrote an anonymous letter to the editor while the Paiutes were performing before the gaslights at the Metropolitan:

I did wonder, when I saw the accounts in the newspapers of the city, that Winnemucca—his daughters and braves, were exhibiting pantomimic scenes of Indian Life, if it could be the veritable Old Chief who was stooping from his dignity to become a common actor, for a "star" I knew he could never be, try however much he would. But now the secret is out. In passing down Kearny street, I met three Indians, who I knew belonged to the Piute tribe and Winnemucca family. . . . I concluded to go into the hotel and see the Chief, whom I had not seen since the Indian war of 1860. Glad was the old man to see me, and the young squaws, both of whom recognised me on the moment.

Well, as soon as I could hear myself speak, (for their chatter was not unlike that of a flock of magpies in spring time) I asked the chief why he had taken the white man's ways to show himself? Then came the story of his people's poverty, their suffering for food, and the cause of the distress now upon them. For this reason he had condescended to make a show of their habits, their pastimes, and among them, their time honored dances: and his object in so doing is to raise money to buy food and blankets for his people. But he sees, even now, that these exhibitions will not accomplish the great object he has at heart. . . .

The fact is that Winnemucca's tribe is starving because of our usurping of their right, and because, of the Chief's kindly feeling toward us. He has firmly refused all offers of assistance for himself and people, tendered as a bribe by numerous tribes more fortunately located, and richer in horses and all else that the Indian prizes. . . .

People of California! People of Nevada! You are those for whom this old chief refused all that would have made his people comfortable. . . . Now will you turn him away empty—tell him to go to his children without bread? . . . I have been acquainted with this aged chief and his family for more than 10 years, and I do not doubt in the least but in every respect his report is true. . . .

The 1st thing to be done is to rescue the Chief, his daughters and his native attenders from the present degrading exhibitions, and provide for their immediate wants. Afterwards such contributions in provisions and blankets should be furnished to his people over the mountains as may seem expedient to the enlightened charity of this community.[9]

We do not know if there was a concerted response to this appeal by a friend of the Paiutes, but it was a foregone conclusion that Winnemucca's debut on the San Francisco stage would produce little for them. The cost of theater rental, traveling expenses, hotel rooms and meals, promoter's cuts, and some minimal payment to the performers had to be deducted from the receipts. Winnemucca's first responsibility was to his own relatives and his band, and he can have done little more than help his needy people with a few sacks of flour and blankets. Still, it helped them to survive another winter.

When the Paiute troupe returned to their homeland, Nevada Territory had just been declared the thirty-sixth state in the union by President Abraham Lincoln. The wealth of Virginia City was needed to help finance the final days of the Civil War. Not much credence was given to Sarah's insistence, while she was in Virginia City, that her father was a friend of the whites and had turned down substantial offers from neighboring tribes who had asked him to participate in a general war. After all, Captain Wells from Fort Churchill was available to subdue the

Indians by the awe-inspiring presence of his cavalry. The four-year truce since the Pyramid Lake War perhaps could not be expected to last forever, but the following remark on Sarah's interview by a reporter in Virginia City reflected the attitude of many of the citizens, who felt secure because of the superior forces:

> While it is well enough to keep an eye open upon the movements of the savages there is no occasion for the slightest alarm. Two or three thousand men fully armed and equipped could be raised almost at a moment's warning in this city alone, and perhaps it would be a good thing in the end if the opportunity could be had to give these redskins a lesson that would last them for a generation or two.[10]

There was no inclination to be concerned about hungry Paiutes.

5
The Pyramid Lake Reservation

In the early spring of 1865, Sarah was in the Indian camp at Dayton, Nevada, when a company of cavalry came through town. The leader, Captain Wells, accused the Paiutes of stealing cattle at Harney Lake in Oregon, and he threatened to kill every Indian that came in sight of his company. He was also looking for the Paiutes who had killed two white miners on Walker River.[1]

Sarah was very frightened for her father's band and lived in dread of bad news in the days that followed. Soon after his appearance at Dayton, Captain Wells and his men moved north onto the Pyramid Lake Reservation. At three o'clock one morning they found an encampment of thirty people on Mud Lake[2] (sometimes called Winnemucca Lake), which is produced by the overflow from Pyramid Lake. The camp was made up of old men, women, and children; Winnemucca had all the young men with him at Carson Sink on a hunting excursion. The soldiers killed all the Numa but one, set the camp afire, and threw babies, still in their baskets, into the flames. Sarah wrote that she had a baby brother killed at this time, who must have been the child of a younger wife of Winnemucca's, as Tuboitonie would no longer have been of child-bearing age. Mary, Sarah's oldest sister, jumped on Winnemucca's best horse and, though the soldiers chased her, made her escape.[3]

During this terrible winter of famine, cold, and unexpected

deaths, Mary and Tuboitonie both died. It is not certain whether they lost their lives as a result of the Mud Lake massacre. Two newspaper articles of the time indicate that both of Old Winnemucca's wives were among those killed:

CAPTAIN WELL'S INDIAN FIGHT

Mr. Gilson, Indian Agent, called at this office yesterday, and in course of conversation admitted that the two wives of Old Winnemucca were killed in the late fight of Captain Wells. He thinks they were killed in this desperate "hand to hand fight" at a distance of half a mile. Captain Wells says nothing in his official report about the slaughter of these women. Mr. Gilson also states that a party of Indians were sent out to bury the dead, and found 29 bodies. No white man has been on the ground he says since the fight.[4]

Another newspaper reported: "Young Winnemucca says Captain Wells did not kill Smoke Creek Indians but says they were some of his people—mostly women and children. It is ascertained on corroborative evidence that the two wives of Old Winnemucca were slain in this 'stubborn and sanguinary' battle, where the killing was all on one side."[5]

The Paiutes at Walker River delivered to Captain Wells two Indians who were supposed to be guilty of killing the miners, but the captain was not satisfied. There were rumors that the Indians in the Humboldt River country were threatening the settlements there, and he led his dragoons to "pacify" that area.[6] On May 20, with thirty-six men, Wells fought five hundred Paiutes, Bannocks, and Shoshonis, according to his report. The cavalry lost two men killed and four wounded. One of the soldiers who fought in the battle probably portrayed the number of Indians present more accurately: "They must have had fifty or sixty guns, perhaps a great many more; they used no bows or arrows."[7]

In the Paradise Valley, north of Winnemucca, the citizens were concerned about the Indian scare. They slept together in one cabin at night for protection, and, thinking that they had evidence of the presence of hostile Indians, one man decided to get military assistance. He happened onto the temporary camp of Colonel Charles McDermit, who sent some of his Nevada Volunteers to the settlers' aid. A group of the volunteers met a body of Indians in the valley, and, though the Indians raised a white flag, the commander concluded that they were not friendly. The sergeant ordered a charge, and in the battle that followed twenty-three Indians died. Five of them had taken cover in a house that caught fire; they were shot to death when they ran from the burning building. One citizen and one soldier were killed in the battle, and several whites were wounded.[8] Soon after, Colonel McDermit, who was in command of the Department of Nevada, was shot in ambush, presumably by an Indian, near Quin's River Station (which later became Fort McDermit).[9]

The Indian difficulties on the Humboldt River and northward to the Quinn, or Queen's, River halted a stagecoach line that some private companies had organized to service the new mines that were expanding in southern Idaho. As stations were destroyed, stock run off, and whites murdered, a war of extermination began. One writer of the time said, "I have seen many Indians by the wayside, where they fell by the unerring bullets of the Henry rifles in the hands of citizens."[10] Most of the depredations that were committed in the Paradise and Quinn River valleys and along the Oregon-Idaho border were executed by Black Rock Tom and his Smoke Creek band of Paiutes, joined by some Shoshonis and Bannocks.[11]

The continuing destitution of the Paiutes, the breakdown of peaceful relations with the whites, and above all the untimely deaths of Sarah's sister, mother, and little brother caused Sarah to remove herself at this time as far as possible from white society. Her recourse was to return to the Pyramid Lake Reservation and find a home there with her brother Natchez and his family.[12]

During the winter of 1865–66, Sarah and Natchez heard of the battles in the north and the decimation of the Numa. Their father had sent word after the deaths of his relatives at Mud Lake that he was taking the remainder of his band into the mountains, where he planned to stay for the rest of his life.[13] Sarah was fearful that the band would be surprised by the cavalry and forced into a battle, in which the Indians would be no match for the dragoons in the deep snow. When they were cornered, the Paiute women fought alongside the men. The soldiers seldom took captives. Instead they would leave the women and children to fend for themselves in the bitter cold, or occasionally they shot them down too.

The *Humboldt Register* described such a battle in January, 1866:

Life on the reservations was always difficult for the Paiutes. Here women and children pose in front of a summer shelter. (Courtesy of Special Collections, University of Nevada, Reno.)

At the close of the battle 35 dead Indians lay on the field with their bows and quivers still clutched in their hands. All were large, powerful men—a picked company of braves, prepared for battle. But 5 squaws were in the band, and they were acting in capacity of pack train. Two of these were killed in battle by mistake; the other three were furnished with some provisions and left unmolested.

Scouting parties made the entire circuit of the field and found that no living thing had escaped, as the snow was 3 inches deep and there were no tracks leading from the camp."[14]

In March the same newspaper described another battle:

At half past nine the order was given to charge. Right merrily the men obeyed. The Indians stood up bravely, fighting sullenly to the last—asking no quarter; but the charge was irresistible. The boys rode through the Indian ranks, scattering and shooting down everything that wore paint. At length the Indians sought shelter under a bluff of rocks. . . . Loss of the enemy, 80 warriors and 35 squaws. The latter were dressed the same as the bucks, and were fighting—and had to be killed to ascertain their sex. . . ."[15]

Captain Sou had been the leader of the raid on Williams Station that triggered the Pyramid Lake War,[16] but now he was working for the soldiers. He led many forays against his brother Paiutes, for which he was acclaimed as "the New Winnemucca" by the whites on the Humboldt River, who signed a petition on his behalf. His actions ensured the safety of his own band at the expense of other Paiutes.

The Humboldt River citizens' petition was published in the *Humboldt Register* on May 5, 1867:

> Whereas, It having been satisfactorily proven that Old Winnemucca, the late Chief of the Piutes, has turned traitor to his tribe, deserted his Country and joined the hostile Indians of the North, and is now instigating and inciting said Indians to continue the war, for the avowed purpose of exterminating the whites and their allies, the friendly Indians; and Whereas Captain Sou has often attested his fidelity to his white brethren on the battle field, and has always been a devoted friend to peace and progress; and Whereas Every inhabitant of the State of Nevada manifestly has an interest in who shall govern and advise the Piute Nation: now, therefore, in order to secure a Chief faithful to the white inhabitants, and to prevent further hostilities in our midst.
>
> Be it resolved, By the citizens of the State of Nevada (the friendly Piutes concurring), that Captain Sou be nominated and chosen Chief of the friendly Piutes to be known by the title of "Winnemucca", and to have supreme command of the Piute Nation; and that we the undersigned citizens of Nevada, and good Piutes, will sustain Sou in that exhalted position which he is by nature so well fitted to adorn.
>
> (Numerously signed, and done up fantastically with the seals of the county (Humboldt) office.)[17]

The citizens' attitude toward Old Winnemucca was especially undeserved, as he had never harmed a white man, nor had he directed his people to do so, except perhaps at the time of the Pyramid Lake War. He had suffered great personal losses from actions led by the military and by white citizens while still keeping the peace.

Captain Sou made a speech to his people in which he argued that the whites were a friendly people, that they killed coyotes but did not eat many rabbits, that they discarded good clothing and threw out much good food, and, best of all, they kept away mean Indians. The whites, he concluded, had become a necessity to the "good" Indians who collaborated with them, and they should be encouraged to remain.[18]

This was a dark time in Sarah's life. She was not only hungry, for there was little to eat at the Pyramid Lake Reservation, but also most of her family were dead or gone. With regard to bands other than Captain Sou's, the "Humboldt code" had been adopted by the whites: "kill and lay waste everything pertaining to the tribes, whenever found—no trials, but at arms; no prisoners; no red tape."[19] Chief Winnemucca was hiding with his small band in the mountains of southeastern Oregon. Even Sarah's sister Elma was gone, for she had been adopted by a French family in Marysville, California.[20] Soon this younger sister would marry a white man, John Smith, with whom she would make her home first in Montana and then in Idaho, never to return to the Indian life. Natchez's main concern at this time was hunting and working to keep his young family alive through the harsh winter. His wife sometimes went to the house of the local subagent, Hugh Nugent, to wash clothes and clean house. She was paid in flour, which helped supplement the rabbits and fish that Natchez could bring in.[21]

There were about 600 Paiutes living on the Pyramid Lake Reservation at this time, including 250 Quinn River Indians who had been brought in by military authorities after their surrender on the Oregon border. All the Paiutes on the reserve were near starvation. Agent H. G. Parker in Carson City complained that because of bad weather he could not get goods distributed to the Indians at Pyramid Lake. Yet in February calico and blankets were provided for Captain Sou's band at the Big Meadows on Humboldt River in payment for some Paiute scalps that Sou had helped deliver.[22]

When spring came, the white men's cattle were herded in droves onto the reservation without any benefit to the Indians. A promised sawmill to produce lumber for houses did not materialize. Natchez and Sarah became convinced that life on the reservation did not hold promise. A ten-mile strip along the Truckee River had been removed from the reservation for the new railroad, and efforts were underway to reduce the reservation still further.

The 22,000 acres of land set aside for the needs of the Paiutes had been known as the United States Timber Reserve. Several entangling agreements had been made by the Interior Department with white lumbermen concerning the property.[23] The sawmill had been sold, along with all cut logs and lumber, on May 27, 1865, for $30,000, which was to have been paid to the Indians in lumber.[24] The lumber was never received.[25] Subsequently, the Central Pacific Railroad ran through the timber reserve and claimed alternate sections, and in 1867 the Nevada legislature passed a resolution that the United States Congress set aside the remainder for school lands for the state of Nevada.[26] Warren Wasson reported at the time that the timber reserve was worth over $100,000,[27] but the legislature decided that it was worthless to the Indians because they would never live on it. White settlers persisted in staying along the Truckee River on the most fertile reservation land despite their promise to Governor Nye in 1862 to quit the area. One might ask why the Paiutes did not force the squatters off the land that rightfully belonged to them, but they knew full well that, if they did so, they would pay with their lives.

The situation was very tense. A Paiute was shot and killed by one of the agent's men for possessing gunpowder (which had been purchased from the subagent, Nugent). Sarah's people were very angry. The relatives of the young man threatened to kill Nugent for his wrongdoing. Sarah and Natchez understood the peril that the band faced: if the subagent was harmed, there would be nothing to keep the soldiers from wiping out all the Paiutes on the reservation, for they needed little excuse.

Sarah tells us that she and Natchez saddled their horses and rode from the Paiute encampment to Nugent's house, crossing the Truckee River, which was swollen from spring storms. As her horse climbed the steep bank on the opposite side of the stream, Sarah fell into the swirling water, but Natchez jumped from his horse and pulled her to safety. She mounted again, and they hurried to Nugent's house, where they warned the subagent that some of their people were threatening to kill him and that he should leave at once.

Nugent did not care to listen to advice and instead told his men to get their guns ready. "We will show the damned red devils how to fight," he yelled. Natchez and Sarah pleaded with him, but he told them vehemently to go away. When the two returned to camp, Natchez called a council. He told the people that ten young men must guard the river crossing to Nugent's house, and, if any of the Paiutes tried to cross the river, they must try to catch them. He admonished, "If there is more than one kill them if you can; by so doing we will save ourselves, for you know if we allowed our people to kill the white men we should all be killed here."[28]

Later that night Natchez called the people together again. He looked very troubled as he told them that he had had a dream. In it the warriors who were coming to kill Nugent had instead killed two white men at the Wells and stolen many horses. The Wells was a whiskey shop about thirty miles from the reservation on the way to Virginia City. No one doubted Natchez's dream. Sometime later a runner came in and confirmed Natchez's vision. The messenger also brought the awesome news that Nugent had gone to the soldiers at Fort Churchill and would probably return with them ready for battle.[29]

While Natchez took thirty of his men toward the Wells, in hopes that they could intercept the killers, the subchief sent out scouts so that the Paiutes would be aware of the approach of the soldiers. Meanwhile, the men in camp prepared to fight. Late in the night two Paiutes brought a written message to Sarah from Fort Churchill:

Miss Sarah Winnemucca,—Your agent tells us very bad things about your people's killing two of our men. I want you and your brother Natchez to meet me at your place to-night. I want to talk to you and your brother.

Captain Jerome
Company M., 8th Cavalry.[30]

When Sarah had deciphered the writing she did not know what to do, as Natchez had not returned. The Paiutes urged her to talk to the soldiers "on paper," but there was nothing to write upon and no pen and ink. Finally she resorted to using a sharp stick dipped in fish blood, writing on the back of the original message:

Hon. Sir.—My brother is not here. I am looking for him every minute.

We will go as soon as he comes in. If he comes to-night, we will come some time during the night.

Yours,
S. W.[31]

The messenger had not been gone long before Natchez arrived with his men who had found many horse tracks near the Wells. Sarah told him that they must go speak to the captain. Natchez ordered two fresh horses, and the two of them rode with twenty men to the soldiers' camp, rushing "like the wind" through the dark night as Sarah reported later. When they arrived, Captain A. B. Jerome and a few of his men stepped away from the fire to meet them. He listened attentively while Sarah recounted the full story of how Nugent himself had sold the powder and how the subagent's own man had then killed the Indian possessing it. She explained how she and Natchez had begged Nugent to leave and that he had refused, talking to them in an insulting manner. The agent stood beside the soldiers and heard what Sarah said without refuting her.[32]

Captain Jerome inquired of Natchez how many horses he thought the Paiutes had stolen. "Maybe sixty or more," he said, "judging from the tracks." The captain then asked them to stay the night, but, since Sarah was afraid to do so, they returned to the Paiute camp. They promised that they would have another talk on the next day.

The Numa did not sleep well that night with the soldiers so close by, though Natchez told them they were their friends and that there would have been many more if they had planned to attack.[33] In the morning the Paiutes waited with apprehension as they watched the cavalry ride slowly to the camp and dismount. After blankets had been laid on the damp sand, another council was held. Captain Jerome told the Indians not to be afraid, that if they wanted more protection he would send for his company from Fort Churchill. Sarah and Natchez promptly told him that their people's biggest fear was the soldiers and not to send for more troops.[34]

When the captain investigated the condition of the Paiutes, he saw they had nothing to eat, though the Indians were waiting expectantly for the *cui-ui* fish *(Chasmistes cujus)* to come up the Truckee River to spawn. Jerome was determined to do something about this situation, and two days later the band received word that he was sending three wagonloads of provisions. While the flour and beef were distributed, Agent Nugent came around and offered to sell some cattle to add to the issue. The captain angrily told him to "be off."[35]

Sarah writes that while the Paiutes on the reservation were still enjoying the bounty from the soldiers, five dragoons came from Fort Churchill with a message from Captain Jerome. He asked for Natchez and Sarah and told them that he had received a letter from his commanding officer inquiring after the whereabouts of Chief Winnemucca. Sarah could not hold back her tears. She described her reply in her autobiography:

> I told him father had not been in since the soldiers killed my little brother. I told him that he sent word to us some six months ago that he had gone to live in the mountains, and to die there. I was crying all the while I was talking to him. My people were frightened; they did not know what I was saying. Our men gathered all round us. They asked brother what was the matter. He told them what the officer said to me.[36]

Jerome told Sarah that his commanding officer, Capt. Dudley Seward of the Eighth Cavalry, wanted her and Natchez to go to Camp McDermit, where they could scout for Winnemucca and his band and bring them in. He said that the band would be fed and well treated, but Natchez and Sarah were dubious of the offer. When they consulted with the Pyramid Lake Paiutes, many said that the soldiers might kill Chief Winnemucca: "You and your sister know what liars the white people are. . . . His blood will be on you." Natchez said, "I believe what the officers say, and if father comes in they will take good care of us." They replied, "Well, it is your father, and you two know best what to do. If anything happens to him you will have no one to blame but yourselves."[37]

More serious trouble with the whites was to come before Sarah and Natchez would contact their father. A brother of Winnemucca's, Truckee John, had industriously started a farm at Pyramid Lake. He had built a cabin and fenced land, where he raised horses, grass, and grain with the help of an irrigation ditch that he had dug. On July 7, 1867, he was murdered by a white man, named Alexander Fleming. The excuse that Fleming gave was that he had recognized John as the Paiute who had killed his brother during the Pyramid Lake War.[38]

On the following day two Paiutes were shot and badly wounded on the road ten miles east of Virginia City. The settlers, fearful of Paiute retribution, left their farms on the Truckee River and assembled for defensive purposes. Franklin Campbell, a farmer on the Walker River Reservation, talked to the Paiutes and found that they had no intention of retaliating, but were worried that the whites would continue the violence.[39] As was the custom, the widow of Truckee John burned her house.

Young Winnemucca, wishing to hunt off the reservation, had used sensible caution. He stationed fifteen of his men on their ponies outside of the town of Susanville, in eastern California, before riding into town to show the hunting permit that he had received from Agent Parker. He was met by mounted citizens with Henry rifles, who chased his Paiute escort away and threw him in the local calaboose for several hours.[40] From then on the young chief attempted to survive living on the reservation.

6

Camp McDermit

When Sarah and Natchez accepted Captain Jerome's invitation to Camp McDermit it was in the heat of the summer of 1868. After an arduous journey to the Oregon border, the accompanying soldiers took them to Captain Dudley Seward, who advised them to bring in their father before Old Winnemucca's band was waylaid by General George Crook.[1] When Crook had taken command of the Department of the Columbia in 1867, his method of combating the numerous small bands of Northern Paiutes had been to establish Camp Harney in south-central Oregon at the center of their stronghold. Most of the Indians had been starved out or exterminated. When they did surrender, it was only after they had been reduced to eating their horses.[2]

By the summer of 1868 most of the bands had been accounted for to the army's satisfaction, but Winnemucca had not yet come in. Sarah explained to Seward that her father had wanted nothing to do with the whites since the Mud Lake massacre. The captain was sympathetic but firm. He advised Natchez to go with a company of cavalry to find his father. He would be paid five dollars a day while doing so. Sarah would remain at Camp McDermit as an interpreter and was offered sixty-five dollars per month for the position.[3]

The Quinn River Paiutes were already in the camp. When

Sarah and Natchez found that they were well treated, clothed, and fed, Natchez was willing to go for Old Winnemucca. He did not take the dragoons with him, however, for he was afraid his people would believe that the soldiers had come to fight them. He took only five Quinn River Indians who would testify to the kindness of the soldiers at the camp. He held a letter from Captain Seward for safe passage among the whites.

Natchez had left with the understanding that his sister would stay with the Quinn River women in the Indian camp. Sarah had many misgivings about finding herself in that situation. It had been years since she had seen many of the so-called "wild Indians," and now she was expected to live with the Quinn River women, who knew only a primitive life. Fortunately, they were very solicitous of her. Of necessity she requested that the commanding officer make the Indian camp off limits to the soldiers, and, when he complied, she rested much easier during Natchez's absence.[4]

Early in July, Old Winnemucca and 490 other Paiutes came into Camp McDermit, guided by Natchez.[5] The men, dressed in tattered clothing, were followed by groups of exhausted women, who were burdened with the baskets that held their few possessions. A scattering of almost naked children came with them. Old Winnemucca met his daughter with open arms. There were no words for those who were gone; one did not speak of the dead.

The soldiers found warm clothing for the men from their own issues, and the people were highly pleased, even though the blue uniforms did not fit properly. There was nothing with which to clothe the women and children, but Sarah suggested that, since the Paiutes were given ample food, they should sell some of it to the camp sutler. Thus they were able to buy yard goods and sewing notions to make their clothing.[6]

In council Old Winnemucca told the people that the band should continue to find their own food. In the summer there would still be deer and rabbit, and the women should continue in the old way to dig roots and gather seed. He was rightly concerned that the Numa would become dependent. Brevet Lieutenant Colonel James N. McElroy, who was in charge of the Paiutes at Camp McDermit, agreed to Winnemucca's request that the men be allowed to hunt and arranged for them to purchase ammunition at the sutler's store.[7]

Fort McDermit, in 1887, with snow on the hills. The long building on the left was the horse barn. The two-story structure on the right in the background was the hospital where Sarah served as matron for a time. (Courtesy of Nevada Historical Society.)

Both Sarah and Natchez were employed as scouts to bring other wandering bands to Camp Harney, Camp Smith, and Camp McDermit. This created enmity among certain segments of the Paiute population, who believed that the Winnemuccas exposed their people to surprise attacks.[8] Meanwhile, the army was criticized by some white citizens for harboring and feeding the Paiutes, who they felt should have been killed outright.

Sarah was asked to bring to Camp McDermit the bands who had surrendered at Camp Smith. At the time Colonel McElroy offered her several companies of soldiers, but, according to her account, Sarah took only her half brother Lee, who was also working as a scout, to accompany her. She and Lee found the starving bands collected at Camp Smith, and after parley they agreed to removal to Camp McDermit. Sarah sent for fifteen wagons to transport the children, and they were furnished rations for the two-day journey, which was made without incident.[9] Over eight hundred Paiutes were given issues every day at McDermit. Each family was furnished a canvas tent. The women lined up in the morning to receive their family's rations, and Sarah helped with the distribution.

General Crook claimed to have made peace with all the hostile Indians from the Humboldt River on the south to Fort Hall on the north.[10] He selected We-ah-wee-wah, a leader from the Malheur Lake area of central Oregon, as the principal chief. Since Paulina, the notorious leader of many fights against emigrant trains in Idaho, had been killed, his band was led by Ocheo.[11] In December, 1868, a peace treaty was negotiated with the Paiutes near Fort Harney by Superintendent J. W. Huntington. Though it was never ratified by the Senate,[12] Crook let most of the Indians return to their old places.

While the surviving Paiutes around Camp McDermit were encouraged to come into the military post for safety and sustenance, the Paiutes in Nevada at Pyramid Lake became increasingly dissatisfied, and many left the reservation. An epidemic of measles from infected cast-off clothing hit those who remained. The agent did nothing for these sick Indians and even refused to reimburse an army doctor who out of humanity had brought vaccine to the reservation. More than one hundred individuals died on the Pyramid Lake Reservation,[13] and about the same number died at the Walker River reserve from ague, typhoid fever, and consumption.[14]

Meanwhile Agent Parker at Pyramid Lake reported to his superior in Washington that the Indians "were never so happy, or so well provided for."[15] In reality, no produce had been raised on either reservation, so that there was no food available except from hunting and seasonal fishing. Later an epidemic of smallpox decimated the Indians who were living nearer civilization on the Humboldt.[16]

The Paiutes were greatly affected too by the new steam locomotives that crossed the iron bridge over the Truckee River into the growing town of Wadsworth, which was flourishing on productive land that formerly had been part of the reservation. Wadsworth was a typical railroad town with saloons and gambling halls. Its presence was felt by the Paiutes, whom a white neighbor had described only a few years earlier, in 1864, as follows: "As yet they [the Paiutes] have resisted the baneful influence of intoxicating drinks and have preserved with great tenacity the native virtue of their women."[17] Some Indians worked on the railroad. They were hired en masse, along with the Chinese, by Charles Crocker, who, it was said, never paid names and faces, but only counted numbers at the beginning and end of a day's work. Indian *nobees* were a permanent part of the landscape on the fringes of Wadsworth.

Paiutes could apply for free passage on the tracks, and whole bands might climb aboard empty flatbed cars. Thus ponies were no longer a necessity for the Humboldt River Indians in their wanderings. Women and young girls could sell their baskets and beadwork to gawking tourists along the railroad, and the men transported fish and game from Pyramid Lake to Lovelock or Winnemucca for the best market. For the Paiutes who were close to civilization, subsistence of a kind was available in the towns, though certainly not on the reservations.

In the fall of 1869, Major Henry Douglass was assigned as Indian superintendent to Nevada, under a policy of President Ulysses S. Grant that replaced civil agents with army officers after the Civil War.[18] Douglass was of a different stripe from his predecessor, Parker; for a true interest in the welfare of the Paiutes emanated from his agency office in Carson City. To the

A Northern Paiute family in Wadsworth, Nevada. (Courtesy of Nevada Historical Society.)

satisfaction of Young Winnemucca and his followers, the major ousted all the white fishermen from Pyramid Lake. Until then the Indians had been compelled to fish from boats while the nets of the white intruders had extended across the Truckee River in at least twenty places. Most important, Douglass learned after a council with the Paiutes of Young Winnemucca's band that they would agree to remain at the Pyramid Lake Reservation if they were assigned individual farms, and if they could expect protection from intruders while receiving guidance in learning to plant and harvest.

In his pursuit of the Paiute point of view Douglass wrote to the commanding officer at Camp McDermit. Colonel McElroy in turn laid Douglass's questions before his Paiute interpreter, Sarah Winnemucca. She wrote Douglass on April 4, 1870, and he was so happily impressed with her letter that he sent it on to E. S. Parker, the commissioner of Indian affairs in Washington. Sarah was very critical of the reservation system: "If this is the kind of civilization awaiting us on the Reserves, God grant that we may never be compelled to go on one, as it is much prefferable [*sic*] to live in the mountains and drag out an existence in our native manner." She did, however, write:

On the other hand, if the Indians have any guarantee that they can secure a permanent home on their own native soil, and that our white neighbours can be kept from encroaching on our rights, after having a reasonable share of ground allotted to us as our own, and giving us the required advantages of learning &eo, and I warrant that the savage (as he is called to-day) will be a thrifty and Law abiding member of the community fifteen or twenty years hence.[19]

The letter supported Douglass's plans to bring the wandering bands onto the reservation to work in agricultural pursuits and establish permanent homes where they could sustain themselves. The major wished to stem the tide of the white citizens who said that the reservations should be opened for settlement since the Paiutes did not live on their lands year-around or cultivate them. The letter was shown around in Washington circles, and in May, 1870, an article on Sarah appeared in *Harper's Weekly*.[20] Her letter was paraphrased in the article, and it was suggested that she should be given serious consideration: "If it should turn out there is no Sarah Winnemucca, and that no such letter was ever written, its statements will still remain as the plea and protest of thousands of the Indians." Later Sarah's entire letter was published in a popular book that received wide circulation, Helen Hunt Jackson's *A Century of Dishonor*.[21]

A Boise, Idaho, editor did not react favorably to the publicity that Sarah was receiving:

Miss Sarah, says Harper's Weekly, "has written(?) a very sagacious letter to Indian Comm. Parker, in which she has eloquently portrayed the wrongs of her race." What infernal noodles some of these Eastern people are. If we are not very much mistaken we had the pleasure of seeing some years ago, Miss S. at Camp McDermitt, Nev. She and a few other interesting relics of the "noble red man" were being fatted at the fort during that winter for the spring campaign against Idaho emigrants. The emigration having stopped for the season "there were no other worlds to conquer," so Sarah and her tribe were about to fare badly, as the supply of dried scalps, grasshoppers and lice had been exhausted. Their condition excited the sympathy of Uncle Sam's boys at the Fort, so they were taken in and cared for until spring when they resumed their favorite pasttime of stealing and murdering. But it is our recollections of Miss Sarah we propose to recite. Sarah was at that time sweet 16 or 20—it would be difficult to judge of her exact age from her appearance owing to a careless habit she acquired of never washing her beautifully chiselled features.

The article continued in the same vein, describing Sarah as an ungroomed, tattered, hungry Paiute. It was a general vilification of her and her father, saying, for example: "Mr. Winnemucca, Chief of the Paiutes, whose gallant exploits in stealing horses and cutting the tongues out of defenseless emigrants will long be remembered by the people of Nevada and Southern Idaho with feelings of just pride and admiration." The following description of Sarah was typical of the piece: "Her raven tresses, which had been permitted to coy with the sportive breeze, unbound, unwashed and uncombed, from her earliest childhood, stood out in elegant and awry confusion from her classically shaped 'cabeza', which contributed to her contour an air of romantic splendour." The article was reprinted in the *Humboldt Register* on May 28, 1870.

Douglass accompanied Natchez to Camp McDermit to induce the Numa there to come to the reservation at Pyramid Lake. He looked forward to meeting Natchez's sister, about whom he was curious after their correspondence. Soon after the encounter with Sarah he wrote:

Some Eastern newspapers . . . have greatly exaggerated her attainments and virtues. She is not by any means the Goddess, which some of the Eastern people imagine her to be (judging from their love letters to her and erudite epistles on Indian affairs), neither is she "a low, dirty, commerce Indian," as the papers of this country describe her to be, in order to counter the Eastern romance. She is a plain Indian woman, passably good looking, with some education and possesses much natural shrewdness and intelligence. She converses well and seems select in the use of terms. She conforms readily to civilised customs, and will as readily join in an Indian dance.[22]

Agent Douglass spoke to the separate Paiute bands, trying to convince them to come to Pyramid Lake. His efforts were not successful, as they were content to remain in their own territories and afraid of encroaching on Young Winnemucca's established hunting grounds.[23] Also the Paiutes could not expect to find *better* conditions on the reservation. Its-a-ah'-mah, the leader of the Quinn River Indians, said:

I was taken to the reservation three years ago with 250 other Indians from here. We had nothing to live on. Measles got among us—many suffered and died. I would not now take what few Quinn River Indians [are left] from here to Pyramid Lake. . . . Here are plenty of Antelope, game, roots and everything to live on. . . . I will stay here and lay my bones here with my dead children.[24]

Douglass's plans for improvements on the reservations under his charge were beginning to get underway when, a few months after his trip to Camp McDermit, he was suddenly informed that the American Baptist Home Mission Society had been given the authority to staff his agency with their own people. In his final report he wrote of his accomplishments and listed some of the problems facing the new agent. He had never been supplied with a map of the Walker River Reservation showing its boundaries. Thus it was extremely difficult to keep out white squatters and fishermen. He also explained that the former subagent under Parker (Nugent) had rented the reserve to cattlemen for $1.00 per head and collected $15,000 for his own pocket. The major suggested that this money would have been better used by the Paiutes. In conclusion he wrote:

It was my purpose next summer had I continued on duty, to organise two schools, one on Truckee [Pyramid Lake] and one on Walker river reserve. . . . It was my intention to place the first school on Truckee river reserve, and employ "Sarah Winnemucca" as instructress; the good elementary English education she has received, and her knowledge of Indian language and character, would make her invaluable as an instructress.[25]

If future agents on the reservation had possessed the integrity and foresight of Major Douglass, much of the problems and heartaches experienced by Sarah and her people would not have come to pass.

7

Marriage and New Agents

In 1870 rumours circulated among the soldiers and Indians at Camp McDermit that the fort was to be closed. Because of the attention of the public to her first letter to Agent Douglass, Sarah decided to write another, this time directly to the commissioner of Indian affairs in Washington.[1] If the military post was vacated, she was fearful that the Paiute bands who were sheltered there would have difficulty in finding safety and sustenance. She exaggerated the Paiutes' warlike intentions in order to make her point:

It will be not only criminal in the authorities to remove the troops now, but it will be far more expensive to the government to restore order and quiet after the Indians have once broken out, and it does not require much provocation to make them do so. I know more about the feelings and prejudices of these Indians than any other Person connected with them & therefore I hope this petition will be received with favor. Sir I am the daughter of the Chief of the Piutes I am living at Camp McDermit and have been in this employ of the U.S. government for nearly three years as interpreter and guide I have the honor to be, Sir, your

most obedient servant
Sarah Winnemucca
Camp McDermit Nev.

PS please answer this short Epistle if you consider me worthy and I promise you that my next letters will be more lenghty [*sic*]. Direct to Camp McDermit Nev.

Sarah Winnemucca
August 9th 1870[2]

A few weeks later Sarah was found in the railroad town of Winnemucca by a correspondent from the Sacramento *Record*. The newspaperman interviewed her and found her to be a well-informed, wide-awake young woman

> . . . and I think the most handsome Piute of her sex that I ever saw. She conversed freely on the condition of her people and their future prospects. . . . She said: I am glad to see you, although I have not now a parlor to ask you into except the one made by nature for all. I like this Indian life tolerably well; however, my only object in staying with these people is that I may do them good. I would rather be with my people, but not to live with them as they live. I was not raised so; . . . my happiest life has been spent in Santa Clara while at school and living among the whites.[3]

During this interview Sarah asked that old school books be sent to her at Camp McDermit, as she and her father and brother were interested in starting a school there for the Paiute children.

Despite those remarks, Sarah's concern for the Paiutes, which all her life had overshadowed her destiny, was placed in the background at this time. She was now twenty-six, but, since she was a woman of two worlds, it had been doubly difficult to find a mate. While the Indian men did not share her experience or education, the whites were mostly repugnant to her, because she knew that she often represented an exotic, available woman to them. She was not available in that way, and she made that clear on several occasions that were reported by the press, as we shall see.

One newspaper writer stated that Sarah was married for a time to a German, named Snyder, who died on a visit back to his home country.[4] We know from Sarah's account that a white man named Snyder was a friend of Captain Truckee and present at his deathbed. In any case, this early marriage has not been confirmed, and Sarah did not mention it in interviews or in her autobiography.

Marriage entered Sarah's mind in 1870 because a man had stolen her heart: First Lieutenant Edward C. Bartlett, who was

more expensive to the government to restore order and quiet
after the Indians have once broken out. and it does not require
much provocation to make them do so. I know more about
the feeling and prejudices of these Indians than any other
Person connected with them & therefore I hope this petition
will be received with favor. Sir I am the daughter
of the Chief of the Piutes I am living at Camp
McDermit and have been in the employ of the U.S.
government for nearly three years as interpreter and
guide. I have the honor to be, Sir, your

most obident Servant
Sarah Winnemucca
Camp McDermit Nev

P S please answer this short Epistle
if you consider me worthy and
I promise you that my next letters
will be more lenghty Direct to
Camp McDermit Nev

Sarah Winnemucca
Aug 9th 1870

Excerpt from Sarah Winnemucca's letter to Commissioner of Indian Affairs E. S. Parker, who was himself of American Indian descent. (Courtesy of National Archives.)

a native of New York and a fine horseman. Bartlett had been attracted to Sarah from the first time he saw her. He liked her flashing eyes and quick temper and was drawn to a woman who could mount a horse gracefully and stay in the saddle all day, not expecting any special consideration. He knew that she had a good mind and a keen interest in the politics and the events that were determining the future of her people.

Unfortunately Sarah had lost not only her heart but her senses too. Bartlett, though well liked by his men, was an irresponsible drunkard who took advantage of people with his charming manners and handsome face. Sarah knew this and had heard the story of Bartlett's short-lived command at Camp McDermit, where Captain Henry Wagner had placed him in charge of the soldiers during a brief absence. The lieutenant, instead of taking the responsibility seriously, had gotten drunk and, in a "frenzy of intoxication," had ridden through the Indian camp shooting off his revolver and shouting that the Paiutes had formed a conspiracy and were planning to massacre all the whites. His fellow officers, familiar with his condition, had rounded him up, undressed him, and put him to bed.[5]

Sarah and Bartlett took the stagecoach from Camp McDermit to Winnemucca, where they boarded the Central Pacific Railroad for Salt Lake City. There they were married by a justice of the peace on January 29, 1871. They could not have been legally married in Nevada, where there were laws against miscegenation. Bartlett turned out to be absent without leave from his company, and Sarah had not consulted Captain Wagner before her departure. The marriage was quite unacceptable to Chief Winnemucca and to Sarah's brother Natchez as well.

While still in Salt Lake, after some of her romantic delusions had been torn from her, Sarah knew that the marriage would not work and that she could not prevent Bartlett from drinking away any money that they might possess. From her work at Camp McDermit she had some savings and had bought some good jewelry, which her husband began pawning. A few weeks later, when she was most desperate, Natchez appeared at her hotel in Salt Lake City.[6] Perhaps Sarah had written him to come and bring her home again.

The army registers show that First Lieutenant Bartlett resigned from the army on November 15, 1871, within a year after his marriage. Sarah returned to her position at Camp McDermit and continued her work there, though from that time on her unsettled marital status would add to her personal problems and bring out more of her fiery nature.

A Baptist minister, George Balcom, was slated to take over Major Douglass's position in the Indian Service in Nevada. He arrived with his daughter, Flora, in early March, 1871. His first concern was to find suitable accommodations in Wadsworth for his large family. The house would also have to serve as a church in which to preach the gospel. He made plans for a day school and "sabbath school" at Pyramid Lake Reservation. They were to be established in a storage shed that Douglass had built. He sent a flurry of letters to Washington asking for subsidies to bring the remainder of his family from New York to Nevada, to buy furniture for a home and office, and to acquire a horse and conveyance for his transportation.[7] His letters were always faithfully signed, "Yours with Christ."

On his first visit to Pyramid Lake, Agent Balcom called the Indian men together, and about seventy-five knelt with him while he and his daughter sang hymns and prayed for the souls of the heathens. He used Natchez as his interpreter, but found that many of the Paiutes understood English. He reported to Commissioner Parker in Washington: "I told them I was born and raised a practical Farmer till about thirty years of age was then converted to God 'The Great Spirit' and belonged to Him ever since, and that now in the change of Administration our Governmental father at Washington had sent me to be their Minister and Agent and gave them quite an idea of work, Morality and Religion."[8]

Balcom was not aware that at this time on the Walker River the Paiute shaman Wodziwob was prophesying the return of the Paiute dead. In his trances Wodziwob was receiving signs that great changes would take place for the Indian peoples. He collected many followers, among whom was a Paiute, named Tavivo, who taught his son Wovoka some of the precepts of the new thought. As the prophet of the ghost-dance religion, Wovoka in turn would become a spiritual leader who influenced many

Indian tribes. Thus the Paiutes' discontent with their white-dominated life found a release in a religion of the Indians' own choosing.

On his next visit to Pyramid Lake Agent Balcom discovered that the Paiutes were holding a traditional "fandango," a dance celebration that was religious in nature. Thus Woziwob's influence was spreading. At the same time the preachings of Balcom may also have affected the Paiutes. About twelve hundred of them were encamped at Pyramid Lake in the spring of 1871. Balcom went two evenings and one afternoon to talk, pray, and sing for them. He wrote:

> They got impressed with the idea that "God was coming" and are very susceptible of religious things, and very serious even in their monotonous dance, modifying it very much. Their criers go about the circular camp crying "God is coming" and all Indians must stop sinning against Him, by swearing, lying, gambling, chewing tobacco, smoking or keeping dogs. And all promise to break off as fast as possible. . . . Any quantity of them are ready to work to send their children to school. So I increase the rations somewhat, and will take the preliminary step to form a school District and school to begin May 1st."[9]

Unfortunately, Balcom was a naive, impractical man and did not know how to deal with the problems that confronted him as Indian agent. At the time of his arrival the settlers on the Truckee River were disgruntled over a dam that Douglass had built. Though it had a fish ladder, it still seemed to prevent the trout from moving up the river to spawn in Pyramid Lake. On March 27, 1871, Balcom hurried to the telegraph office at Wadsworth with an urgent message to the commissioner: "Two men from Reno have torn out part of dam what shall I do?"[10] Upon closer inspection the agent found that the dam was not materially damaged, even though giant powder had been used.

Two weeks later the agent received a threatening letter from white fishermen in Reno: "Will come down with force enough to take out the Dam and clean out the Indians, there is about 150 men armed and ready to turn out at any moment. . . . etc. N. B. This is no boys play. If you wish to reply address H. C. Reno."[11] Balcom sent for troops and was hopeful that the soldier guards would arrive before any trouble.

On April 29, Balcom sent the following telegram: "About twenty wild indians drove us from reservation House last night soldiers wanted."[12] Then, after sending this missive, Balcom's terror turned to sheepish apologies as he reported in a letter to Parker the explanation for the happenings of the previous night. The agency house had been surrounded by twenty Indians on horseback, who were shooting guns and yelling, "You go away, all." Two farmers, named Bass and McCormick, had been with Balcom inside the building, and the three whites had soon discovered that their own guns were gone: "One my 16 shooting improved Winchester costing me $45," complained Balcom, "the other McCormicks double barrelled shotgun well loaded for any emergency." Balcom confessed:

> I locked myself into one room and held the door while the other men parlied with the Indians . . . but I utterly refused to leave (though I confess to the greatest fears of my life) until both the white men come and said they were going and had our horses saddled, so then I left, but as I was passing around the corner of the house an Indian shot at me, no more than 12 feet distant, but I recd no harm. I mounted the Govt horse who took me a mile pretty quick, but in going up a steep hill my saddle girt gave way and let me off dangerously, the horse kicking the saddle off and ran back until caught by friendly Indians who had gathered.[13]

Balcom hid in a "friendly" Indian camp until morning and asked for six escorts back to town. Later in the day Sheriff Doyle of Reno arrived with the missing guns and the explanation: Nugent, the former subagent on the reservation, had furnished the powder and the men to play the part of the wild Indians. They were opposed to the dam and the Indian fishing business.[14] Nugent was only reprimanded over the fiasco.

Agent C. A. Bateman, another Baptist missionary, arrived soon after Balcom's misadventure. His destination was the Walker River Reservation, where he had been assigned to find his field of Christian endeavor. After determining the immediate needs of the Paiutes there in a businesslike way, he made plans for buildings, sought out suitable farm land, and put to work as many Paiutes as he could afford to pay. It was apparent to him that because of a drought the grass seed and pine nuts would not provide sufficient food:

Indian women with their laundry at Hot Springs, Nevada. (Courtesy of Nevada Historical Society.)

No sooner than I commenced operations here in opening irrigating ditches—improving lands and planting etc. etc., than I found three times as many wanting to work as our monthly allowance of supplies would justify . . . and though we were obliged to turn many away before we were aware we found some of them with tools in their hands hard at work that they might thereby receive something to satisfy their cravings for food.[15]

Though Bateman and Balcom were brothers in the American Baptist Home Missionary Society, they did not see eye to eye on many issues. Bateman was distressed to find that Balcom had already overspent the monies available for the agency by $1,500. Balcom had made a trip to California to buy furniture, built a summer kitchen, privies, and a well at Pyramid Lake, and set up a school with a blackboard and a few desks. Bateman had starving Paiutes uppermost in his mind and was particularly upset that he could not purchase more of the supplies that were direly needed. Bateman confided to Commissioner Parker in Washington that the Indians at Pyramid Lake did not like Balcom and therefore came to Walker River to add to his own burdens.[16]

Many of the Paiutes who were normally at Pyramid Lake were observed by the military on the Fall River, in Big Valley, and near Camp Bidwell in northeastern California, collecting roots and hunting game.[17] General E. O. C. Ord, who was commander of the Pacific division, noted, "I think if the Indian Department of Nevada is powerless to give food to the starving Indians, military commanders should be authorized to issue to such in limited quantities, as much less expensive than having to fight them."[18]

At this time Sarah was still concerned about the possible closing of Camp McDermit. She and Natchez therefore made a trip to Carson City. Getting no satisfaction from the Nevada officials, the brother and sister then traveled to San Francisco to interview General John McAlister Schofield. The general was polite and sympathetic, but said that he could not provide a home for the Paiutes at Camp McDermit because only the politicians had the authority to determine what the Bureau of Indian Affairs might do with the Indians in the northern part of Nevada. He concurred with Sarah that Balcom had spent money unwisely on a schoolhouse and the salary of a teacher while her people were starving. He recommended that she and Natchez contact Senator John P. Jones at Gold Hill, Nevada, who would be better able to help them.[19]

Sarah and Natchez returned to Nevada and took the stage up Mount Davidson to the mining town to seek out the wealthy senator. Jones received them. He was apparently concerned, because he asked polite questions, but he made no commitments to help them. Upon their leaving he gave them a twenty dollar bill. Perhaps this salved his conscience, for the portly gentleman did not manage to do anything else for the Paiutes.[20]

While she was still in San Francisco, Sarah had written a letter to General Ord that caused a sensation in Nevada. There were repercussions in Washington as well, as Balcom and Bateman had difficulty explaining the allegations that Sarah made against them. Bateman replied to the inquiries of the Indian commissioner that Sarah was a fake and not the daughter of Old Winnemucca, that she had not been on the reservation and had never held a council with the Paiutes there.[21] Balcom was even stronger in his vehemence against her, questioning her moral integrity rather than addressing the points of her argument.

This was the letter that understandably raised the agents' ire:

E. O. C. Ord. Esq.
Sir:

I have visited your City through the persuasion of my Indian Brothers and Sisters, for the purpose of asking if there is not some way by which our Indians can be provided for during the coming winter, as the dry season has caused a scarcity of Fish and other food which the Indians chiefly live upon. I being Chief Winnemuccas daughter they look to me for help, and I am afraid if there is not some notice taken of this appeal that there will be an insurrection amongst our people.

We held a Council at the Pyramid reservation and there were present sixteen hundred and ninety adults and it is to prevent this trouble if possible that I ask aid. We have asked the Agents of the different reservations to help us, but all to no avail, only to be put off with another promise, so that many of the Indians of the Pyramid reservation having become dissatisfied and being on the borders of starvation, have left their homes and wandered we know not where but they say they will not work for these Agents for by doing so they enrich these Agents, and come to absolute poverty and degradation themselves, and we would all much rather be slain and put out of our misery than to be lingering here,—each day bringing new sorrows—and finally die of hunger and starvation.

We know full well that the Government has been, and is still, willing to provide us with all we need, but I must inform you that it never gets past these Agents' hands, but they reap all the benefit whilst we have all the suffering.

Your's respectfully,
Sarah Winnemucca

San Francisco
July 1, 1871[22]

At about the time when the two agents were required to answer Sarah's charges, Agent Balcom explained to the commissioner that he wished to resign, for his position was not compatible with his higher call as a missionary. He wished to leave Nevada as soon as possible so that he could save his homestead on the Solomon River in Kansas. He hoped to settle his affairs speedily, draw his pay, and then rejoin his family.[23]

After Balcom's departure Bateman did not spare criticism of his administration, for he found that the Indians at Pyramid Lake had been criminally neglected. One Paiute died while he was present, and he ordered a physician to tend the others. He also found the dam broken and the crops beyond saving, though a few Paiutes were bringing in sand by boat, trying to repair the damage. He distributed clothing to them, as they were in tatters.[24]

The attending physician, E. S. Coleman, later noted that Bateman called a "council" of six old Indians on the reservation to make a show of inquiring into Sarah's assertions. The doctor thought it a little singular that Sarah had no notice of such a council, nor did Young Winnemucca, though the chief was at the time only five miles from the council house. Doctor Coleman wrote, "The report of the council is doubtless a curiosity."[25]

Young Winnemucca died in the fall of that year, on October 28, 1871. The agent first claimed that the Paiute leader had heart disease, but changed his story six months later, when he admitted that the chief had died of a lingering consumption.[26] In the *Sacramento Union* of May 16, 1872, Doctor Coleman wrote: "The Chief Winnemucca went up from the Reservation to Wadsworth, laid down in the sagebrush and died there for want of medicine and care. The Indians have no houses, not a single one and in case of sickness are exposed to rain and sun, with no one to care for them." Thus Young Winnemucca—who had held high hopes for the justice of the whites for his people, who had preached peace but was forced to lead his Paiutes in an unwanted war against the whites—had died in destitute and demeaning circumstances.

When the farmer Franklin Campbell at Walker River had become acquainted with the preachings of the shaman Wodziwob, he had told the Indians and the whites that the philosophy was good and no harm could come from it. Indian emissaries visited the reserve from Idaho, Oregon, and the plains states to observe and learn about the new religion. Campbell visited the Indian camp and watched the Indians gather around the shaman while he lay in a trance. They joined in a song that guided the spirit back to the body. When he awoke, the shaman gave a long account of his visit in spirit form to the "Supreme Ruler," who he believed was then on his way with all the spirits of the departed dead to reside again upon this earth and change it into a paradise. Life was to be eternal, and no distinction was to be made between races.[27]

The Paiutes would not preach insurrection. That was against their conservative way of life and not feasible. Still they desired equality and justice, both of which were to be attained, they believed, in the new era to come. In the quiet of the desert, where there were few whites, and where the rugged Sierra loomed large against the baking sun of noon or the low-hanging stars of a clear night, the spirits could seem near, very near, to them.

8

The Modoc War

Sarah continued working at Camp McDermit for almost a year after the breakup of her marriage in 1872. She was no longer employed as a scout but served as the hospital matron, with W. P. Corbusier as attending physician.[1] There are indications that Sarah made attempts to contact Edward Bartlett during this time. Perhaps there was even an effort at reconciliation.[2] Sarah's fall out of favor with her father because of her marriage took a great emotional toll on her. Chief Winnemucca and her people were the focus of her interest and love.

After an argument with Captain Wagner, the commander at Camp McDermit, with whom she had never gotten along very well, Sarah moved in 1873 to Winnemucca, which was eighty miles south of Camp McDermit on the Central Pacific Railroad.[3] She was in need of work, since her ill-fated marriage had taken so much of her funds. As she had a reputation for fine glove making and millinery, she relied upon those skills to support herself. She also acted as interpreter at Battle Mountain in the Shoshoni country of Nevada, while an issue of goods was distributed there.

Sarah ridiculed the agents for the meager issue, calling it "the saddest affair she ever saw," and she noted the abundance of ready-made clothes that were destined to go on farther east to the Indians on the borders of the state. During the issue Bateman arrived and gave the Shoshonis one ton of flour, which was more than Sarah had ever seen him give to the Paiutes. She said to him in front of the Shoshoni agent: "You come up here to show off before this man. Go and bring some flour to my people on the Humboldt River, who are starving, the people over whom you are agent. For shame that you who talk three times a day to the Great Father in Spirit-land should act so to my people."[4]

Sarah's criticism was warranted, but she did not know that in that year of unusually deep winter snows Agent Bateman found himself without funds for the Paiutes because of former Agent Balcom's overspending. Bateman had no response from Washington to his urgent pleas for help, and shipments could not get through the heavy snows in the Rocky Mountains in any case. He had no emergency budget. He did call on General Schofield to help the hungry Paiutes at Walker River Reservation, where the Indians had congregated in large numbers to hear of the coming apocalypse from the shaman Wodziwob. Bateman was given army flour to supply them.[5]

When Sarah returned to the town of Winnemucca, her fiery temper got her into difficult situations. The following article appeared in the *Humboldt Register*:

We witnessed a settlement of a slight misunderstanding between two of the gentler sex of the Piute persuasion, the other day. It seems that one of their sisterhood had been slandering the virtue of Mrs. S. W. Bartlett, who came here to attend the Piute dance. Mrs. Sarah caught her out, and went for her, and such scratching, biting and pulling of hair, we never did see; until, at last, Mrs. Bartlett got her traducer down, and sat upon her, bounced upon her, and at every bounce gave her a lick in the face, exclaiming, "there, talk so about me to white folks, will you?"[6]

Only a couple of weeks later Sarah again made the news. This time she did not wholly succeed in trouncing her foe, for it was a waiter at the Travelers Home:

The trouble occurred in the dining room of the hotel, with no one but the combatants themselves to witness the affair, consequently we can but give the sequel to the transaction. The young man got off with a black eye, and Salley [*sic*] with a severe jolt in the mouth, which split her lip badly, and caused the claret to flow most profusely. The barkeeper interfered and stopped the muss. Sally rushed across the street to procure a warrant for the arrest of her adversary, but before the papers could be made out, she went into spasms, and soon after was taken in charge by the Indians and carried off to camp. The whites, however, had her conveyed from there to a room at the French Hotel, where she lay for two days in a stupor, apparently more dead than alive. At one time her life was despaired of, but at last accounts however, she was rapidly convalescing. There are, of course, all sorts of rumors afloat. Some say Sally was the agressor, and others that she was not. Some say that she was drunk, while others contend that she never drank. Some who claim to know all about such things say she was drugged, while others who claim to be equally wise, say it was nothing but an overdose of "mad" that caused the stupor. Up to this time there have been no arrests, but it is expected there will be as soon as "Sally goes marching around."[7]

Sarah's volatile nature had been subdued in her earlier years. It was a facet of her personality that would be called upon to help her contend with the stresses of living in two worlds, an unhappy marriage, and the defense of her honor in a frontier society. She was essentially on her own, and she was an object of admiration or contempt, depending on the viewer's attitude toward race and the role of women. As an Indian she had no legal protection of her person or property. At this time she started carrying a small knife for protection.

Because of her prominence in Indian affairs in Nevada, Sarah had become a personage well known to the residents of the state. In the *Nevada State Journal*[8] a writer described her in February, 1872, as a woman of medium height:

. . . Rather stout, but not too much so, and graceful in all her movements. Her jet black hair hangs in heavy curls, and her sparkling black eyes forbid anything tending to too much familiarity. She dresses very tastefully but not extravagantly—a la Americaine, upon this occasion, in a tight fitting suit of black alpaca, very prettily trimmed with green fringe—in all making a very attractive appearance.

When asked about the delicate question of her age and place of birth she laughed and said that was almost more than she knew herself. This I do know, I was born near the Humboldt Lake. As to the time . . . that it was during Captain Fremont's visit to California when my Grandfather, Captain Truckee accompanied him and took part in the Mexican war then going on.

After brief questioning on her work as a scout and interpreter with the army, Sarah was asked about the reservations. She described the agents as follows:

[They] are too anxious to keep the people down, or from doing anything to help themselves. If let alone they would go to work, as quite a number have done already. Our agent is continually promising farming implements, but they never come. He don't want them for should my people raise their own provisions his place would be worth but little. Then again, I know that the agent has been in the habit of renting the reservations to stockraisers, putting the rent in his own pocket. Last Fall, when I was there, there was an immense number of sheep pastured there. It seems to me high time that the Government should look into these matters, and see that my people shall not suffer that these agents may put money in their pockets.

When questioned about her marriage, Sarah replied:

My folks were very angry at my marriage, my father especially—he says he never will forgive me. They all knew the character of the man—he was nothing but a drunkard. He kept continually sending to me for money after my return home, and I supplied him as long as I could; but what makes me now so bitter against him is the fact that he finally sold all my jewelry. I never want to see him again.

The interview continued as follows.

Reporter—How long since you have seen your father—Winnemucca?

Miss W.—I have not seen him for two years, though he was at Camp McDermit the first of last month. He was so angry at my marriage that, though living but a short distance from me he would never send for me.

Reporter—There has been a report in circulation that he has gone to help the Modocs in Oregon; at any rate, that he has mysteriously disappeared from the reservation with a number of others. Do you know anything of this?

Miss W.—But little. During the late Indian fight in Oregon a cousin of ours, Jerry Long, was reported killed, and my father immediately wrote to my uncles to send him some of the best young men to go over there with him. . . . Quite a number went to him, and I think they went over into Oregon to join the Modocs. The death of Jerry seemed to raise quite a bitter feeling among some of the tribe.

Reporter—Could you have no influence with your people in this matter?

Miss W.—Very little; when once they imagine an insult they seem to lose all reason. . . . I have now told many of the utter foolishness of their taking part in this trouble, and am confident many have remained here through this. I cannot say that I know my father and his braves have gone to the Modocs, but that seems to be the general impression among us.

Old Winnemucca now subsisted with his small band in the Steens Mountain area of southern Oregon (which was known then as Stein's Mountains). He seldom came into Camp McDermit except to council with the soldiers, as rations were no longer provided to the Indians there.[9] There was unrest among the Paiutes, partly because of the recent arrest of two of their people.[10] Natchez was hired by cattlemen from southern Idaho to talk with Winnemucca when it was claimed that depredations had been committed by his band in the area around Steens Mountain.[11]

By the time of the interview with Sarah early in 1873, the Modoc war had raged for over two months. It was an embarrassment to the United States Army, for about 175 Modocs (two-thirds of them women and children) were holding off troops from their stronghold in the Lava Beds in northeastern California and causing many casualties among the soldiers. The Modocs were resisting a return to their reservation at Klamath, where they claimed that they had starved. They wanted their old tribal lands on the Lost River, Oregon for a reservation, but these were denied them.[12]

Both the military and white citizens were apprehensive that other tribes would revolt when they saw the Modocs' success. The interview with Sarah, which indicated that Old Winnemucca might join the Modocs, did not ease anyone's fears. Captain Jack, the Modoc leader, was known to have sold guns and ammunition to Paulina's band of Paiutes in 1865.[13] Would the Paiutes help him now?

A Nevada newsman observed:

> For some time many of the old settlers who are familiar with the Indian character have believed that the Piutes, or a portion of the tribe, at least, were secretly aiding the Modocs. They knew all about the death of Canby and the Peace Commissioner within 24 hours after it occurred and before the San Francisco papers, with a detailed account of the affair, reached here. Whether the Piutes have assisted the Modocs or not, it is certain that by a system of telegraphing known to the Indian, they have kept themselves thoroughly posted on their movements and doings.[14]

Lieutenant Colonel Frank Wheaton, commander of the District of the Lakes, recognized Winnemucca's authority among the Paiutes and said that, though the chief was old and feeble, he was the acknowledged head of all the "Piute Snakes" tribe: "I have reason to believe that runners frequently pass from the Klamath Lake Basin to communicate with the heads of Winnemucca's different Bands, and I know they are promptly advised of everything of interest to them that occurs at Military Posts in Southern Oregon."[15] He pleaded for reinforcements at Camp Bidwell, as an unusually large number of Pyramid Lake Indians were in the Surprise valley:

The settlers in all the valleys between Yainax and Camp Harney are reported by several reliable parties to be greatly alarmed and excited dreading an outbreak of the several bands of Pi-u-tes off and on reserves in Southern Oregon. . . . Suspicious conduct of several bands, warrants me in suggesting that Camp Harney be largely reenforced at an early date and that there should be one company at Camp Bidwell as protection to Surprise and Goose Lake Valleys.[16]

One of the officers at Camp Warner in southern Oregon met with the Chief Ocheo, whose Paiutes had left their reservation at Yainax, Oregon (Ocheo had taken over the leadership of Paulina's band in 1867, when that chief was killed). The Paiute assured the Camp Warner representative that his band was not friendly with the hostile Modocs.[17] The officer reported: "We have thus far no occasion to doubt his sincerity, but it is thought his future conduct may be governed in some degree by the attitude assumed by Winnemucca the prominent chief of the tribe."

Sarah had commented to the *Nevada State Journal* reporter in February: "I cannot say that I know my father and his braves have gone to the Modocs, but that seems to be the general impression among us." Her remark was taken up by a Portland, Oregon, paper in April, but much distorted: "Mr. Jones, recently from Camp Warner, reports that Sally Winnemucca, an educated squaw and Government Interpreter at Warner, stated that her father's band (Winnemucca's) was in constant communication with Jack, and that it was agreed that if the soldiers did not whip Jack all the Indians would join in a general war of extermination."[18]

Lieutenant Colonel Wheaton had read the article in the Nevada paper and recognized the original context. He wrote to the assistant adjutant general of the Department of the Columbia:

The Indian Squaw referred to is not and never has been an interpreter at this post [Camp Warner]. . . . I understand she was at one time employed in that capacity at Boise or McDermit in 68 or 69. . . . Her home is near Winnemucca on the C. P. RR and February last I heard of her being in Reno Nevada. . . .

The nearest residence or settlement to Camp Warner is D. R. Jones' stock ranch in Warner Lake Valley, 18 miles from the post. The Indian referred to [Jones] is apt to know her further opinions, as she is living with him or was in March last.[19]

If Sarah was living with an Indian named Jones at this period in her life, she may have married him in an Indian ceremony, but not with any white formality. In a later interview in the *San Francisco Call* of November 2, 1879, she did relate that she was married to an Indian for a short time.

Wheaton's letter continued:

I cannot learn that any proposition has been made to O-che-ho to join other Piute Chiefs in any projected outbreak, but I believe the young men of the different Piute Bands to be greatly excited and elated at the delay in exterminating Jack's, renegade Modocs, and that if Egan their most popular and influential War Chief, or O-che-ho, probably the next best chief among them choose to become disaffected and lead them a very expensive and bloody war would ensue. . . . This Chief, Egan and We-ah-wa all Piute Snakes, Lalake the Klamath Chief, and the renegade Modoc Jack are all firm believers in the Smoholla or new Indian religion which instructs them that the time is not far distant when all dead Indians will be restored to life and that through their aid and the magical efforts of their Chief Medicine Men all white men will be Spirited away and the Country restored to its original Indian occupants.[20]

The curly headed Doctor the principal medicine man of Jack's Modoc Band induced and has through his influence on Jack kept up the Modoc War. O-che-ho cannot be convinced today that a bullet shot at his chief Medicine Man would harm or injure him in any way, and only a few weeks since, he kept a party of incredulous Klamaths waiting three days at his camp while his medicine man was arranging with the great Spirit to catch all bullets fired at him.[21]

On May 15, 1873, Captain Wagner's command from Camp McDermit met Chief Winnemucca at Steens Mountain. Captain Jack's surrender was only two weeks away, and the Modoc shaman's influence over his tribe had been broken by their losses in battle. Winnemucca appeared to have very few followers with him—only about twenty men—but they were young and capable warriors. He reiterated his desire to remain at peace with the whites, but seemed impatient and restless. He asked why troops were moving toward Camp Warner, saying, "There are no Indians that way." Wagner became suspicious that a runner had been dispatched to notify Winnemucca's friend Ocheo that the troops were coming near. There had been continued bad feeling between Winnemucca's band and the settlers around Steens Mountain. Winnemucca asked Captain Wagner to keep the stockmen away because local whites had threatened him.[22]

On June 1, Captain Jack of the Modocs surrendered. After a trial by a military tribunal at Fort Klamath in southern Oregon he and three of his followers were hung for the death of three United States peace commissioners. The remaining Modoc prisoners were sent to the Quapaw Reservation in Indian Territory. General W. T. Sherman telegraphed to General J. C. Davis: "I will submit [prisoners] to the War office for reference to the highest authority with a view to what disposition is to be made of prisoners according to law and Justice. Some should be tried by court martial and shot others to be delivered to the Civil authorities and the balance dispersed so that the name 'Modoc' should cease."[23]

9

Law and Order

Natchez had made a name for himself among the white citizens in western Nevada as a capable Paiute leader who spoke good English and was an excellent interpreter. He helped the Storey County authorities stop Chinese liquor sales to the Indians, and he adjusted difficulties not only between whites and Indians but also between Paiutes, Washos, and other Indian tribes.[1] He aided John Wesley Powell of the Smithsonian Institution in collecting Northern Paiute material goods, such as baskets and hunting paraphernalia, for museum specimens. He also transmitted an extensive Paiute vocabulary to Powell and explained Paiute customs, including burial methods and the marriage ceremony.[2]

In the fall of 1873 the Shoshonis were brought to a big council at Elko, Nevada, so that Agent Bateman could persuade them to go on a reservation. The tribe appeared to be seriously considering the proposition when Natchez spoke to a newspaper reporter about the foolishness of choosing reservation life: "The Truckee reservation [Pyramid Lake] is a cold, unhealthy place and we Paiutes can't be forced to stay there. The Paiutes never receive presents and do not expect any from Agent Bateman."[3] Natchez had observed that the Shoshonis were issued beef, potatoes, blankets, combs, utensils for cooking, and various trinkets. Distribution of goods was now a subject of controversy between Natchez and Bateman, as it had been between Sarah and Bateman.

The Paiutes heard that Agent G. W. Ingalls was distributing blankets at Stone House, a Southern Pacific Railroad stop in the Shoshoni country, nineteen miles west of Battle Mountain. Some of the Paiutes took advantage of the free rail transportation and went there to receive their share. They were perhaps testing the agents to see what would happen. Ingalls told them to go see Bateman.

When they did, Bateman told them that he would have nothing to do with them and that they should see Ingalls. The Paiutes could not understand why they should be so pushed about and get nothing. When they asked for an explanation from Bateman, he forgot his "Christian character and allowed his evil spirit to rise." Natchez "got his injun up" too, and high words passed between them. It seems that Natchez threatened to go to Washington with other Paiute leaders if Bateman would not distribute goods to them as the agents had done to the Shoshonis. Bateman told Natchez that he would have him arrested and sent away from his tribe where he would never come back.[4]

Natchez, worried by that threat, spoke to the editor of the *Humboldt Register* about the altercation. The newspaper people told him that they thought no harm would come of it. Bateman, however, informed General Schofield that Natchez was inciting the Indians against him. Under instructions from Schofield, Captain Wagner came from Fort McDermit, obtained evidence to issue a warrant for Natchez, and then arrested him and delivered him to Fort Alcatraz in San Francisco Bay.[5]

The white community of eastern Nevada came to Natchez's defense. Newspapers headlined the story, blaming Bateman for the trouble:

> We have no doubt that the arrest of Natchez was a very needless if not outrageous piece of official tyranny. . . . We suspect the trouble is that Natchez knows too much to suit the purposes of Mr. Indian Agent Bateman. . . . He is not to be galled by any humbuggery of the Agency to which the affairs of his tribe are referred. An Indian Chief . . . who has kept his people in such good relations with the whites, deserves better treatment than he has had—unless, indeed, it is going to be held by the Department that an Indian has no rights that an Agent is bound to respect.[6]

Petitions signed by citizens in behalf of Natchez were forwarded to military headquarters.[7]

Bateman kept up his side in the controversy by passing a petition around Wadsworth. It was signed by about forty residents, and in it Natchez was termed "a pretended chief": "[He is] considered by all a troublesome Indian. . . . and his late arrest by the military was not for the reason of prohibiting him from exercising his rights but for appearances and actions indicative of evil. . . . Said arrest was by the unanimous voice of this community."[8]

On February 9, 1874, Natchez was released from Alcatraz. He came home from the escapade with the new aura of chieftainship about him. He said that he had been treated well at the fort, where he had enjoyed complete liberty. He held a high opinion of General Schofield and all of the officers at the fort. As soon as the Indians heard that Natchez was back, they flocked to see him, and a big celebration was held. Even some Shoshonis came down from Battle Mountain. The Indian community had a new hero, and Bateman had lost face. He was advised by some local newspapers to "bag his head and leave the country."[9]

At the beginning of the new year, 1875, Natchez helped his father and Sarah from a carriage onto a street in San Francisco. Although the noonday traffic was busy, many pedestrians stopped to stare at the dark, wrinkled face of Chief Winnemucca, who was dressed conspicuously in a blue uniform with gold epaulets and braid and a top hat decorated with a feather. He marched straight-backed up the steps with his daughter and Doby John in pursuit. Natchez paid the coachman and followed. Sarah's brother was a tall, good-looking fellow who spoke English well and made friends easily. Sarah must have made amends with her father over her marriage to Bartlett, for now the Winnemucca family trio were in San Francisco to interview General Schofield and advise him of their latest ambitions for the Paiutes.[10]

By this time the general had had previous dealings with all three of the Winnemuccas. He listened while Natchez explained on his father's behalf that the old chief would much rather be supervised by the military than live on a reservation where the agents abused their power and stole what rightfully belonged to the Indians. Every winter had brought some new crisis to the Paiute bands who were no longer cared for by the army. They were forced from the reservations, where little or no food was provided. After one band leader, Ocheo, had agreed to go to the Yainax Reservation in southern Oregon, twenty-five of his people had died there. Captain R. F. Bernard, the commander at Fort Bidwell, could not see how this small band could survive another winter unless the commissary issued rations at the fort.[11]

Chief Winnemucca asked that land be given him near Camp McDermit, where he could look to the soldiers for protection. The old leader wanted the government to give him a start by providing implements and seeds for raising grain. He promised to settle down happily to farming with his people.[12] Schofield, of course, could make him no such promises, and he reminded his visitors that the politicians made all the decisions regarding the future welfare of the Indians. Again it was suggested that the Winnemuccas go to Senator Jones in Gold Hill, Nevada.[13] Sarah remembered how Jones had turned her and Natchez away with a twenty-dollar bill for their trouble several years earlier. Back in the hotel, however, she and Natchez agreed that they would return to the senator. Schofield had been their one hope in San Francisco, and he seemed to be powerless to help them.

On the return train the old chief sat stolidly watching the landscape of the Sierra, as they traveled over the mountains to Reno. His head dropped, and he snoozed occasionally. He had not been able to sleep in the stuffy, noisy hotel room in San Francisco, where vehicles rattled by on the streets. The floor had been uncomfortable where he had insisted on spreading his blankets.[14]

Natchez and Sarah parted company with their father at Reno and took the stage up the mountain to the Comstock diggings. When they were finally admitted into Jones's office, they found that the bewhiskered senator was more rotund than ever. He amiably offered them velvet-covered chairs. This gentleman was the owner of the Crown Point Mine and was reputed to be worth $100 million.

The Winnemuccas repeated the same request with which they had confronted General Schofield: they asked that the Paiutes be alloted land for which they could receive title and that they be taught to be farmers. They used their brother Tom as an example. He had worked in California for some years, and, since he had returned to Nevada, he had done well on his small ranch with the knowledge that he had gained.[15] They suggested that the reservation system be abolished in Nevada and that the Indians be under the sponsorship of the military, who were honest and concerned for the welfare of the Paiutes. The senator was enthusiastic about their suggestions, and he so favored their opinions that he promised to advocate them in Congress.[16]

While in Virginia City, Natchez was invited to dine with several gentlemen. Sarah was interviewed by a reporter of the Virginia City *Territorial Enterprise,* who described her as a "handsome well-formed, intelligent-looking petite young lady with dark flowing hair, spanish eyes and complexion who made use of the 'best English.'" The reporter thought that she looked twenty-two years old rather than the thirty-one that she professed to be. He commented that he had seen her mingling with her tribesmen as they were seated on the ground "engaged in playing the traditional game of 'poker'": "On such occasions she never hesitates to partake of their primitive and homely fare. . . . The friendly feeling manifested by herself towards them has greatly endeared her to the children of the desert."[17]

When they had visited Senator Jones, Sarah and Natchez had represented the Paiutes who did not choose to live on a reservation. At this time others were already committed to reservation life at Pyramid Lake, and they were worried by the recent news that the Central Pacific Railroad planned to sell the best reservation land on the open market. The railroad had acquired every other section of land along its route by an act of Congress, and, as has already been noted, the tracks ran through the most fertile part of the reservation. The company planned to sell this land to settlers: "All the improvements, buildings, ditches, fences and even the lake where the fisheries were found were included in a diagram of the area claimed by the Central Pacific Railroad," according to the report of U.S. Indian Inspector William Vandever to Indian Commissioner A. C. Barstow.[18] White squatters who had been chased off the reservation in past years were now baiting the Pyramid Lake Indians, telling them that they would soon return and take back fields and pastures for their own. Commissioner Barstow, on visiting Pyramid Lake to work out a compromise agreement with the railroad company, found few Indians on the reservation. There was an almost complete absence of houses; no teacher, preacher, blacksmith, or carpenter;

A Paiute camp near the tailings of the Ophir Mine, Virginia City, Nevada. Stove pipes emerge from the traditional smoke holes of the karnees. (Courtesy of *Bancroft Library, University of California, Berkeley.*)

and, worst of all, no agent. Unbeknownst to the Bureau of Indian Affairs, Agent Bateman for sometime had been living 150 miles away, near Sacramento, California. He had left his son Cephas as farmer in charge of the agency.[19] Soon after that was disclosed, Bateman resigned and nominated a Baptist compatriot, A. J. Barnes, as the new Indian superintendent for the state of Nevada. Barnes proved to be a crook of the highest order; he swindled Indians and citizens alike and was later forced out of office.

After the Winnemuccas' diplomatic efforts with politicians and military officials in San Francisco, Gold Hill, and Virginia City had not secured food for the starving bands, Chief Winnemucca and Sarah came into Camp McDermit with sixty of their people, asking for rations for the Paiutes. Sarah interpreted Winnemucca's long speech to Captain Wagner, and he in turn reported it as follows in a letter to Assistant Adjutant General Samuel Breck in California:

> In a treaty entered into in 1867 between his [Winnemucca's] people and General Crook, the General had promised them food and clothing as long as they remained peaceable. They had, he said, been placed on Reservations, but that the Agents had failed to supply them with the promised food, and that some, in consequence, had left the reservations in search of game and other food. That the officers had always failed to keep their word in the treaties he had made with them, although he had never broken faith with them. That when they had been fed by the military it was as "prisoners of war" and that they had never received anything at the Indian Agencies. He said also that as he was growing old and was held responsible by his suffering people for the nonfulfillment of the promises made them, & he begged of the "Captain" (me) to use his influence to procure food for them. He did not ask this himself but for his people his women and children. . . . His people were now in a starving condition, and had only the choice between two evils left them, either to starve or to steal cattle and be shot by the soldiers. He asked again for help, all former wars, he said, had their origin in want of food; he wanted no more slaughter of his people, he was about to return to his home in Steens Mountains, but before leaving he wished to ascertain if his people would be provided for and would ask the Captain to say "Yes" or "No."
>
> I replied to him that I had given heed to everything he had said, that I felt for the condition of his people, but that I was powerless to help them, as it was not within the province of the military to provide

for the Indians, but only to protect white men and good Indians and to punish the bad. That the Government supplied the Indian Department with large sums of money to feed and clothe Indians and no doubt if they went to the Reservations and stayed there they would be well cared for. . . . There was no money from which the army could furnish their wants.

But that recently I had received instructions to issue bacon or pork to those who were starving and was now prepared to issue bacon accordingly.

Sarah, at this juncture, asked them if they would eat pork to which they gave a decided negative, adding that so long as there were plenty of cattle in the Valley, they would not eat it and that as a matter of self preservation they would have to help themselves to the cattle.

Sarah then reminded me of experiences with Pork: they had either thrown it into the Creek or used it in their fires. I replied to her, that it was to be presumed, if they were actually starving, they would have eaten the pork, that white men and soldiers had to eat it. To which she answered "I eat it too but I cannot get my people to eat it." She further proceeded to say that her poor people were starving as they had failed to collect roots or seeds last fall, under the impression that they would have been fed by the Government during the winter, and if they could only be fed for a few months it would be a matter of humanity. Her people years since had taken care of poor whites who had come among them, and they looked now to the Government or to the Community for help and if they failed in their appeals, they would be forced into the commission of depredations, in which she would join them, she was quite willing to throw off the garments of civilization she now wore and mount her pony. She remembered the time when the hills surrounding this very camp were swarming with hostile Indians and then and there the officers talked very sweetly to her.

She appealed for her people to those who had the influence, but feared that the majority of those in power would rather spend millions upon some scheme of their own than a few hundreds where humanity called as in the case of her people. She referred to the Modoc war where she said it required several hundred soldiers to defeat about 50 Modocs, and that the soldiers would never have succeeded had the Warm Spring Indians not assisted them.

I again reminded her that her people must not commit any depredations, that I and my command were here for the sole purpose of protecting the settlers and their stock, and would do so at all hazards.[20]

Later, however, Captain Wagner wrote to Breck:

Nothing has occurred which would indicate preparations for hostility on the part of the Indians. Sarah Winnemucca left here a few nights ago on the stage for Winnemucca and Chief Winnemucca accompanied by "Doby John" a sub-chief of the Humboldt band of Indians, departed here on Sunday, the 21st inst. for the north, and as I was informed by them for the Malheur Reservation, Oregon.[21]

After Sarah's departure there was a flurry of letters between General Schofield in San Francisco and his army superiors in Washington, D.C. Since the only surplus army food was pork and bacon, which made the Indians ill, it was finally decided that they would be allowed to barter it for flour with the post trader at Camp McDermit. It would then be baked into bread for the Indians at the post.[22]

On his return from San Francisco, Natchez had gone to Lovelock, Nevada. He resumed making a living for his large family by catching fish in the Humboldt River and selling them in Winnemucca, or he hired out as a ranch hand. Old Winnemucca continued his nomadic life in Oregon. Sarah stayed in Winnemucca, where within a few weeks the *Winnemucca Silver State* commented on her activities. She had gotten into a jealous tussle with another Indian woman.[23] Soon after, she was accused of cutting one Julius Argasse with a knife on the sidewalk in front of the Winnemucca Hotel.[24] Sarah had felt that her dignity was threatened because a man had touched her without permission. He had soon found that she was very able to protect herself.

The "Piute Princess," as the newspapers of the day chose to call Sarah, was put in the county jail overnight. She called in as her defense attorney M. S. Bonnifield, a man who had often befriended the Winnemuccas and the Paiutes. Her case was to be tried next day in the court of Judge Job Davis. The charge against her was assault with intent to do bodily harm. Although a large array of witnesses was subpoenaed for the defense, including several doctors and prominent church members, the case was dismissed before its merits could be evaluated because the knife, upon examination, was found to be of the smallest size.[25]

Some of the Paiutes awaited the decision outside the courthouse. When Sarah and Natchez appeared on the steps of the building, they both talked at length to those who were assembled about white justice and the merits of the court system. Sarah must have been bitter that Indians did not have the right to use the courts in a criminal case nor to testify against whites.[26] Possibly she explained to the waiting Paiutes that that was one reason why the case against her had been dropped: she would have won hands down if it had gone to trial, but, since she was an Indian, the white authorities would not deal with her case.

10

The Malheur Reservation

While riding to Camp Harney in late April, 1875, to spend time with her father, Sarah was thrown from her saddle and dragged through the sagebrush. She sustained no serious injuries.[1] At Camp Harney she stayed with the Paiutes in Old Winnemucca's lodges, enjoying the gambling games at night and the gossip of the women. One night her half brother Lee came from the Malheur agency with a letter for her. It was an invitation from Agent S. B. Parrish to become the interpreter at the Malheur Reservation.[2]

Sarah's first reaction was to say no to the proposal. She wanted no more to do with agents and reservations. Lee told her that Agent Parrish, known as "Sam" Parrish, was a good man who did well by the Paiutes at Malheur, and he encouraged her to take the position. Sarah turned to her father and asked him if he would go with her. He replied that he would, and on the next day they made the long trip over broken terrain to the Malheur agency, which was fifty miles to the east. The Malheur Reservation had been established in 1872, and it was the home for three Paiute bands under Chiefs Weahwewa, Watta-belly, and Egan.[3] Chief Winnemucca and his band of 150 had occasionally spent time there. Sarah gives us the details of the unfolding events at the Malheur Reservation in her autobiography.

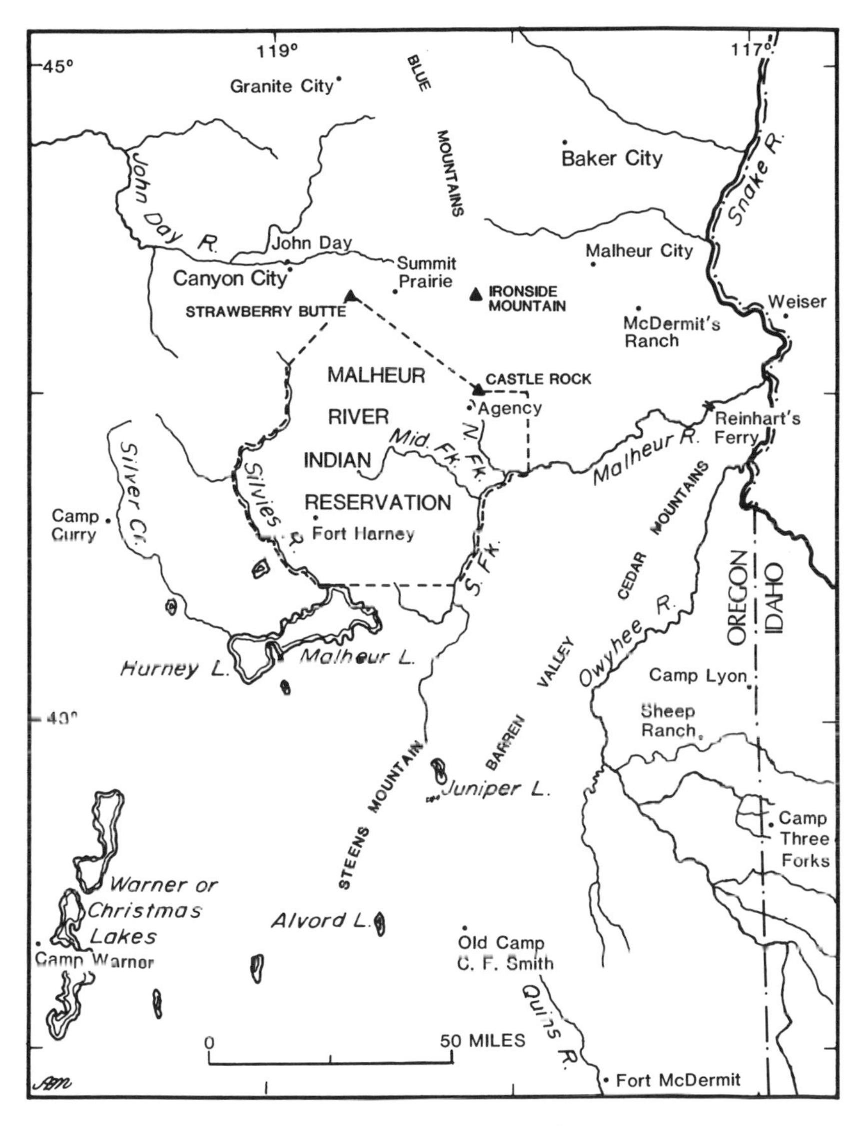

Map 2. Malheur Reservation and Vicinity

Agent Parrish was pleased to see Sarah. He gave her a nice room and a salary of forty dollars a month, which she gladly accepted.[4] Soon after her arrival Sarah observed how Agent Parrish treated the Indians. He called a council at which she acted as interpreter while the Paiute men, women, and children crowded around expectantly. Parrish told them that he had come to show the Paiutes how to work. He said that he could not kneel and pray for sugar, flour, and potatoes to rain down, as he was not a preacher. He drew a picture in the sand with a stick to show them his plans for building a water ditch to irrigate their fields, and he told them that crews would be needed for ditch digging and for going to the woods and cutting down trees for fences. Under his guidance the Indians would raise potatoes, turnips, and watermelon and would plant grain as well. They could raise barley and oats, but not wheat, as there was no grist mill at that time. When the crops were mature, they would belong to the Indians, because the land had been given to them by the government. Sarah saw that her people were delighted with the agent's words.[5]

Three young men were needed to learn blacksmithing, and three others to learn carpentry—trades at which they would be able to earn a living. A schoolhouse was to be built so that the young ones could learn to read and write. Parrish said that all the Numa should come to the reservation, where the government had given them a store, food, and clothes, and where they could work and earn a living. "Send out your men everywhere and have them come to this place," he told them.[6]

When the agent was finished speaking, Chief Winnemucca asked the people, "What do you all think of what this man, our new father, says?"

Chief Egan said, "I think it is very good, if he will only carry it out. There has been so much said that has never been fulfilled by our other agent."

Chief Oytes was a shaman and a follower of Smoholla, the prophet of the Dreamer religion. He considered himself to be bulletproof and kept himself apart from white ways. He announced: "I am not going to work. I and my men have our own work to do, that is, to hunt for our children."

When Sarah had translated what each leader had said, Parrish answered Oytes's statement by saying, "All right, Oytes,—you can do just as you like."

Chief Winnemucca rose and said, "My son, Natchez, tells me that if we do not work as we are told by the white people, we will not get along at all. . . . We will all work at whatever our white father says we must work at."

On the next morning all the Indians were ready to work, even those of Oytes's band though their leader was nowhere in sight. Everyone joined in, even old men, women, and children. Most had never done this kind of labor before, and there were not enough tools to go around. In the end people were on their knees, digging with their bare hands. The work continued thus for five days, until Sarah was told by Agent Parrish to bring the people again to a council.

Parrish complimented the Indians on what they had done, but told them he did not wish the old men and women to go to the fields, as it was too hard on them. He must have been aware of a new law passed by Congress that all Indians had to earn their rations (effective March 3, 1875), but he ignored it in the case of the old men. He expected the women to be preparing the meals for the workers.

At the end of six weeks the ditch was 2½ miles long and 10 feet wide. When the task was completed, Sarah again called the Paiutes together. Parrish said to them:

> All my people say that you won't work; but I will show that you can work as well as anybody, and if you go on as we have started, maybe the Big Father at Washington will now give us a mill to grind our corn. Do all you can, and I know [the] government will help you. I will do all I can while I am with you. I am going to have a schoolhouse put up right away, so that your children can go to school, and, after you have cut your hay, you can go out hunting a little while and get some buckskins; I know you will like that.

They all agreed happily and went to shake the hand of Sam Parrish and his brother, Charles, as well. Charles Parrish was the reservation commissary. His wife would soon be hired as the reservation teacher.[7]

Samuel Parrish was a hard, efficient worker, and he expected results from the work of the laboring Indians. He was the son of

S. B. Parrish, a pioneer of 1840, who won the Paiutes' esteem on the Malheur Reservation. (Courtesy of the Oregon Historical Society, Portland.)

one of the early Methodist missionaries to the Indians of Oregon. He believed that the Paiutes could better their lot in the space of a few years if the white man kept his word by them, treated them with respect, and cultivated their natural interest in learning.

Sarah's autobiography tells us that the Paiutes next built a road, so that supplies could be hauled in for the winter. Summer had come and gone, and the hay had to be cut. At about this time some Indians from the Columbia River came onto the reservation to trade with the Paiutes for furs and buckskins in exchange for horses. The Paiutes were afraid of being cheated, but wished to have permission from Agent Parrish to trade the hides that they had collected, especially their beaver pelts, which were quite valuable. Oytes was all for trading without permission, and he had swapped for three horses before the day was over.

In the meantime Chief Egan told Sarah of the presence of the Columbia Indians, who, he said, often made trouble and should not come near the reservation. Winnemucca also talked to Parrish about the matter and reminded him how the Paiutes were afraid of Oytes. The shaman had told the Numa the winter before that he had the power to make them ill if they did not follow his wishes. Winnemucca said, "Last winter we had some kind of sickness, and a great many of our children died. He said it was he who was making us sick, and he told us to pay him or else we would all die. Every one of us paid him, but a great many died anyhow."[8]

Parrish discovered that Oytes had taken thirty men from the reservation and joined the Columbia Indians. The group remained away from the Malheur for almost a month. It was soon after Oytes's return that Parrish called a council to pay the laborers for their work. Parrish was liberal, paying the haymakers one dollar a day for their labor, as well as telling them that the hay that had been cut was theirs. He explained that six horses and two mules belonged to the Paiutes on the reserve. He bought the grain that was raised, paying Chief Winnemucca and Egan for it in accordance with his agreement with the people. He announced: "Now I want to tell you something more. If you work for me or any of my men, we are to pay you for it. If you cut or pile wood, we will pay you for it. If I send you to Canyon City for myself or my men, you shall be paid for it." When he asked them if they liked his law, the Paiutes all said, "Truckee, Truckee," which meant "very well."

Parrish reminded them that their potatoes would be ready to dig when they returned from hunting. Then he distributed flour, a can of gunpowder, lead, and caps to each man except Oytes. That night the people were very happy and held a fandango, a celebration of dancing and singing. They were happier than they had been for a long time. Sarah joined them in the hand game and was as deft as any of the players at hiding the sticks while moving them from hand to hand in accompaniment with a rhythmical chant.

After the big hunt the ponies of the men were laden with dried venison. All came in to the reservation but Sarah's father and a few of his people. Winnemucca sent word to Sarah that he was going to the Pyramid Lake Reservation to see the Paiutes there and to encourage them to come to Malheur. Sarah was sorry to see her father leave, for she was afraid of Oytes, as were most of the other Paiutes.[9] Oytes acted strangely. He made signs with his hands and peculiar bowing motions, while he chanted nonsensical sounds and stared at people in an odd way.[10] He shared the belief, along with the followers of young Wovoka on the Walker River Reservation and other Dreamers, that there would be a resurrection of all Indians, at which the wrongs committed against them by the whites would be righted. The Dreamers believed that the mother earth should not be plowed and therefore one should not work as a farmer. Wovoka, however, willingly worked as a ranchhand in Mason Valley, Nevada.

On the day when rations were distributed, Oytes came to Sarah and said: "I want you to talk to your father, as you call him. Tell him I and my men are going to live with our brothers; that is, the Columbia River Indians. I cannot call that white man my father. My father was black, like myself, and you are all white but me, and, therefore, tell him I quit my country."

Sarah said to Chief Egan, who was nearby, that she would go. He offered to go also. When they had ridden a distance from camp, Sarah looked back and saw Oytes. She told Egan, "I am so frightened of that man." "Don't mind him," Egan said. "If he can make you frightened of him that is all he wants, but if you are not afraid of him he will be one of the best men you ever saw." Oytes continued to follow along behind.

When they stopped at the agent's house and went in to talk to him, Sarah told Sam Parrish everything that Oytes had said. Parrish turned to Oytes:

> I am heartily sorry that you have such a bad heart. Let me tell you, Oytes, if you want to get your young men into trouble, you can. I have not come here to make you do what you don't want to do. I came to tell you all that government is willing to do for you, and if you will not do it I cannot help you. I have men here to teach you all how to work, and now you want to take your men away with those Columbia River Indians. They are just like you. They don't want to work like other people. Now the sooner you go the better. I don't want to say anything more to you.[11]

The agent told Chief Egan that on the following Monday the Paiutes would be issued rations and that it would then be time for the potato digging. A pit would be dug to store the potatos for future use. An issue of clothing was also made, with which Sarah was delighted. Ten yards of calico plus ten yards of flannel for underwear were given to each woman, and unbleached muslin as well. Pantaloon goods were given to the boys, as well as handkerchiefs, shoes, stockings, and blankets. The men received shirts, pants, hats, looking glasses, and shoes, and they were able to choose the colors of the blankets and shirts that they received. The Northern Paiutes had never been treated in such a fashion before, and they never forgot their kind "father," Agent Parrish.

Although Oytes had not yet left the reservation, he received nothing. Neither did Sarah because she was on salary. Oytes came to her and complained bitterly, and later the same night he threatened the others if they would not give him some of their goods. In March, 1874, Indian Agent H. Linville had sent to Camp Harney for troops and permission to arrest Oytes because he had threatened to massacre the whites on the reservation at that time.[12] Now Oytes told the other Indians that he would kill Agent Parrish. When Sarah heard that threat, she ran to the agent and warned him. The whites on the reserve numbered twelve in all, including children. They prepared themselves for a vengeful attack. As Oytes made no move during the night, Agent Parrish sent for him the next morning. Chief Egan brought him up to the agency house.

Parrish stepped from the porch and told him: "Oytes, I have

three hundred dollars. If you will let me shoot at you, if my bolt won't go through your body the money is yours. You say bolts cannot kill you." The agent then stepped back with his gun cocked.

Oytes fell on his knees and cried: "Oh, my good father, don't kill me. Oh, I am so bad. I will do anything you say. I will do just as my men are doing [and go to work] . I will not go away if you will forgive me."

Parrish replied: "All right, Oytes; don't let me hear anymore of your talk, do you hear? You shall not fool me, and don't say anymore to your own people."

Oytes replied, "No, good father, I will not say anything more," and he and Parrish shook hands. The agent then took him to the store and gave him a blanket and a new set of clothes. He told him to return the goods that he had taken from the others.[13] After that, things went well for Agent Parrish and his charges, and there was mutual trust.

Soon after, General O. O. Howard, military commander of the Department of the Columbia, visited the Malheur Reserve. He was accompanied by his daughter, Grace, who had just graduated from Vassar College. This was the first time that the general met Sarah, and he was favorably impressed with her perfect English, her attractive appearance, and her "air of great self-respect."[14] During the night that he stayed at the reservation, the Paiutes assembled for a fandango and kept up their singing, dancing, and drumming so that the general had many wakeful hours. He was particularly worried for Grace's safety and called Sarah to the agency house to ascertain if the Indians were giving a war dance. She laughed and replied that they were merely celebrating his presence on the reservation and were performing the ritual in his honor. Howard rested more soundly during the remainder of the night.

Reporting on his observations at Malheur, Howard sent a telegram to the adjutant general: "Have just visited Malheur Indian Agency. Think it very important that present Agent be continued. Indians whites and army officers commend Parrish for successful management of remote and difficult agency. Please inform Commissioner of Indian Affairs."[15]

Despite the commendation of Howard and the warm acceptance of the Paiutes, Parrish received criticism from other quar-

Old-style nobees *alongside canvas tents in a Paiute encampment.* (Courtesy *of Nevada Historical Society, Reno.)*

ters. He had extended the limits of the reservation to ensure that the richest farming land, two hot springs where the Paiutes had traditionally bathed, and the land claimed by Chief Egan and cultivated by him would be a part of the reservation. Settlers' petitions to senators complained of the loss of land to the Indian Department, and anonymous letters of criticism in local papers did not help the standing of Parrish.[16]

Through the winter the Numa continued to work. They dug another ditch, which was 2½ miles long. One evening, when they had about half a mile to finish, Parrish called a council and told the people that they had 292 enemies in Canyon City. G. B. Curry was the leader of a group who wished to take the west end of the reservation for their own. Parrish told them, "These white men have talked to your Father in Washington, saying that you are lazy, and will not work."

Leggins and Egan said: "Our Father, you are here to talk for us. Tell our Big Father that we don't want to give up any of our reservation. The Pyramid Lake Reservation is too small for us all, and the white people have already taken all the best part of it. . . . We do not want to have white people near us. . . . We know what they are, and what they would do to our women and daughters."[17]

Parrish promised to write Washington and see what could be done. In the meantime work progressed on the school house. The carpenter finished the building in early spring. The Indian Department complained of the large number of employees on the reservation. The agent had hired his sister-in-law, Mrs. Annie R. Parrish, as teacher and Sarah Winnemucca Bartlett as her assistant.

Parrish defended his expenditures in a letter to Indian Commissioner E. P. Smith:

> The number of scholars as you will observe is increasing and the indians are all taking a great deal of interest in the same. We have added an industrial branch to the school in which the boys can learn something about farming and the girls can learn to sew and make up their own clothing in good shape. My intention hereafter is, instead of making issues of cloth, to compel the women and girls to come to the school house and make up all their clothing there under the immediate instruction of the teachers and I think that enough can be saved to the

government from material thus saved to almost pay the salaries of the teachers.[18]

He wrote the Department of Indian Affairs that Sarah was especially needed, as she could speak both languages.

The official opening of the new school house was on a glorious day in May, 1876. Mrs. Parrish, the well-loved teacher, brought her organ into the new building, and, with the windows thrown open, the people who gathered outside could hear the singing of the children. All the white employees sang as well. It was a joyous crowd.

Little Mattie, an orphan child and a niece of Chief Egan's, was especially enthralled by Mrs. Parrish.[19] Though she could not as yet understand the English language, Mattie recognized her as a kindhearted woman and a good teacher. The "white lily," as Mrs. Parrish was called by the children, brought to the classroom bright pictures of animals and natural scenes, upon which the students of various ages feasted their eyes. When she used a large wall map to introduce the children to the idea of the United States, the students thought that the land must be red, green, yellow, and blue, as it was on the map. Once Chief Egan himself came to the classroom and told the students that they should listen well to the teacher because it would help them greatly to speak and understand English and to know more about the white world.[20]

Sarah observed and learned a great deal from Mrs. Parrish's teaching methods. In her autobiography she explains that, after teaching in the morning, she and Mrs. Parrish cut out dresses and skirts in the afternoon for all the women of the tribe, and the women were occupied in making them up. Each of the young schoolgirls made a dress and a skirt for herself, as well as garments for the blind and those who were too old to do for themselves.[21]

Parrish was very proud of the Paiutes and what they were accomplishing. Ninety acres of newly plowed fields had been sown, and fences now protected the fields from roving stock. When a letter critical of Parrish appeared in a local paper, the agent wrote to General Howard that the "alias," or anonymous, writer was misinformed about the number of Indians on the reservation and that it was utterly false that the Paiutes had stolen horses:

> Now General, you will pardon me for saying anything about the above mentioned correspondence but when I am laboring faithfully and doing the best I can to raise up and improve these indians, and make them a home that will be a comfort to themselves and a pride to the Department, it makes me mad to have some irresponsible person under an alias assail me in the daily prints and virtually call me a thief.[22]

Seven days later President Grant appointed W. V. Rinehart, former army officer, as the new agent for the Malheur Reservation. When Parrish told the Paiutes that he was leaving, they were distraught. Oytes got up and said, "We will not let our father go; we will fight for him. . . . We have made no complaints against him. We will all stand by him. He has taught us how to work, and that's what we want, and the white lily is teaching our children how to talk with the paper, which I like very much. I want some of the young men to go and tell our father Winnemucca to come here as soon as he can. I know he will think as I do. I say once more, we will not let him go."[23]

Sarah told Parrish everything that was said by the Numa. In reply he told her to tell them that it was not because he had done anything wrong that he was being sent away, but because he was not a Christian, and all the reservations were to be under the Christian men's care. "Before I go," he said, "I am going to plant for you, and help you all I can. I will give Egan and Oytes land for peas; Oytes, just on the other side of the river for him and his men, and Egan at the Warm Spring . . . and . . . Jerry Long [*sic*] and Sarah Winnemucca, and others, on this side of the river. . . . Your new father will not be here until the first of July." Jerry Long was a blind cousin of Sarah's. She had asked Parrish to take him on as interpreter in her stead because he had a family to support and could not do other work. She meanwhile was employed as Mrs. Parrish's assistant in the school house. The Numa set to work. Parrish told them that they could plant whatever crops they desired.

When Chief Winnemucca arrived from Pyramid Lake Reservation, Sarah took him to Parrish. The old man took the agent's hands and said, "My good father, you shall not leave me and my people. Say you will not go."

He answered: "It is not for me to say. I would like to stay, but your Big Father in Washington says that I must go, and that a better man is coming here. You will like him, I know."

Winnemucca told him: "I do not want anyone but you. I am going to see the soldier-father tomorrow. I know they will keep you here for me, or I think they can if they wish to."

Parrish said, "They can do nothing against the government."

Winnemucca sat for a long time without saying a word. Then Parrish said, "Come with me, Winnemucca, I want to give you some things."

Sarah accompanied them to the storehouse, but when they got there, she noticed her father standing in one corner of the room as if he were lost. When Parrish asked him what kind of clothes he wanted, Winnemucca replied: "I don't want anything if you are not going to stay with me. I don't want anything from you, because it will make me feel so badly after you are gone."[24] Sarah had to explain to her father that the agent would not understand if he did not take the gifts, for that was the way of white people if they were to part; the whites even kept pictures of those who had died. The old man then accepted the clothing.

On the next day Sarah, Chief Winnemucca, Egan, and Oytes went to see the officers at Camp Harney. Sarah and her father stayed with a friend, a Mrs. Kennedy, until they could speak to the commanding officer, Major John Green. When the major received them, he thought that they had come to complain about their agent in the same way that they had about the previous one. Instead Winnemucca said:

> We all like our good agent Parrish. . . . There can be no better man than he, and why send him away? Oh, my good soldier-father, talk on paper to our Big Father in Washington, and tell him not to take him away. I have a reservation at . . . Pyramid Lake. For so many years not one of the agents ever gave me or my people an old rag. I am just from there. My people have nothing to live on there but what little fish they catch, and the best land is taken from them. A great many of my people . . . say they will come here to make homes for themselves.[25]

The major agreed to send a letter to Washington and tell the officials what the Paiutes had said. Then he turned to Sarah for more information. Although he was quite sympathetic with the

Indians' plight, there seemed to be little that he could do. He did, however, make the following report on May 26, 1876, to the assistant adjutant general of the Department of the Columbia:

> I have the honor to report that the Indian Chief Winnemucca paid me a visit yesterday, and the first question he asked was whether I knew why Mr. Parrish (Indian Agent) was to be removed: I told him I did not know the reason. He then went on to say that Mr. Parrish was doing so much for the Indians in the way of teaching them how to raise crops, that he thought it would be a great wrong to remove him when he was doing so much good. He described how much work had been done at the Agency since Mr. Parrish had assumed control. Winnemucca also says: That if they had had such an agent as Mr. Parrish, the war with General Crook would not have occurred; that all the Indians like him except two. . . . It seems to me strange to remove an agent who is doing so much for the Indians and one whom they are so unwilling to lose.[26]

Sarah and her father returned to the reservation and told Parrish what had transpired. He laughed, but Sarah was apprehensive about what might come. On June 28, 1876, Major Rinehart arrived, and, after Parrish had spent a day showing him the reservation and the plots of land belonging to their various owners, he said good-bye to the Numa. That was the last they saw of him.

11

Trouble at Malheur

During the summer of 1876, Sarah concerned herself with the problems that inevitably were to come between the Paiutes and the new agent at Malheur. She also attended to some personal business. She had married Edward Bartlett more than four years before, and in all that time they had lived together less than one month. Now she had fallen in love again, with a man named Joseph Satwaller, and she had decided to file for a divorce from Bartlett. Little is known of Satwaller except that he was a resident of Grant County, Oregon, where the Malheur Reservation was located.

Sarah started proceedings against Bartlett on July 10, 1876. A summons for her husband was printed in the *Dalles City* (Oregon) *Mountaineer* for a six-week period, since Grant County had no regularly published newspaper. Bartlett did not appear, and on September 21 the divorce was granted in the circuit court of Grant County. Charles Parrish, the former agent's brother, acted as Sarah's counsel. Although Sarah had not been allowed her day in court in the assault case in Winnemucca, Nevada, she was able to file divorce proceedings. Civil cases involving Indians were regarded differently from criminal cases, which were traditionally handled by the federal government.

At the divorce proceedings Sarah testified that she had sent

Bartlett money through the Wells Fargo & Co. express, but he had never written her, and that he never sent her money. She was quoted as saying: "We never quarrelled any before we separated. I was kind to Defendent, during our marriage and he was kind to me only he spent my money. And Defendent took my jewelry worth about $700.00 and pawned it for $200 at a pawnbrokers shop and spent it. I never got a cent of it. This was jewelry I had before I was married."[1] Sarah paid the court costs of $69.62 to regain the name Sarah Winnemucca.

Major W. V. Rinehart was an old soldier who had been in command of Fort Klamath in 1865, when the first Northern Paiute bands had accepted a treaty and agreed to live on the Klamath Reservation.[2] He was a proponent of an extermination style of warfare. In later dealings with General O. O. Howard, Rinehart spoke derisively of the "religious idiocy" of Howard's lenient policy toward Indians.[3] Rinehart believed in following the letter of the law and would not budge in his fervor to keep the Paiutes subservient to his disciplined administration. Authority was the principle tool with which he knew how to deal with others, and, when his authority was breached, even by a child, he became irrationally brutal. He pulled the ear of a young boy, knocked him down, and kicked him because he had laughed in response to an order. Sarah explained that the child did not understand English, but that was irrelevant to the major. Soon another boy was imprisoned and threatened with hanging because he had showed disrespect.

At the first council that Rinehart held, Egan and the other tribal leaders learned that Rinehart's attitude and policies toward them would be very different from those of the well-loved Agent Parrish.[4] Major Rinehart told them how he had come to make them good people and that the land on which they lived belonged to the government and not to the Paiutes. The government would, however, give them money for their labor, paying them one dollar a day for men, women, and boys. Rinehart said, "This is what the Big Father in Washington told me to tell you."

Egan protested, "The man who just left us told us the land was ours, and what we do on it was ours, and you come and say it is government land and not ours.[5] According to Sarah, Rinehart then became angry and said, "Egan, I don't care whether any of you stay or not. You can all go away if you do not like the way I do."

The Paiutes then went to work to test the agent and see if he would pay as he had promised. At the end of the week, on Saturday, the people walked right from the fields to the agent's office to get their money. They soon learned that Rinehart meant to pay in goods, not cash as he had promised, for he started putting up signs: blankets, six dollars; pants, five dollars; shoes, three dollars; and so on. He told Sarah, "The rations they have had are worth about four dollars a week, and then they have two dollars left to get anything they want out of the storehouse."[6]

When the Numa saw how they were to be paid, many got up and left. The white employees meanwhile were walking around in new clothes from the storehouse. Egan rose and said:

> Why do you want to play with us? We are men, not children. We want our father to deal with us like men. . . . Don't say you are going to pay us money, and then not do it. If you had told us you wanted us to work for nothing, we would have done it just as well [as] if you had said, "I will pay you." . . . You did not say anything about the clothing nor about what we ate while we were working. I don't care for myself, but my men want their pay, and they will go on with their work just the same. Pay them in money, and then they can go and buy whatever they like, because our Big Father's goods are too dear. We can go to our soldier-fathers, and get better blankets for three dollars than yours. You are all wearing the clothes that we fools thought belonged to us, and we don't want you to pay anything."[7]

Rinehart lost his temper and cried: "If you don't like the way I do, you can all leave here. I am not going to be fooled with by you. I never allow a white man to talk to me like that!"

That night in council many of the leaders said that they wished to go to Camp Harney to complain about their new agent, but Sarah advised that they wait a while. The council reluctantly agreed. Soon after, Egan and Oytes's men came to have a talk with Rinehart. Egan said, "My children are dying with hunger. I want what I and my people worked for; that is, we want the wheat. We ask for nothing else, but our agent Parrish told us that would be ours."

Rinehart replied, "Nothing here is yours. It is all the government's. If Parrish told you so, he told you lies."

Sarah then asked Rinehart why he had not spoken up when Agent Parrish had been there and was showing him around. Parrish had told Rinehart where each Paiute had land and had raised crops. She had been present and had not seen Rinehart make any objection to Parrish's arrangements. "Why, if you take the government wheat, you rob the government," Rinehart replied.[8]

Egan rose and told Sarah, "I want you to tell everything I say to this man. Then he made the following speech:

> Did the government tell you to come here and drive us off this reservation? Did the Big Father say, go and kill us all off, so you can have our land? Did he tell you to pull our children's ears off, and put handcuffs on them, and carry a pistol to shoot us with? We want to know how the government came by this land. Is the government mightier than our Spirit-Father, or is he our Spirit Father? Oh, what have we done that he is to take all from us that he has given us? His white children have come and have taken all our mountains, and all our valleys, and all our rivers; and now, because he has given us this little place without our asking him for it, he sends you here to tell us to go away. Do you see that high mountain away off there? There is nothing but rocks there. Is that where the Big Father wants me to go? If you scattered your seed . . . there, it will not grow. . . . Oh, what am I saying? I know you will come and say: Here, Indians, go away; I want these rocks to make me a beautiful home with! Another thing, you know we cannot buy. . . . We have no way to get money.[9]

When Egan sat down, Rinehart replied, "You had better all go and live with the soldiers. What I have told you is true, and if you don't like what the government wants you to do, well and good; if I had it my way I could help you, but I cannot. I have to do government's will."

The uneasiness and misunderstanding of the Paiutes increased when Rinehart began giving only vouchers instead of giving goods or rations in payment. His supplies fell very low because the Indian Department did not process an order that he had placed soon after his arrival until after the first snow had fallen.[10] Starvation was imminent, and it appeared to be the result of Rinehart's evil doings.

Sarah took a short trip into Canyon City before the snows were too deep for her to travel. She was accompanied by Joseph Satwaller to the courthouse, where they obtained a license and were

W. V. Rinehart, the last Indian agent at Malheur, whose tactics increased the discontent of the Northern Paiutes. (Courtesy of Oregon Historical Society.)

married on the same day, November 13, 1878,[11] in the home of Charles Parrish. Sarah did not write of this short-lived marriage in her autobiography, nor does it seem to have been generally known that she had married again. "The white Lily," Annie Parrish, was a witness, and the three Parrish children watched the ceremony, which was performed by a justice of the peace. Apparently Sarah returned to the reservation after only a short honeymoon, for she, Egan, and some other Paiutes rode to Camp Harney in the middle of November to complain about Rinehart to Major Green.[12]

When the major came to investigate the Paiutes' condition at Malheur, Egan was the chief spokesman. He told Green that the Paiutes had to work for all their issues and asked if this was the new rule of the government. He also said that no blankets were available at the agency, nor clothing of any kind, and people were very cold. They had been promised sugar for the sick, but received none. Egan observed that they never knew what to expect of the government.[13]

Major Green then explained that it was the law that all male Indians between the ages of eighteen and forty-five must work for all the goods and food that was issued to them. He told them that they ought to send their children to school so that they could learn to read and understand the law themselves. Then they would not have to depend on others to explain it to them. If they went to the agency doctor, they could get sugar if he prescribed it.[14] Most of the Indians preferred the remedies of their own medicine men.

After the council and investigation the major wrote his superiors that he could find no fault with Agent Rinehart except if "it be a fault that some of the Indians do not like him. Egan came to my tent after the interview, and said he was glad I had come, that he believed I had told them the truth and that he would go to work again with a good spirit."[15]

There was no school for the children to attend as Major Green had advised. It had been closed soon after Rinehart's coming, and Sarah no longer worked there. The agent had fired Sarah shortly before she had gone to Camp Harney with the chiefs to lodge a complaint against him. He found that she had written several letters against him, and he felt that she had kept the

Paiutes discontented. Her cousin Jerry Long was hired as interpreter in her place.

Sarah stayed at Malheur for a few weeks, trying to sell a stove for which she had paid fifty dollars. In the end she had to leave it to Rinehart, who enjoyed its warmth but would not pay her for it. He wrote a letter to General Howard complaining that Sarah was an unfaithful employee who had counseled and encouraged disobedience to the law: "The want of supplies at the Agency and the protracted delay in procuring more was easily turned to account by her in the attempt to engender dissatisfaction among the Indians. . . . Most of the real trouble and all the reported or imaginary threats of the Indians are believed to have originated with this unfaithful employee."[16]

In Sarah, who had worked diligently in the interests of her people, Rinehart had found a scapegoat to blame for his agency's troubles. Meanwhile, as she left the agency to join Joseph Satwaller, she undoubtedly held high hopes for her new marriage. It was not to be a success, however, though no details of the relationship have come down to us. Rinehart indicated in a letter to General Howard that she and her husband lived at the Warm Springs agency for a time.[17]

In the following months Agent Rinehart became increasingly concerned about the bands of Paiutes who refused to come to live on the Malheur Reservation and those who worked as farmhands on white ranches. It was an embarrassment to his administration that he had so few Paiutes on the reserve when he was supposed to be issuing to at least 700 people. He went himself to Steens Mountain to talk to Chief Winnemucca, but the old chief would not return to the Malheur. He proudly showed Rinehart a letter that had been written for him on buckskin by Judge Bonnifield of Winnemucca. It stated that he desired a new home on the Owyhee River in eastern Oregon, where he proposed to engage in farming and stock raising with all his people. The agent wrote the Indian Department: "In his visions of the new El Dorado on Owyhee the old man is very enthusiastic and will likely lead most of his people away from this Reservation for a time at least, as they seem to imbibe the spirit of his adventure and partake of his hallucination."[18]

In June, in northern Oregon, Chief Joseph and his Nez Percé

tribe refused life on a reservation, and war ensued. At Malheur, Agent Rinehart, frightened by the prospect of hostilities, collected guns and ammunition and sent his employees to safety. The Paiutes were also alarmed. They returned to the reservation in considerable numbers. It was unsafe away from the agency during wartime because the frontiersmen needed little excuse to take a potshot at an Indian.

Chief Winnemucca, however, still did not return to Malheur, and rumors circulated that his band had crossed the Snake River and were on their way north to join the hostile Nez Percé.[19] The cavalry companies at Fort McDermit were ordered to the front. There was considerable speculation that there would be a local Indian uprising while the soldiers were occupied elsewhere. The settlers took some comfort in the knowledge that Natchez was staying on his ranch near Lovelock and working as usual. The big Indian sent a telegram to General McDowell, saying: "No truth in reports of Piute hostility. Winnemucca my father at Idaho wants me and Chiefs talk with you danger that whites may make trouble for their own benefit—Pay expenses of me & chiefs to come and talk at San Francisco—answer immediately."[20]

General McDowell declined to send for Natchez, explaining that he had no resources to pay his fare, but he thanked him for confirming his own judgment that the Paiutes would remain peaceful. In the meantime, in Idaho, Old Winnemucca conferred with Governor Mason Brayman and told him of the Paiutes' peaceful intentions. He and some of his men were feasted by the governor as guests of honor.[21] Winnemucca returned in triumph to Oregon, but he was immediately challenged there by Oytes,[22] who was jealous because Winnemucca had paraded himself among the whites in Idaho as the chief of all the Paiutes. The old man had never been accepted very wholeheartedly on the Malheur Reservation by Oytes's band, who looked down upon Winnemucca's people as the "rabbit hunters" of Nevada. Oytes was a shaman of the Wadatoka band, whose wanderings had always been centered in the vicinity of Malheur.[23] He was sympathetic to Chief Joseph and the Nez Percés. Rinehart wrote to the commissioner of Indian affairs:

> It appears that those bands who have lived along the Blue Mountains [in northern Oregon] and followed the deer, antelope, and bear chase for a livelihood are disposed to look upon the rabbit hunters of the sage

plains of Nevada as an inferior people, and treat them accordingly—telling them this is not their country. Prompted by a feeling of independence of their less civilized Snake Brethren, the Piutes under Winnemucca are looking out for a new home of their own.[24]

One of Winnemucca's biggest objections to living on the Malheur was the presence of Oytes, who, as we have seen, threatened other Paiutes with the power of his Dreamer cult and the practice of witchcraft, which they generally believed could cause sickness and death. Winnemucca's interpreter at this time, Charlie Thacker, had been raised and educated by a white family, but he, also, shared Winnemucca's respect for Oytes's magical abilities.[25] Rinehart sent a special agent, William M. Turner, to seek out the old chief in another effort to get him back to the Malheur. Even though Turner promised that Agent Rinehart would put a stop to Oytes's 'black art,' he too could not convince Winnemucca.[26]

Still pursuing his old dream of land on the Owyhee River, Chief Winnemucca once more visited San Francisco, accompanied by Natchez and several other Paiute leaders from Virginia City and Churchill County, Nevada. He was still vigorous; his hair, cut short, was only slightly sprinkled with gray. While interviewing General McDowell, he wore a soldier's uniform coat with a double row of buttons, cavalry pants with broad yellow stripes down the sides, a pair of huge epaulets, and his usual felt hat adorned with a large, black plume.[27]

Through Natchez, who acted as interpreter, Winnemucca explained that he was now an old man, too old to fill the onerous position of chief of a tribe numbering over 700 people, and that he wanted the government to grant him a reservation for himself and about 40 of his tribe, who were willing to cast their lot in with his. In addition to this he wanted a company of cavalry stationed on the reservation to keep the peace between him and the other Indians and between the Indians and whites. Since he was too old to fight, he would have to stand between the two factions and let them fight over his head. He wanted to have land given him, so that he could plant grain and raise stock. He had always been a good friend of the white man and had used his influence on the side of peace on all occasions when trouble seemed imminent.[28]

General McDowell told Winnemucca that he already had an

agent, Rinehart, and he would have to apply through him to the Indian Department for the land that he wanted; the military authorities could do nothing. There were at this time two companies of cavalry and one of infantry at Camp Harney; they represented all that could be spared for the region. The general advised the chief to return to his reservation at once.[29]

When the party returned to Winnemucca, Nevada, Natchez was interviewed by a reporter of the *Daily Silver State.* He observed "No Indians can get anything from the government if they behave themselves." The reporter agreed that "the Piutes for years have been peaceable and it seems that because they are so, they receive no favors from the Indian Department."[30]

Winnemucca's band and that of his friend Ocheo of Surprise Valley, California, continued to show their unwillingness to come onto the Malheur Reservation. This rankled Rinehart, who claimed that they were pulled away by the free food at Fort Bidwell and Fort McDermit and the nightly fandangos, which he called a "species of brothel-dance."[31]

These allegations of Rinehart's quickly solicited responses from the officers stationed at Bidwell and McDermit. They testified that the Indians had not been given subsistence at the military camps for years and that they seldom saw Ocheo and Winnemucca. Captain Wagner of Fort McDermit wrote, "For the past three years the 'Old Chief' with his personal band of about 50, all relations, camped portions of the time on the Owyhee River near the Idaho line—there they subsist by fishing and hunting."[32]

Wagner called in Ocheo, who made a sympathetic appeal "to be let alone," which Wagner reported as follows:

> He was harming no one, he asks for no assistance from the Government or the settlers, this is his home, he was born at this very creek—pointing to a creek east of the garrision—his father and mother are buried but a hundred yards from here. He has a ranch about four miles from here, with land fenced in and under cultivation, whereon he was raising potatoes and grain: during the winter he was hunting game in Warner Valley and Mountains. General Crook and all the former officers at Camp Warner and this post told him that he was all right as long as he behaved himself. He does not want to go on a reservation, and will not go.[33]

General Crook confirmed Ocheo's statement. He warned McDowell that this band of Surprise Valley Paiutes was well armed and that the country they occupied was difficult of access. If they chose to resist, they would be as determined and as difficult to overcome as the Modocs. McDowell suggested to the War Department that they be slow to yield to any efforts that might be made toward the military to coerce Ocheo's band onto the Malheur Reservation.[34]

As for Winnemucca, he visited the Malheur once again and asked that Rinehart work on his behalf for the land he coveted on the Owyhee. Rinehart would not support him in his purpose and told the old chief, "Since you are not satisfied at Pyramid Lake Agency and do not like Malheur, now your people are vagabonds without homes or property and they soon will be without friends and regarded as worthless." He did offer him a location at the confluence of the north fork of the Malheur River with the main river, fourteen miles below the agency. Winnemucca indicated that he would consider the offer if he could have the use of agency teams and tools to build a road to the place. Rinehart agreed. On the next morning the agent discovered that Winnemucca's band had suddenly left the reservation. Oytes had as usual threatened the old man and his people. As a result it was unlikely that he would ever bring his band to the reserve.[35]

All the Paiutes on Malheur Reservation were seriously discontented. Their unhappiness was not caused by the connivings of Oytes, who was avoided as a shaman of power, but by the administration of Rinehart. The latter never deviated from his policy of giving issues only to working Paiutes, no matter how great the need.

Chief Egan expressed his animosity to a saddler in the cavalry at Fort Harney, who passed on the information to United States Senator Newton Booth, who he thought might take an interest in the Paiutes' plight. He wrote:

> From what I have been able to learn, not alone from the Indians themselves, but from white men as well, the cause of the discontent in this locality, is due to the rascally treatment the Indians receive at the hands of the Agent Rinehart. . . . The Agent has upon his "Rolls" between 600 or 700 Indians, for which he draws "Government Allowances" that of this number, he issues scanty allowances to such as work for him (the Agent) upon his farm. . . . Ehgan, the "War Chief" of the Payutes. . . . cannot speak english [*sic*] very well, but from the interview I had with him, I am Strongly inclined to the belief that he does not

Camp Harney, Oregon, during the winter of 1872. (Courtesy of Oregon Historical Society.)

propose to bear this sort of treatment much longer. I could read his determination in his countenance.[36]

In mid-April, 1878, after a church service conducted by Rinehart, several tribal leaders, including Egan, accused the agent of concealing from them the state of affairs at the Fort Hall Reservation in Idaho. Oytes told the agent that the Paiutes were afraid that soldiers would come and take away their guns and ponies as they had those of the Bannocks at Fort Hall. Rinehart replied that General Crook was at Fort Hall investigating the trouble and that, if they wanted, he would send for him. He said that they should not listen to the reports of trappers and squawmen, but wait for the full report from the general.[37]

Meanwhile the intruders' stock were grazing on the Malheur Reservation in large numbers, and the ranchers made no secret of their intention to take up residence on the Malheur.[38] At the request of the Indian Department, Rinehart reluctantly produced figures that showed that squatters maintained 545 horses and 10,720 cattle on the reservation and that they had also cut eighty tons of hay.[39] Winnemucca, Oytes, and Egan were aware that the citizens of Harney Valley had signed a petition to acquire the most fertile land on the western boundary of the reserve.[40] The chiefs complained that the area was their only source of the camas root, a staple much like potato on which the Paiutes depended; the settlers' contention that the Indians had no use for this part of the reserve was absurd. The chiefs again took their complaint to Camp Harney.

Finally, under pressure from the military, the Indian Department requested the removal of the settlers and their stock. When news of this decision reached the squatters, Rinehart found that the ranchers, not surprisingly, were suddenly interested in leasing the land. First J. W. Scott came forward and offered $100 as a deposit on a lease for Harney Valley. On the same day a Mr. Devine of Todhunter and Devine, who had signed the settlers' petition, upped Scott's offer by a proposal to rent 500 square miles of the reservation at $200 annually. The proposal included all of Harney Valley and the Crow Camp country.[41] Two days later J. W. Scott was back with a better proposition than Devine's: $1,500 per annum, paid in advance, for the use of the same acreage that Devine had requested for a five-year period.[42] Rinehart recommended that the department accept the terms of Scott's lease because the Indians had no immediate need for the land except for hunting, root digging, and fishing, and the cattle would not intrude upon those activities. A day later Rinehart granted authority to Peter French to cut the timber on the reservation, which was to be used for building and repairs at Camp Harney.[43]

For all his faults, Agent Bateman on the Pyramid Reserve had at least consulted Young Winnemucca and other Paiutes when there were major decisions to be made regarding the reservation. Such a course never entered Rinehart's head. He considered that his charges were incapable of making such decisions concerning the land that was their home, and he maintained that they were on the reservation only "through the courtesy of the United States Government." But, as it turned out, sudden events were to lead to a new crisis, in which the eviction of squatters, or the leasing of land to cattlemen, became of minor consequence to Agent Rinehart.

12

The Beginning of Hostilities

In April, 1878, Sarah was visited by a delegation of three Paiutes from the Malheur Reservation. She had not been living with Joseph Satwaller for some time and was working for a Mrs. Charles Cooley at the head of the John Day River near Prairie City, Oregon.[1] The men told her: "We are worse off than when you were at the Malheur, if that is possible. There is so little food, the children are dying of hunger." Sarah could see the poor condition of the men themselves.

Mrs. Cooley invited the hungry men into the house, and a meal was set before them such as they had not eaten for a long time. They asked Sarah: "Please come to Camp Harney and tell the officers that we are hungry, for Jerry Long, the interpreter, is in with Rinehart; he gets plenty to eat. You are our only voice!"

Sarah reminded the men how little she had been able to help them when she had complained to the officers at Fort Harney. She told them that she would do all that was within her power, but she could not leave at that moment. Toward the end of May six more delegates came from the Malheur and begged for Sarah's help again. This time she promised she would come as soon as she could get over the snow-covered mountains with her wagon.

On the first of June two gentlemen from Canyon City came to

Sarah and asked if she would take them to the Malheur Agency, for they had heard that she was going there. One of the men, a Mr. Morton, had a daughter named Rosey, a pretty little girl of twelve, who would be making the trip. Sarah agreed to take them to Malheur for $20. They left Mrs. Cooley on June 4. After making their way over the mountainous wagon trails, they arrived at the Malheur Agency on the next evening. Sarah dropped her passengers at Rinehart's house and went on to stay with her cousin Jerry Long.

Jerry told her that many Bannock Indians were now on the reservation and that there was trouble afoot. He sent for Egan, Oytes, and Bannock Jack to come speak with her. Jerry had no food, and, when the others came in, they had none either.

"Did you bring any salmon or anything to eat? Sarah went to bed without anything to eat. We have not anything at all down here," Jerry told them. "We have not caught any salmon for ten days and therefore we had nothing to bring. What does that praying agent mean by not giving us our rations?" Egan complained bitterly.

Jerry replied, "I was there yesterday to see if I could buy some flour of him, but he won't sell me any. He told me to tell you and Oytes that he has written to Washington about the wheat, and just as soon as the order comes he will send to your people."[2]

Sarah went to the council tent with Jerry and was introduced to the Bannocks. Bannock Jack asked if she had heard of the trouble at Fort Hall, and she replied that she had not seen a newspaper for a long time. He then told her what had happened. Two girls had been digging roots when white men came and caught one and used her shamefully. The brother of the girl, Tambiago, got drunk and killed a white man in retaliation. The Bannocks were told to bring in the Indian within ten days to serve white justice. When the fugitive was found, the Indians returning him to the fort discovered that Colonel John Smith had already taken away all the Bannocks' ponies and guns in retaliation against the tribe. Jack complained that it was not as if they had not tried to bring in Tambiago, and the guns and ponies were not the government's to take. He asked Sarah to write it all down and send it to Washington, which she agreed to do.

Egan rose and made a long speech about Agent Rinehart and

how he had wronged them. He spoke with dignity and authority. He was dressed like a white farmer in a cotton suit and straw hat, with his hair cut short at the neck.[3] His appearance was in sharp contrast to that of the Bannocks, whose long, braided hair was arranged in a pompadour at the forehead, while feathers and beads hung from their fringed leather garments. Sarah noticed that all of the council looked to Egan as their leader. Oytes listened attentively to him, while crouching quietly in a corner.

Egan said that Agent Rinehart had never issued clothing since he had been at Malheur. He had taken all the stray horses and penned them up for his own and shot the Paiutes' horses if they chanced to go into his grain fields. He allowed his employees to play cards and gamble with Jerry Long and the mail carrier so that they lost any money they had earned. "Now one and all of you, my men, give our mother what little money you have. Let her go and talk for us. Let her go right on to Washington, and have a talk with our Great Father," Egan implored.

He collected $29.25 from the council and gave it to Sarah, who promised she would make the long trip for them to Washington, D.C. She told them that she would sell her horse and wagon in Elko, Nevada, where she could board the train. She had agreed to take Mr. Morton and Rosey to Silver City, Idaho, en route to Elko. The party left the agency on the morning of June 8 by way of the Barren Valley.[4]

Sarah did not know that word had been received at Fort Harney of new trouble with the Bannocks on Big Camas Prairie in southern Idaho. The warrior chief Buffalo Horn had attacked and wounded some white freighters. The Bannock chief had served as a scout for the whites under General Howard during the recent Nez Percé war, but now he was embittered because the settlers had not fulfilled their promises to remove squatters and their cattle from the Camas Prairie, as had been agreed by treaty in 1868. He had 300 or 400 warriors who were well mounted and anxious to fight.

At Malheur, Rinehart was aware that all was not right on his reservation. He was suspicious of the Bannocks who had recently come from Fort Hall, and he would not issue to them, though Egan begged that the visitors be given food. Then a courier arrived reporting the Camas Prairie depredation, and this messenger was followed a few days later by a second, who reported that the Bannocks on the Snake River had stolen government wagons loaded with ammunition. Rinehart moved his employees off the agency. When he found that his own Paiutes had left to assemble at the southeastern corner of the reserve in Barren Valley (even Jerry Long, his interpreter, had gone with them), the agent hurriedly left for the settlements in the John Day River valley.[5]

General Irvin McDowell was apprised of the trouble in Idaho. He telegraphed to Camp McDermit for confirmation from Natchez and Chief Winnemucca that they would help keep the peace. Both professed their continued friendship for the whites and announced their intention to leave for the Malheur Reservation to talk to the Bannocks there.[6]

Jim Crowley and his son were cattlemen in Barren Valley, along with J. W. Scott, who was now the beef contractor for the Malheur Reservation. These men talked with the Bannock and Paiute chiefs at the ranch of a man named Thomas Davidson. The Indians asked Scott if he would write their grievances on paper to send to Washington. If so, the Paiutes promised to return to the reservation despite all that had occurred with Rinehart. The chiefs dictated, and Natchez interpreted what Scott should write for them. When they had finished, not having much confidence in Scott's integrity, they took the paper and gave it to Crowley to read.

They found that Scott had not voiced their grievances, but "had painted the Indians as 'demons' and the agent as an 'angel.' " Natchez and Old Winnemucca could barely restrain the Indians from killing Scott on the spot.[7] Subchief Leggins of Winnemucca's band made an earnest speech in the whites' behalf, reminding the others that he had invited the white men, and, if they were killed, he and the Paiutes would be blamed for it. He declared that they would have to kill him first. Since the Bannocks wished to influence the Paiutes to join them, the issue was not pressed.

The whites stayed until darkness. When they attempted their escape, they were chased by the hostile Indians for fifteen miles.[8] While being pursued, Natchez leaped from his exhausted horse and hid in the sagebrush. Thus he finally eluded his pursuers. Old Winnemucca, however, was captured and held prisoner by Oytes, who had become the new leader of the Malheur Paiutes.

Chief Egan too had lost his authority, for the voices of moderation were no longer tolerated.

Crowley rushed to warn the troops at Fort Harney of a new Bannock-Paiute war alliance. Already most of the cavalry at Harney were marching eastward toward Idaho, and only a skeletal force remained at that fort. Rinehart returned with a few employees to the Malheur agency to check on its condition. When he heard the report from Crowley, he telegraphed Commissioner E. A. Hoyt to ask for troops to protect the public property because he was abandoning the agency.[9] Levi Gheen, a farmer at the Duck Valley Reservation near the Nevada border, also sent a telegram to the commissioner: "The Bannocks are murdering and plundering through the northern country— They have run the Shoshones off the Duck Valley reservation and taken possession of everything. A Shoshone just arrived [in] great excitement. I am here without means. What shall I do!"[10]

Sarah says in her autobiography that, as she, Rosey, and Mr. Morton traveled through Barren Valley, they knew nothing of an Indian war, but they did notice that the few houses along the road were vacant. On the morning of June 12, as they were coming to the summit before the descent to Fort Lyon on the Oregon-Idaho line, they met a man on horseback, who stopped to warn them that the Bannocks were warring with the whites and killing everyone in their way. He said that they had chased the stage driver as he was coming from Elko and that they had killed him and wounded a passenger, who fortunately got away on one of the stage horses. The Bannocks had captured guns and ammunition. The messenger told Sarah's party that they should hurry on to Stone House, where the settlers had congregated for some protection.

Sarah's pony, which had been trotting neatly, was now rushed ahead. The three passengers in the wagon held on, while keeping a cautious eye out for hostiles. When they drove up beside Stone House, men came out of the building with guns, wanting to know who they were. Sarah explained that they had just heard of the war from a man on the road.

Captain Reuben F. Bernard's cavalry company had followed Buffalo Horn's trail from the Camas Prairie in Idaho. They arrived at Stone House on the same day as did twenty volunteers from Silver City, Idaho, who had recently engaged the Bannocks in battle near South Mountain in Idaho. One of the volunteers, Piute Joe, claimed that he had killed Buffalo Horn in the fight, but the soldiers were skeptical of the Paiute's story. Sarah noticed that the soldiers were looking at her as if she were some fearful animal, and she felt very uncomfortable. After Bernard spoke to the captain of the citizen scouts, he introduced himself politely to Sarah and said, "The citizens say that you have a good deal of ammunition in your wagon."[11] Sarah's heart "almost bounded into her mouth." She said: "Captain, they must know or they would not say so. . . . If you find anything in my wagon besides a knife and fork and a pair of scissors, I will give you my head for a football. How can I be taking guns and ammunition to my people when I am going right away from them?"[12] The tall, black-bearded captain had been active in the campaign against the Modocs and was now in charge of Fort Bidwell. He told Sarah that he believed her.

Sarah knew, of course, that her trip to Washington, so recently proposed by Egan, was now postponed indefinitely. She asked Bernard if she might be of service to the army, as she had been employed before as an interpreter and scout and was familiar with those duties. Bernard replied that he would telegraph to General Howard at Fort Boise and see what the general proposed. He asked if Sarah knew the country well, and she informed him that she did. Later, when Bernard moved on to a place called Sheep Ranch, he assured Sarah that, if Howard wished her services, he would let her know.

Sarah had a difficult time that night, for the people at Stone House still accused her of smuggling ammunition.[13] She cried and told them to look in her wagon. Finally a Captain Hill of the volunteers spoke for her: "I know your father is a friend of the whites. If I can do anything for you, I will be most happy to do it. If you want to go to the command, I will give you a horse."[14]

On the next morning Sarah took leave of Rosey and Mr. Morton. She claims in her autobiography that Morton had proposed marriage to her and that she had declined, saying that she could only marry for love (that she was still married to Joseph Satwaller was apparently not discussed). Sarah had decided to join Bernard at Sheep Ranch and saw the opportunity to go there with some couriers who were headed in that direction because telegraph lines had been pulled down. When they arrived, Captain Bernard informed Sarah that General Howard had accepted her as a scout. He also told her that her brother Natchez was reported to be killed or captured by the Bannocks. Numb with grief, Sarah also learned that her father and other tribesmen were held unwillingly by the Bannocks. She immediately made up her mind to go to them.

Bernard reported to Howard, "Sarah Winnemucca is in my camp; she wants to go to her people with any message you or General McDowell might desire to send; thinks if she can get to the Pi-Utes with such message she could get all the well-disposed to come near the troops, where they could be safe and fed; says there is nothing at the Malheur agency with which to feed them."[15]

Howard answered: "Send Sarah with two or three friendly Indians straight to her people, and have them send a few of their principal men to you. I will see that all who behave well and come in are properly fed. Promise Sarah a reward if she succeeds."[16]

Sarah tells us that she was sent off from Sheep Ranch the next morning with two Paiutes, George and John, who reluctantly accompanied her into the hostile zone. She had been offered $500 for the return of her people. Bernard had given her a helpful note at the last: "To all good citizens in the country—, Sarah Winnemucca, with two of her people, goes with a dispatch to her father. If her horses should give out, help her all you can and oblige. Captain Bernard."[17]

The trio traveled fifteen miles to the Owyhee River crossing. There they found citizen scouts, who gave Sarah a fresh horse and something to eat. They soon struck the Bannock trail and traced it down the Owyhee for some miles to the spot where the Bannocks had camped. Sarah knew that the Bannocks had been mourning the death of Buffalo Horn, for she found broken necklaces, torn clothing, and remnants of cutoff hair along the trail. Then she found that the Indians had turned toward Barren Valley. The three traveled all day through the rocky, dry country and did not stop to rest even when daylight ceased. Finally, Sarah called a halt when their horses gave out.

George and John alternated watch while Sarah slept with her saddle for a pillow. Her horse, tied to her arm, kept waking her but there were no trees to which to stake mounts in the wasteland. At daybreak Sarah mounted and hurried on, as both the animals and their riders were almost dead for water. Heading for Jim Crowley's ranch in Barren Valley at a hard gallop, they discovered on arrival that the house had been burned to the ground. Chickens were still running around in the yard, and John suggested they catch one for breakfast, but Sarah insisted it would not be right. She drew water from the well for their coffee and found a burned-out tin can in which to make it, while the two men watered the horses.

They rode hard all day over alkali flats and tumbled lava rocks following the trail through country that was destitute of wood, water, and grass. It was at least sixty miles to any white habitation, and, when Sarah spotted a discarded clock on the trail, she knew that the Bannocks must still be ahead. They soon found a fiddle without a bow, which Sarah tied onto her saddle. Later that same day they spotted a mountain sheep, which John had the luck to kill. They were happy to take some of the meat, but in the excitement of the hunt Sarah had lost her fiddle. Five miles farther they noticed two figures on a hillside. Sarah took her handkerchief and waved, and, as the riders drew nearer, there was a call from the mountainside: "Who are you?"

"Your sister, Sarah!" Sarah replied. She had recognized Lee Winnemucca, who ran down the mountain and joined them. He told them:

> Oh, dear sister, you have come to save us, for we are all prisoners of the Bannocks. They have treated our father most shamefully. They have taken from us what few guns we had, and our blankets, and our horses. They have done this because they outnumber us. . . . Here I am standing and talking to you, knowing the great danger you are in by coming here. . . . Take off your hat and your dress and unbraid your hair, and put this blanket round you, so if they should come down they would not know who it is. Here is some paint. Paint your face quick. Here, men, hide your guns and take off your clothes and make yourselves look as well as you can.

All of this was accomplished quickly.

"Where is our father?" Sarah asked.

"We are all up over that mountain. We are but six miles from here. . . . but you will be killed if you go there . . . our brother Natchez has made his escape three days ago."

When Sarah heard that last piece of news, she was overjoyed.

Juniper Lake, Oregon, with Steens Mountain in the background. Here Sarah Winnemucca successfully brought her father and other Paiutes out of a Bannock war camp, which was located in a valley beyond these precipitous slopes. (Courtesy of Robert Canfield.)

She told Lee that she had to go to their father because she had come with a message from General O. O. Howard."[18]

Lee led the way over the rocky, steep mountainside, which they had difficulty ascending. At last Sarah looked down into the hostile stronghold and was overcome with the sight. There were about 327 lodges below, and 450 warriors were in Little Valley, catching and killing cattle that they had herded before them in their plunder through the countryside. As a civilized Indian woman Sarah thought it a beautiful but terrifying sight. She asked:

"Brother, is our father's lodge inside the line? We must leave our horses here and go on foot."

Lee replied, "If you are discovered, how will you get out?"

"Oh, well, our horses are almost given out anyway; so, dear brother, we must trust to good luck. . . . Let us go quick and be back, for I have no time to lose."

They hurried down the mountain and were not distinguished from the other Paiutes by the Bannocks.[19]

Before Sarah entered her father's lodge, she waited excitedly until Lee had announced her presence. Old Winnemucca then took her in his arms and said, "Oh, my dear little girl, and what is it? Have you come to save me yet? My little child is in great danger."

Everyone in the tent whispered, "Oh, Sadie, you have come to save us!"

Sarah told them: "Yes, I have come to save you all if you will do as I wish you to and be quiet about it. Whisper it among yourselves. Get ready tonight, for there is no time to lose, for the soldiers are close by. I have come from them with this word: 'Leave the hostile Bannocks and come to the troops. You shall be properly fed by the troops.' Are you all here? I mean all the Malheur Reservation Indians?"

"Yes, all are here, and Oytes is the chief of them."

"Father, you tell the women to make believe they are gathering wood for the night and while they are doing that they can get away."[20] While Sarah was yet talking, the women left one by one with ropes in their hands, with their babies on their backs and their little ones by their sides.

Lee directed the men to catch as many horses as they could after dark and drive them to Juniper Lake. Winnemucca gave similar orders to his nephews, George, Jim and James. Now that it was night, they all left the tent. Sarah felt as if she were in a dream. She could not get along, and her father had to help her. When a horse came running, they all fell to the ground. When it stopped nearby, the rider called softly for Chief Winnemucca.

It was Lee's wife, Mattie, with a horse for them, which Sarah was very thankful to mount. They hurried back up the mountain to where they had left their horses and, upon finding them, rushed down again toward Juniper Lake, where the women were cooking the meat of the mountain sheep that had been killed earlier. After eating quickly, they hurried on their way. Children were tied to their mother's backs so that they would not fall off in their sleep.

Lee came to Sarah and told her that he was going back for more people. Jerry Long was held a close prisoner, and Egan and many of his people had not come.

Sarah replied, "Get all the people you can."

Winnemucca, Mattie, Sarah, George, and John led, while six men brought up the rear and watched to see if they were pursued. At daybreak they came to Summit Springs and called a halt. They unsaddled their horses and prepared to lie down to rest. Winnemucca insisted that Sarah have something to eat. Just then came a warning alarm. Sarah and Mattie rode bareback on their horses to meet the rider, whose mount was almost falling from under him.[21] He told them, "We are followed by the Bannocks."

Sarah told him to jump up behind her, and they hurried back to the camp with the news. The rider said that Egan and his whole band had been overtaken and forced back. He had looked back and saw Lee running. The Bannocks shot at him, and he supposed that he was killed.

Winnemucca said, "If my son is killed, I will go back and be killed by them too. If we are to be killed off for what the white people have done to them, of course we cannot help ourselves."

Sarah pleaded with her father to save himself and the others with him. She told him that she was determined to return to General Howard. Her father then agreed to continue their flight and asked that she send the troops to them as fast as possible. Mattie cried out to Sarah, "Let me go with you. If my poor husband is killed, why need I stay?"[22]

Away the two women dashed on their horses, galloping through the desolate country without water. At noon the same day they finally came to a stream called Muddy Creek, where they let their horses rest and found some white currants to eat. Then, jumping their horses across the stream, they sped on toward the soldiers' camp. At three o'clock they were at the crossing of the Owyhee River, where they were given fresh horses and hard bread by the white volunteers. Then they were off again to Sheep Ranch, whipping their mounts into a lather. Upon their arrival Captain Bernard helped them from their horses.

Sarah was so fatigued and excited that she burst into tears and could not speak for a time. Captain Bernard, Lieutenant Charles E. S. Wood, Lieutenant John Pitcher, and General O. O. Howard received her report. Sarah told them that Chief Winnemucca was on his way and that he wanted soldiers for protection from the Bannocks, who had forced back Chief Egan. She noted that the officers looked at each other as if she was lying; Lieutenant Pitcher winked at Lieutenant Wood. In contrast, General Howard had such confidence in her story that he changed his plan of operation.[23] Piute Joe was sent with the captain of the volunteers, Colonel "Rube" Robbins, and all Robbins's men to bring in Chief Winnemucca and his band. Within a few days forty of the band were found and were sent safely to Camp McDermit.[24]

The whole round trip, from 10 o'clock on June 13 to 5:30 on June 15, in the saddle day and night over hard terrain, had been a grueling ride of 223 miles.[25] Sarah was justly proud of having helped her father and her people from the hostile camp, though the Paiutes who were left behind or recaptured by the Bannocks, including Egan, had lost any chance to escape. Sarah's raid of the camp had caused them to show their true colors to the Bannocks, and they were closely held prisoners through the remainder of the war, which had only just begun.[26]

13
The Bannock Indian War

Brigadier General George Crook, Department of the Platte, was interviewed early in the Bannock War of 1878 by a reporter from the *Omaha* (Nebraska) *Herald:*

Reporter: There is much serious apprehension in regard to trouble with the Indians.

Gen. Crook: There are good grounds for it. As long as the muzzle-loading arms were in use we had the advantage of them, and 20 men could whip a hundred, but since the breech loaders came into use it is entirely different; these they can load on horse-back and now they are a match for any man. In regard to the Bannocks I was up there last Spring, and found them in a desperate condition. I telegraphed and the agent telegraphed for supplies, but word came that no appropriation had been made. They have never been half supplied. The agent has sent them off for half a year to enable them to pick up something to live on, but there is nothing for them in that country. The buffalo is all gone, and an Indian can't catch enough jack rabbits to subsist himself and family . . . What are they to do! Starvation is staring them in the face, and if they wait much longer they will not be able to fight. . . .

Reporter: It seems to me that it would be cheaper to treat the Indians justly.

Gen. Crook: Of course it would be cheaper. All the tribes tell the same story. They are surrounded on all sides, the game is destroyed or driven away, they are left to starve and there remains but one thing for them to do—fight while they can. Some people think the Indians do not understand these things, but they do and fully appreciate the circumstances in which they are placed. Our treatment of the Indian is an outrage.[1]

The Department of Indian Affairs could not let this censure go unnoticed, especially as it was fighting for its very existence at this time. Congress was considering the transfer of the Indians to the War Department from the Department of the Interior. It was publicly pointed out by Indian Commissioner E. A. Hoyt that all of the congressional appropriations for Indians did not amount to more than 4½ cents per day per Indian for subsistence.[2] That was the ready retort of Agent Rinehart also, whenever his administration of the Malheur Reservation came under fire.

Ironically three wagon teams loaded with desperately needed flour finally arrived at Malheur soon after the start of the outbreak.[3] The delay of a few weeks had brought calamitous results to the Paiutes and Rinehart. The Malheur agent had telegraphed General Howard for troops to protect the agency, but the general had replied that Rinehart should employ citizen guards for this purpose. When Rinehart then asked the Indian Department for further instructions, he waited five days without a reply.[4]

He proceeded to Canyon City and tried to employ a small guard on his own, but found it impossible to procure arms or men. He then asked Captain Evan Miles, who was en route to Camp Harney, for a small detachment of men to guard the agency. This plan was frustrated because all of Miles's men were needed by Bernard, whose company had driven the Indians beyond the agency.[5]

When he thought that danger from the hostiles was past, Rinehart sent for all his employees to return to the reserve. He found, however, that Major Joseph Stewart and his company were ensconced at Malheur, and they were soon followed by General Howard and his staff. Howard instructed Stewart to take charge of all public property, and Stewart's officers were to account for all the stocks that they took from the agency for the use of the soldiers while the agency was used as a depot for army supplies and prisoners. Rinehart was instructed to act as a guide and scout, pointing out the hiding places of the Indians. The agent grumblingly gave up his quarters and had to sleep in the haystacks. As it turned out, General Howard and his staff remained only a few hours; the officers and their men hurriedly arrived at the agency and just as hurriedly departed. Meanwhile Rinehart tried in a frenzy to inventory the agency's goods before the soldiers had depleted the stocks. He finally had to leave his third attempt to his employees, after which he and they left the reservation for Canyon City.[6]

Sarah meanwhile was kept busy as a scout. She traveled with Mattie. On one occasion the two women heard some soldiers on the road. When one soldier commented, "Oh, look, they have Sarah Winnemucca a prisoner," the two women laughed.[7] When Sarah's party reached the agency, the news had just arrived that the hostiles were heading for Harney Valley and it was likely that Captain Bernard's company would overtake them. Sarah and Mattie were charged by General Howard to go to Camp Harney, accompanied by Howard's aide-de-camp, Lieutenant Melville C. Wilkinson, and two other soldiers. When they reached the last stage stop, they had to replace Mattie's horse, and they took time to eat. The lieutenant followed them into the stage house, and a white woman serving coffee looked at Sarah and said: "Well, I never thought I should feed you again. I hope they will not let you off this time."

Lieutenant Wilkinson interrupted, "You don't know what you are talking about. This is Sarah Winnemucca."

She answered: "I don't care. Rope is too good to hang her with."

The lieutenant told Sarah, "Never mind her, she is crazy," but Sarah could not eat her food.[8]

The group reached Camp Harney the next morning. Both women were so tired that they went to bed without eating. In the evening the wife of the commanding officer, Major G. M. Downey, called on Sarah to see if she needed anything, and, seeing that her dress was worn from traveling, she kindly gave Sarah one of her own.[9]

The next day, June 23, was a Sunday. Lieutenant Wilkinson, who was a minister, planned to preach to the soldiers, but at ten o'clock a courier alerted Camp Harney that Captain Bernard's men were in battle near Camp Curry. Although his company had surprised and charged the Bannocks, the hostiles had

General O. O. Howard, who led the United States Army tracking Chief Joseph and the Nez Percés in 1877. He found himself in a similar pursuit of the Paiutes and Bannocks during the Bannock Indian War of 1878. (Courtesy of Oregon Historical Society.)

rallied, and now Bernard needed reinforcements. Three soldiers had been killed, and three wounded; the Indian casualties were unknown.[10] Sarah, Wilkinson, and Mattie raced their horses to report back to Howard that same day, only to find that they had missed him en route; he had already left for Harney with more troops.

The main command was able to catch up with Captain Bernard near Camp Curry in a few days, but steady movement was required. It became apparent that the hostiles intended to reach the Columbia River region and were hopeful of picking up allies along their escape route.[11] On June 28, Howard made this comment in his notebook:

> Move at 6 a.m. Rough trail. Wagons move 13 miles; arrive in camp 8 p.m. Bernard goes some miles farther, Bernard sends back word Indian pony-tracks just ahead. They turn suddenly and go back. Very cold; snowing all day. Large Indian camp at this place (About 1,500 or 2,000 Indians have been here.).[12]

Sarah and Mattie were sent to interview a Bannock Indian woman who had been captured in the Camp Curry battle. At first she would not talk, but in the end she told them much that was of interest to Howard. She confirmed that Buffalo Horn had been killed at South Mountain (as Piute Joe had claimed) and that Oytes was now the leader. The hostiles were headed for the Umatilla agency because the Umatillas had promised Oytes that they would join in the war. Sarah noticed the woman's blind eyes filling with tears as she remembered her nephew Buffalo Horn.[13]

The pursuing cavalry found itself in the deep canyon of the South Fork of the John Day River. The wagons had much difficulty covering the terrain. They moved along the highest ridges and then slid down the steep descent to the valley floor. Howard later wrote: "What a diversified country! Jagged rocks, precipitous slopes, knife-edged divides, deep canyons with sides steep and difficult, the distance from a crest to the mountain stream that tumbled over the rocks far below being sometimes four or five miles."[14]

As the Indians pushed northward, the settlers who found themselves in the Bannocks' path rushed to the towns or other fortifications for protection. The army seemed to be always behind and unable to check the progress of the Indians. Citizen scouts were enlisted to watch and head them off if possible.[15] The one-armed General Howard was the object of much sarcasm from certain segments of the press and the community. This war was unfolding in a way similar to the Nez Percé War, in which Howard's troops had chased Chief Joseph for hundreds of miles, seldom engaging in conflict.[16]

A dozen volunteers from Canyon City skirmished with an advance of about fifty hostile warriors. One of the citizens was killed in this encounter, and, when the news reached Canyon City, more volunteers rallied to the front. The town itself was in an uproar.[17] Agent Rinehart, who had retreated there from the agency, found his army experience useful in the emergency. He helped build a breastwork and rifle pits for the defense of the town. He had worked about three hours when the drum roll sounded from the courthouse announcing that the Indians were sweeping up the valley.

All was chaos and panic. Over one hundred families left their homes and clambered hastily up a steep bluff west of the town to reach the mining tunnels, which were now converted into a temporary refuge. There were sixty men with forty guns, some of which were only shotguns. Water was brought up the hillside in barrels and buckets. Provisions and bedding were placed in five underground tunnels which were lighted with candles and filled with terror-stricken women and children.[18]

Toward night a messenger arrived with the news that a second party of citizens had struck the Indians twenty miles down the valley and the whites were flying before the enemy. Two men had been killed, and two farmhouses were burned. This information produced a panic that lasted the night. Reports were abroad that 200 to 300 Indians were behind the advance of 50 and that the cavalry was 100 miles away.[19] On the next morning the citizens learned with relief that the main body of hostiles had bypassed the town and were on their way north.[20] The cavalry had finally arrived on the John Day River, and the infantry was only one day's march behind.

During those tumultuous days some American newspapers were sympathetic to the plight of the Indians. The *San Francisco Call* of June 23 took Rinehart to task for starving, abusing, and lying to the Paiutes. It stated that innocent settlers, killed without warning and without any knowledge of the provocation, were paying the penalty of the agent's crimes with their lives and property. The writer was concerned that Rinehart's success in getting away with thousands of dollars' worth of plunder would encourage other agents to imitate his example.

The New York Times predicted that an Indian outbreak might be extended into a larger war, because many Indians were disaffected in southern Idaho, western Montana, and eastern Oregon: "The malconstruction of our machinery for dealing with the red race is more than ever apparent. The War Department and the Interior Department, between whom the responsibility is divided, are seldom capable of effectively assisting each other."[21]

All of the Malheur Paiutes appeared to be with the Bannocks except Old Winnemucca's band of about forty whom Sarah had brought out of the Bannock camp.[22] After a short sojourn at Camp McDermit, Winnemucca had gone to Steens Mountain, where he found a few of Egan's people who had escaped from the Bannocks during the Camp Curry battle. They told him that Chief Egan and his brother-in-law Charlie had attempted to join the soldiers during the fight, but they had been critically wounded. Now the Bannocks were compelling Egan to march with them, and he would probably die.[23] The old chief also found Ocheo and his band on Steens Mountain. They told him that they wanted to go back to Surprise Valley but were afraid of the settlers and soldiers. They had never entered the hostilities, though the Bannocks had come urging them to do so.[24]

While bivouacked near Pilot Rock, Oregon, General Howard received word that some of the hostiles were crossing the Columbia River with a large number of horses. Major J. A. Kress attacked with his men on the steamer *Spokane*, destroying an Indian camp and confiscating blankets and buffalo robes.[25] The *Spokane* continued to patrol the river while Captain Wilkinson with thirty-two men boarded the steamer *Northwest* with a gatling gun and two howitzers.[26]

Sarah and Mattie stayed with General Howard's command, sometimes riding in an army ambulance over the rough terrain. In her autobiography Sarah tells how on July 7 the general asked her if she would go to the Indians and see if they would surrender without a fight. She accepted the assignment, but, after the officers discussed the matter further, they agreed that the risks were too great for her.[27] On the next day General Howard was informed by two scouts that they had located the Indians' main camp about three miles ahead on the heights of the foothills of the Blue Mountains. At this all the cavalry drew up for battle, and Captain Bernard directed them quickly into position. They faced the Indians' stronghold, which was protected by a crest of lava and backed by timber farther up the steep mountainside.[28]

When the cavalry charged, Sarah and Mattie stayed near Howard, who told them to get behind rocks to protect themselves from the bullets that were whistling about. She heard the chiefs' singing as they ran up and down the front line, while the gatling gun and other artillery whanged into the rocky ledge where the Indians fought. Once she thought that she heard Oytes yell, "Come on you white dogs—what are you waiting there for?"[29]

Howard, in describing the battle of Birch Creek, wrote:

> As we reached a high crest we saw the Indians and their ponies among the rocks. They did not act as usual, but kept moving about, some jumping up and down as if in defiance. Their conduct was like Joseph's Nez Percés at the Clear Water the year before, when with blankets tossed high over their heads they danced around, looking and acting like howling dervishes in their frenzied capers, doubtless hoping to inspire terror in our breasts.[30]

Many of the troopers' horses were hit—they lay screaming in pain as they lay on the mountainside—but the cavalry surged ahead. They finally dislodged the Bannocks, who moved on to the next height. Sarah told Mattie, "We will see a great many of our people die today, and soldiers, too." She was numbed by the thought and ran out into the open to take a position by General Howard.[31]

Soon the hostiles were forced from their new battlements. Leaving their horses and camp provisions, they backed into a dense stand of pines on the crest of the Blue Mountains, where they made another short stand. Finally they retreated through the safety of the trees, where the cavalry could not easily pursue. Sarah surmised that the fleeing women and children were moving back to their own country on the best horses.[32]

The Indians' losses during the battle could not be determined, as they picked up their dead and wounded and carried them along. A scout came running to General Howard to say that an Indian was lying tied to the tail of a horse in a stream at the bottom of a deep canyon.[33] The general sent Sarah and Mattie to investigate, but they found nothing.

Five soldiers had been wounded in the battle. About twenty horses had been killed, but 200 or 300 of the Indians' horses had been captured. One of the soldiers, badly hurt, was brought to Mattie and Sarah for them to watch. They asked him if they could do anything for him, but he shook his head. Later General Howard came with a book and read and prayed with him. At four o'clock in the morning he cried out for someone to come, and the two women rushed to his side, hoping to assist him. He looked at them, but could not speak, and died in a few minutes.[34]

In retrospect Sarah wrote:

> Sometimes I laugh when I think of this battle. It was very exciting in one way, and the soldiers made a splendid chase, and deserved credit for it; but where was the killing? I sometimes think it was more play than anything else. If a white settler showed himself he was sure to get a hit from an Indian; but I don't believe they ever tried to hit a soldier, —they liked them too well,—and it certainly was remarkable that with all these splendid firearms, and the Gatling gun, and General Howard working at it, and the air full of bullets, and the ground strewn with cartridges, not an Indian fell that day.[35]

Sarah and Mattie stayed with Bernard's company, who pursued the Bannocks back to the North Fork of the John Day River. Meanwhile General Howard, fearing that some of the hostiles might cross the Snake River into Idaho, took the *Northwest* for Lewiston. While he was on the steamer, an Indian courier from the Umatilla Reservation in northern Oregon reported to him that the hostiles had burned the Umatilla agency, Cayuse Station.[36]

As soon as the Umatilla agent, N. A. Cornoyer, had seen that Cayuse was in flames, he hurried there with thirty-five of his Indians. They found that the whole force of the hostiles was coming down the mountain slopes in their direction. Cornoyer gathered the agency Indians to protect themselves and their stock, but the hostiles appeared to have no intention of attacking immediately. Instead they camped out of sight in a deep canyon.

This delay allowed time for a messenger to go to the troops to request assistance for the agency Indians, who were considerably outnumbered.[37]

Before Miles arrived just at daybreak, eleven Umatillas and about fifty Columbia River Indians had defected to the Bannocks, and, while the soldiers were eating breakfast, the hostiles reappeared, about 400 strong. The Indians hesitated in their charge when they saw the unexpected soldiers, but commenced firing at long range. They continued to do so until the cavalry and some volunteers from Pendleton drove them back into the surrounding mountains.[38]

On the morning of July 14 one of the Umatillas who had joined the hostiles sent word that, if the Umatillas were pardoned, they would send a party of Cayuse Indians to a certain place in the mountains where they would waylay Chief Egan and deliver him into the hands of the army. Miles accepted the terms, and forty-three Cayuses waited at the designated spot.[39]

Chief Egan had been born of Cayuse parents, but had been captured as a child during a Shoshoni raid and had found a home among the Northern Paiutes.[40] Already critically wounded in the Camp Curry fight, and in a desperate state of mind, he and some of his followers were called away from the Bannock camp to the proposed rendezvous by Umatilla Chiefs Umapine and Five Crows. The Cayuses seized and bound him, but a fight ensued against the Bannocks, who had discovered the plot. In the struggle Egan fought to get away and was shot and killed by one of the Umatillas.[41] On the next morning the Umatillas displayed Egan's head on a pole, along with four others. They had killed twelve men and had captured five prisoners and about 300 horses.[42]

In their pursuit of the Bannocks, General Frank Wheaton's forces later came across Egan's body, which was identified by Captain Thomas McGregor. Egan, who had always told the young men that it was folly to defy the whites, had wounds in his chest, wrist and groin. His broken wrist had been bound in willow splints and laid across a pillow on his breast. Dr. J. A. Fitzgerald, the army surgeon who examined the body, decided that Egan would have died in any case of his Camp Curry wounds.[43] The doctor was said to have sent Egan's head as a specimen to the Army Medical Museum at Washington, D.C.

One investigator found that the Army Medical Museum had no record of the head, but acknowledged receipt of the head of Egan's brother-in-law Charlie, whose body had lain nearby: "That the body of Egan was decapitated, there seems to be no doubt. What happened to the head may be conjectured."[44]

On the night when Egan died, Sarah screamed in her sleep and woke Mattie. She had dreamed of his murder. When the women learned a few days later that he was indeed dead, Mattie was unconsolable, for Egan had been her stepfather.[45]

Lieutenant Colonel James W. Forsyth, fresh from General P. H. Sheridan's headquarters in Chicago, Illinois, assumed command of Bernard's battalion. Pushing through woods and mountains, the soldiers struck the Bannock rear guard in the canyon of the North Fork of the John Day River. The soldiers slid down the trails of the gorge, and, while climbing back up, some of the pack mules lost their footing and tumbled into the chasm. About forty Indians were keeping guard at the top of the trail to protect their bedraggled main force, as the latter moved southward. The guard shot three of Forsyth's men, including a citizen courier.[46]

During the commotion of that fight one of the soldiers found an Indian baby lying face down in the dirt. She appeared to be unhurt, and Captain McGregor handed her over to Sarah and Mattie, after he had fed her gingersnaps, sugar, and water. The women were careful to preserve the baby's original clothing and beads so that, if the parents surrendered, they could identify their child. Two women had been taken as prisoners. Sarah asked one of them, whom she knew, if she would care for the child. The woman consented, and Sarah showed her how to give her condensed milk.[47]

In hot pursuit of the Bannocks the army crossed the Blue Mountains into the Granite Creek valley. There, by a strange coincidence, Sarah and Mattie found their former agent Sam Parrish watering his cattle on Little Creek. He looked up in astonishment and came to them, holding out his hands, while tears ran down his cheeks. He said: "Oh, Sarah, little did I think when I left you that it would all come to this. The poor Paiutes. I can't believe it!" Sarah told him all that had happened and rode with him for a while as he drove his cattle ahead.[48]

General Howard and his troops were camping at the crossing of the Canyon City and Malheur City wagon roads, and that night the general asked Sarah if she would go to the Malheur agency to see if any Indians had put in an appearance. Sarah, Mattie, and Lieutenant Wilkinson rode with eight Indian scouts to the agency. They found that the place had been deserted since the early days of the war. On the next day they returned around the east side of Castle Rock only to discover that they had just missed General Howard. Since the women were quite tired, they told Wilkinson that they would rest a bit before returning to the agency, where the general was headed. The lieutenant was reluctant to leave them, and not without cause. Soon three soldiers appeared and announced, "Come, boys, here are the girls, and the lieutenant is not with them." Sarah and Mattie jumped on their horses and had a wild ride back to Malheur. When Howard heard their story, the three soldiers were immediately dismissed.[49]

One of the women prisoners was sent out to find her people and tell them to return to the reservation, where they would be fed by the government. Before the woman left, Sarah said: "Tell them I, their mother, say come back to their homes again. I will stand by them and see that they are not sent away to the Indian Territory."[50] Sarah watched the woman as she rode away on an army horse across the high plateau toward the distant mountains. The woman did find a few of her people and brought them in some weeks later, but, once the Paiute bands were back in familiar territory, they promptly scattered and remained elusive.

On July 27, Sarah and Mattie left Howard's command to accompany Colonel Forsyth. The latter was rounding up groups of hostiles, who would be kept as prisoners of war subject to the order of the department commander. With Forsyth the two women marched to Steens Mountain along the South Fork of the Malheur River, riding sometimes as much as thirty to forty miles a day. Some of the horses gave out in the burning sun, and the soldiers were forced to march without benefit of water over the wasteland. When Mattie's horse became exhausted, she and Sarah took turns riding and walking. When they got to their destination, they found no evidence of Paiutes.[51]

They crossed a forty-five-mile desert to old Camp C. F. Smith, and still there were no signs of Indians. That night, however, the women saw a signal fire of distress in the hills. Colonel

Forsyth wished to know its meaning, and, when Sarah told him that they would find a lone Indian by the fire, he did not believe her. Then citizen scouts went to the area and found the footprints of one man, who was later brought in. He proved to be an acquaintance of Sarah's, who had been a good farmer on the Malheur Reservation when Parrish was there.

Sarah was so close now to Camp McDermit that she could not bear the thought of moving on without seeing her father and other relatives. When she asked the colonel for permission to go, he asked if Mattie could talk English well enough to take her place. Sarah replied that she could. Then Forsyth insisted that she take Lieutenant John Pitcher and two soldiers with her to McDermit. The four rode at a fast trot through the night. Finally, early in the morning hours, Sarah received permission to ride ahead, and with relief she broke into a gallop, arriving at McDermit just before daybreak. We have her account of what happened when she was reunited with her father.[52]

She rode up to one Paiute camp and said, "Here, you are sleeping too much! Get up!"

One of the women jumped up and said, "Who is it? What is it?"

"Where is my brother's camp? Where is Natchez?" Sarah asked. The woman pointed out the camp, and Sarah rode up to the tent. "Halloo! Get up. The enemy is at hand!" she called.

Natchez rushed out and said, "Oh, my sister!" He helped her off her horse and said to his wife, "Jump up, wife, and make a fire, sister is so cold." Sarah had nothing on but a dress. She was given a blanket, and a fire was soon made.

Natchez said to the waking people, "I am afraid, my young men, you are not doing your duty; for I have here in my camp a warrior who has just arrived. Come . . . and see for yourselves."

Winnemucca was the first to come up. He ran to Sarah and took her in his arms. "Oh, my poor child, I thought I never would see you, for the papers said you were killed by the Bannocks. . . . When I heard you, my darling, who saved my life for a little while longer, had gone first, I thought my heart would break!"

Sarah put her face on his chest. Then Winnemucca said, "Look up, dear; let me see if it is really my child." The tears ran down the old man's cheeks, and everybody had tears in their eyes.

Sarah sat at the fire and related all that had happened since the day that they had parted. She told them who had been killed and how many prisoners the United States Army had. She told them about the baby and a blind woman who had been scalped by whites and yet lived; about Oytes and about how Egan had been murdered by the Cayuses, his own people.

The Numa said they hoped that, when the soldiers caught Oytes, they would hang him, for he was to blame for all their misery. When Sarah told them that Umapine, the Umatilla who had killed Egan, was now a scout with Colonel Forsyth, Leggins rose and said, "My brothers, I think we ought to go and kill him. We have never done them any harm, and have always been kind to them when they came on our reservation. We have given them presents. Oh, my brother Winnemucca, and you, my dear Natchez, . . . You and your sister can demand of them to give him up to us."

Then Sarah jumped up and said: "I have not told you all. At the time they took Egan, they also took a great many women prisoners, and most of them are young girls."

When Sarah sat down, Natchez spoke. First he warned the Numa that they would probably never get their women and children back by killing Umapine. He said that he would make the following speech to the Umatillas:

> Friends, we have come to talk to you. Now tell us what our sub-chief, Egan, has done to you that you should kill him, and have him cooked in the way you did. Was he good to eat? . . . For four years you have come on the Malheur Reservation, and told Egan and Oytes to make war against the whites. You have called them fools for staying on the reservation to starve. . . . You are nothing but cowards; nothing but barking coyotes; you are neither persons nor men. . . . Now we cease to be friends, and after the soldiers quit fighting with the Bannocks and with Oytes' men, we will make war with you for the wrong you have done us, if you do not return our women and girls whom you have taken as prisoners. Do you know there is not money enough in the world to make me go and fight a people who have not done me any harm? You have done this year after year against your own people. . . . And what do you gain by it? . . . You are as poor as we are, we, who have never taken our own brother's scalp and fastened it on a pole and danced round it to show our white brothers how brave we are. . . .
>
> General Howard and General McDowell . . . have asked me to fur-

nish them twenty-five of my men as scouts for them. General Howard and General McDowell are my best soldier-fathers; yet they could not give me money enough to take up arms against any tribe of Indians.

Natchez concluded by saying:

> Now, my dear children, I will go with my sister, and I will say all to the Umatillas that I have said to you, right before General Forsythe and all the officers. I think it is right and just, and I also think it is the only way we can get back our women and girls. . . .
>
> I am afraid the soldiers will think we have come to fight them, if they see so many of us coming; therefore I think about thirty of us will be enough to go.

Meanwhile Lieutenant Pitcher had arrived. He agreed that the men could go with him and Sarah to Colonel Forsyth. Winnemucca, who had not spoken, now rose:

> I am ashamed to have to speak to you, my children. . . . Where is one among you who can get up and say, "I have been in battle, and have seen soldiers and my people fight and fall." Oh! for shame, for shame to you, young men, who ought to have come with this news to me! . . . My child's name is so far beyond yours. . . . Her name is everywhere and everyone praises her. Oh! how thankful I feel that it is my own child who has saved so many lives, not only mine, but a great many, both whites and her own people. Now hereafter we will look on her as our chieftain, for none of us are worthy of being chief but her.

14
Yakima

Natchez delivered a speech to the Umatillas with Lieutenant Colonel Forsyth's command, but Umapine, the man who reportedly had killed Chief Egan, was not present. Since the scouts could not find him or his pony, it was presumed that he did not want to face the wrath of the Paiutes and had returned hurriedly to his own country.[1]

Mattie and Lee were now reunited, for Lee had escaped safely from the Bannocks and returned to McDermit along with Winnemucca. He remained with Mattie and Sarah when the rest of the warriors returned to McDermit, and the three acted as couriers for Captain Bernard, Major George B. Sanford, Colonel Forsyth, and Captain W. H. Winters during the next few weeks, as small bands were gathered and brought into the military camps.[2]

On August 13, 1878, Oytes surrendered with a party of sixty at the Malheur agency. This seemed to signal the close of the war, as only a few hostiles were unaccounted for.[3] The Bannocks returned to their country beyond the Snake River, where skirmishes between them and the army occurred as late as September and as far east as the Yellowstone country.

Sarah had been all through the camps at Fort Harney with the Indian baby, and no one could identify the child. At last she found a young couple in mourning who recognized the little one. They were overcome with joy at her return. She had been thrown from her basket on a steep incline, and her mother had not missed her until too late in the confused retreat. The grateful parents named the child Sarah.[4]

Sarah Winnemucca would not have worked so industriously gathering together the Paiute stragglers if she had known what her "kind" soldier fathers were planning. In October orders came to the officers that all the Paiutes who belonged on the Malheur Reservation were to be gathered at Fort Harney so that they could be returned to Malheur Reservation for the coming winter. Sarah was told to go to Camp McDermit and bring all her people to Camp Harney. A company of cavalry was to accompany her.[5]

When Sarah told the people what was expected, they were quite upset. "We know there is something wrong," they told her. "We don't like to go." Meanwhile the officers told them that there was nothing to fear, and Natchez said, "Our soldier-fathers will see that you are all right."

Leggins replied: "Rinehart is there yet. . . . We know how we suffered while we were there."

The Numa felt greatly troubled in their hearts. Were the soldiers going to punish even those who did not go with the Bannocks? Captain Wagner became quite angry with their questions and told them that, when soldiers received orders, they had to obey them, and it was the same for the Paiutes.[6] At the council that night the people agreed to make the trip to Harney, and on the next morning, October 4, 1878, their horses were prepared for the long trek.[7] Families and relatives were parted. All were crying and lamenting that this should happen. Natchez accompanied the 180 Paiutes as far as Camp C. F. Smith, and then he too had to return. He did not go before reaching an agreement that Leggins would be chief in the absence of Winnemucca and himself.[8]

It took seven days for the Numa to arrive at the post. Army clothing was soon issued to the men, who were pleased with the new outfits. Of course, the army could not furnish calico and muslin for the women and children and they had to do without.

The people kept wondering when they would be sent to the Malheur agency. Sarah heard that Agent Rinehart was seen there from time to time and was ordering supplies through the Indian Department.[9] The Indians were well treated at Camp Harney, but they still had an unerring suspicion that all was not

Gathering sagebrush for campfires against the winter cold. (Courtesy of Special Collections, University of Nevada, Reno.)

well. They observed new settlers moving onto the reservation, building cabins, and fencing their herds, while the military did nothing about it.

One day Sarah was called to the office of Captain M. A. Cochran, the post commander. She had such a feeling of foreboding that she trembled before him. Cochran told her that she looked ill and to sit down, because he had bad news. The Paiutes were to be taken to Yakima Reservation beyond the Columbia River.[10] Sarah reminded him that many of the people had done nothing wrong, that many had not gone with the Bannocks. For example, Leggins, who had saved the lives of several whites, had moved his band to Camp McDermit right off. She asked, "If there are any to be sent away, let it be Oytes and his men, numbering about twenty-five in all, and the few Bannocks that are with them." The captain answered that the soldiers would not take Chief Winnemucca's band, but all those who were there at Camp Harney.

"Oh, if you knew what I have promised my people, you would leave nothing undone but what you would try not to have them sent away," Sarah cried. "My people will never believe me again." The major promised that he would write the president and do what he could to alleviate the situation.[11]

Sarah told the sad story to Mattie, who said, "We cannot help it if the white people won't keep their word."

"Our people will say we are working against them and are getting money for all this," Sarah replied.

The disconsolate women walked to the camp in the evening and watched the singing, the dancing, and the drumming. The Numa were happy. Sarah thought, "My poor, poor people, tomorrow or next week your happiness will be turned to weeping." She and Mattie could not sleep.

One evening, a few weeks later, Sarah was again called to headquarters. Mattie said that she would accompany her. Captain Cochran met them and said, "Sarah, I am heartily sorry for you, but we cannot help it. We are ordered to take your people to Yakima Reservation."

Sarah thought her world had ended. How could she tell her people? "What, in this cold winter and in all this snow, and my people have so many little children? Why they will die."

Captain Cochran had no reply, only to say that they should tell no one until a few days before leaving.[12] When the time arrived, Sarah was told to bring Leggins to Cochran's office. The officer then asked who were the worst offenders during the war. Through Sarah as interpreter, Leggins named Oytes, Bannock Joe, Captain Bearskin, Paddy Cap, Boss, Big John, Eagle Eye, Charley, D. E. Johnson, Beads, and a son-in-law of Oytes's called Surger. Those men were sent for and were placed in the guardhouse. Sarah was told to tell them that they were put there for safe keeping because the citizens of Canyon City were coming over to arrest them.

Then Sarah had to tell the whole encampment the decision of the army. The misery and heartbreak of the Numa were immense. The women still had few clothes, and there were no blankets. When Captain Cochran heard that Rinehart was getting Indian supplies at the agency, which was only fifty-five miles away, he wrote and asked if he would come and issue to the Paiutes at Camp Harney, as they were suffering for want of clothing. When he received no answer, he wrote again, but again received no answer.[13] Apparently Rinehart did not desire to break his precedent of never issuing clothing to Indians. They received nothing from him.

Leggins's band were told that they would not go to Yakima and were not put under guard, but Oytes's, Egan's, and Tau-wa-dah's were closely watched. It was just before Christmas, and the people had one week to ready themselves for the journey. On the night of December 25 thirty prisoners of war at Camp Harney broke guard and escaped. The alarm was given before they had time to get far, and the two companies of cavalry at the post were alerted before more could follow.[14] On the next day Lee and Leggins were sent out to bring the prisoners back. Later Sarah and Mattie rode after five women who had gotten away. While the two women scouts were riding hard, Mattie's horse slipped in the snow, and she was thrown to the ground. Sarah wheeled her horse around and jumped down beside Mattie, rushing to hold her in her arms. Help was summoned from the camp, but the surgeon there did little for her.[15] In the days that were left before the trek to Yakima, Mattie lay quietly on the bed, uncomplaining. Her large eyes followed Sarah about the room as she sewed fur caps, fur gloves, and fur overshoes for the two of them. On the day of departure, January 6, 1879, Mattie was carried out to a four-horse wagon.[16] Fifty other wagons were waiting for the women, children, and old people. The men were to follow on their horses.

The journey to Yakima was 350 miles over two mountain ranges in the dead of winter and without adequate clothing. Suffering was inevitable. When the slowly moving column arrived at Canyon City, a telegram waited for Captain Winters. Inexplicably, he was to return for Leggins's band at Camp Harney.[17] The weather turned stormy, and it snowed during the two days that the wagon train waited for Leggins. During this time Mr. and Mrs. Charles Parrish came to speak to the prisoners.

Mrs. Parrish was the beloved teacher, the "white lily," who had been with them during their little time of happiness at Malheur. She remembered the names that she herself had given to the children. She cried when she saw Mattie, one of her best students, in such a helpless condition and she took the young woman's hands. Mattie wept also, for the white woman had been more than a teacher to her. The Paiutes begged Mr. Parrish to help them and not to let them be taken to a country that they did not know where the other Indians would not welcome them. He told them that there was nothing that he could do.[18] On that night an old man who could not manage for himself in the cold was left in a wagon on the road. He had frozen to death by morning when they returned for him. The citizen who owned the wagon threw his body out beside the road.

The captain sent Sarah to instruct Leggins, who had just come up, that he was to help the soldiers guard the prisoners; the "Big Father" in Washington wanted him to do this, and then his people could return to Oregon in the spring. Sarah gave Leggins this message, but he would not speak to her, nor would her brother Lee.[19] They traveled all day in the snow, and that night a woman gave birth to a baby who died soon after. The mother lived another day before she too was left by the road. Three young children died on the trip from exposure to the cold. Another woman gave birth, and she lived, but her baby did not. All this time Mattie was in considerable pain being jostled along on the rutty roads. Sarah knew that there was little hope for her recovery.

After they had crossed the Columbia River on a ferry, the exiles arrived in Yakima on January 31. They made camp thirty miles from the agency buildings, which were at Fort Simcoe. The refugees stayed at this camp for ten days, while the agent, Reverend James H. Wilbur, prepared to receive them. He had not been forewarned of their coming and had no extra food or shelter available at the time of their arrival. Meanwhile Agent Rinehart at Malheur complained because 65,000 pounds of both beef and flour lay unused at his agency.[20]

"Father" Wilbur hastily constructed a large shed 150 feet long near the agency for the 543 prisoners. The work was done by the Yakima Indians, who were regarded as "civilized." It was to this shed that the Paiutes were herded when they moved to the agency.[21] The snow was waist-deep, and there was no wood for fuel. Many more people died. When they saw the conditions in which they were to live, they lost hope.

The Paiute men still had their long, warm soldiers' overcoats, but many of these were soon lost to the Yakima Indians in gambling and trading for horses and buckskins. Leggins had a good many horses with him, and so had the other men, but they kept disappearing. The Paiutes asked the Yakimas to keep an eye out for them until it was discovered that the Yakimas themselves were taking the horses and disposing of them. Sarah's own horse, Meride, disappeared and was later found with pack sores on her back.[22] Agent Wilbur did not try to improve the relations between the two Indian groups. Sarah believed that he did not want to be bothered about the horses or the lost clothing of the Paiutes.[23]

In early spring Wilbur did put the Numa to work planting wheat on their own sixty acres. The agent also told Sarah to report to her people that seventeen wagons of clothes were on their way to them from The Dalles and that they would be distributed. The issuing day came in May. Of the lovely goods that the Paiutes had seen brought into the storehouse from the wagons, only twenty-eight little shawls were given out, plus some dress goods which were so thin that Sarah claimed one could sift flour through them. Two to three yards were given to each woman. One mother was given six yards of cloth for herself and her six children. Some of the men who had worked hardest got blankets, and a few got hats.[24] After the issue the people laughed and said: "Another Rinehart!—don't you see he is the same? He looks up into the sky and says something, just like Rinehart." The goods brought for the Paiutes were sold to whoever had money for them.

During this time Mattie's condition had deteriorated. The agency doctor, a man named Kuykendall, could not help her. (Sarah relates in her autobiography how he would give her a little sugar, rice, or tea for the sick, saying, "Give them something good to eat before they die.")[25] Mattie was unable to assist with the issue of clothing, and she suffered much before her death on May 29, 1879.[26]

Rinehart made a trip to Fort McDermit in late April to talk to Winnemucca and Natchez in an attempt to induce them to come to the Malheur Reservation with their people.[27] He reminded them that Oytes was no longer at the Malheur agency and that the fertile land would be theirs, although Ocheo would be coming also from Camp Bidwell. Winnemucca refused the offer. He was still haunted by the dream of land near Fort McDermit or on the Owyhee. Most of all he was convinced that the settlers of Grant County would kill any Indian, friend or foe, on sight. Already two of the tribe had lost their lives in this manner.[28] Then, too, squatters were on the best land of the Malheur and were determined to stay.

Rinehart seemed to be the only participant in the conversations who was not facing reality. His reservation had been without a single Indian on it for almost a year. Although it was a lost cause, he could not give up such a lucrative position easily, and he persisted for many months in his determination to get the Paiutes to return.[29] He did get Old Winnemucca and Natchez to promise that they would return to Malheur if Chief Leggins and his band were brought back from Yakima.

Leggins and the other prisoners at Yakima were not forgotten by their fellow Paiutes. Chief Winnemucca took the case of Leggins to General McDowell in San Francisco. He explained that his son Lee, who had always been friendly to the whites, was also held prisoner.[30] The general produced letters showing that Lee was not a prisoner, but free to go when and where he pleased. As for Leggins, McDowell promised to inquire into his case. Winnemucca again asked for land of his own, but the general, though he desired to grant the old man's request, had no power to do so.

Again Rinehart met with Winnemucca and Natchez. He threatened that he could compell them to go to Malheur.[31] Then, suddenly changing his tactics, he offered Natchez $100 for his assistance plus $5.00 per head for every Paiute whom he could persuade to return to the Malheur reservation.[32] Natchez refused.

When Natchez was interviewed in San Francisco in June, 1879, he talked to the reporter about the Paiutes' situation at Yakima where his sister and brother Lee were living. He had recently received a letter from Sarah, and she was teaching school. Her sixty Paiute students were doing well. They had a good crop of corn and potatoes, but twenty-one people had died since the previous winter when they had been forcibly moved to Yakima and many more were on the sick list. If General McDowell allowed him to go to Yakima, Natchez planned to take Sarah some pine nuts. She had written him that she had a real yearning for the taste of them.[33]

At Yakima, Methodist minister Wilbur was making plans for a religious revival. Important personages from the East were to come to observe his work with the Indians. Sarah, though she bitterly denounced people who she felt did not behave as professed Christians should, had accepted the religion of the whites and considered herself a Methodist; Father Wilbur and General Howard wrote of her as a Christian woman.[34] She was told by Wilbur to keep the Paiutes out of sight during the revival. She understood that it would be an embarrassment to the agent to explain what had happened to the clothing of her people, who were still scantily dressed.[35] However, when it was time for the meeting, she did the opposite of what Wilbur wanted. She brought the Paiutes right to the agent's house and had them sit on the benches intended for the Christian Indians. In her autobiography she wrote, "I wanted all to see how well we were treated by Christian people." When she saw that some of the Numa came to the revival every day, especially the little children, she stood at the pulpit and interpreted the words of Father Wilbur and Bishop Erastus Otis Haven from Boston, so that the Paiutes might hear the sermons themselves.[36] Despite this confrontation the plight of the Paiutes did not improve under Wilbur.

By August, Natchez's plans for visiting Yakima had not materialized. When Sarah at last received her compensation from the army for her work as a scout and courier during the Bannock war, her people begged her to go east and talk for them. With the means at hand Sarah promised that she would do all that she could and told Father Wilbur that she would like to leave. He at first would not let her go, but then he said, "Well, Sarah, I can't keep you if you want to go. Who is to talk for your people?" She replied, "Brother Lee can talk well enough." Then Wilbur said that she was free to go when the religious revival was over.

Sarah left Yakima in November and went directly to Vancouver to see General Howard at his headquarters. She told him of the misery of her people at the Yakima Reservation, their desire to return to their homes, and her plan to go to Washington to speak for them. Howard encouraged her in her enterprise, giving her a letter of introduction to Washington officials.[37]

She did not know that Agent Wilbur had written to the commissioner of Indian affairs that the Paiutes now under his charge were "contented and happy," saying, "I think it would be a childish course to return them." He reminded the department that they had spent $50,000 in removing the Indians to Yakima. He recommended that the Malheur Agency be broken up and Yakima made the Paiutes' permanent home.[38] Agent Rinehart now had run up against an antagonist with an equal talent for self-aggrandizement.

The "pernicious" fandangos for which Agent Rinehart had such contempt were held several times yearly. The numerous Paiute chiefs would agree upon a time and place, and often as many as three or four hundred people would assemble. It was a time for young people to pursue a mate, and for all the Numa to visit and have a good time storytelling and gambling. By now card playing had become as popular as the rhythmical chanting of the traditional hand game. Older Paiutes would sit around the sagebrush fires in their colorful blankets, the firelight flickering on their painted faces. Little children peeped from their rabbit-skin blankets on the outer edge of the large encirclement of scattered fires, while older children ran and jumped in play, calling to each other in the darkness.

When the first dance was called, some men formed a circle around a cedar tree set up in a large cleared area. They commenced a low chant as they moved with regular steps facing the tree, shoulder to shoulder. Gradually women and children filled the circle, and the chant continued:

Hoe, hoe, hoe, hi-hi!
Hi-yah, hi-yah, hi-hi!
Hoe, hoo, hi-yah, hi-hi!

The chant and dancing might keep up all night. If a dancer tired, another replaced him, most of them with the sacred red paint daubed on their faces. It was a solemn dance of communion and hope, though it seemed monotonous to white observers.

Wovoka (or Jack Wilson, as he was called by the whites) had lain ill in his hut in Mason Valley near the Walker River Reserve. He had fallen into a coma and then into trance, where he was transported to the spirit world and received a revelation. Afterward he had reported to his fellows: "An Indian millennium is to come, when all warlike things are to be discarded and honesty, peace and good will will prevail between men of all colors."[39] In their simple dance at the fandango the Paiutes expressed a longing for the promised new era.

The Northern Paiutes now possessed two leaders who would draw national attention to the plight of native Americans. While

Wovoka, or Jack Wilson, the Paiute shaman who originated the Ghost Dance religion. (Courtesy of Nevada Historical Society.)

Sarah Winnemucca would travel the continent, Wovoka stayed in Mason Valley. The Indians came to him, riding free on the rails, to hear the wisdom of the prophet who heralded a new day.

Sarah Winnemucca would attempt a political change while Wovoka prophesied a spiritual one.

15

The "Princess" Sarah

On her arrival in San Francisco from Portland on the steamer *California*, Sarah found herself something of a celebrity. When Natchez met her, he was accompanied by several reporters, who asked for individual interviews. Sarah was described as a self-possessed young woman who had been in the public eye during the Bannock War; the San Francisco newspapers headlined her as "The Princess Sarah." One writer commented, "The fire-flash in her eyes and the dramatic action of her race invest the simple language she uses with a native eloquence which carries a certain weight with the most cautious hearer."[1] The "princess" wore at her throat a silver ornament that had been given her by Natchez. It was engraved with an inscription by the citizens of Humboldt County who were grateful for the saving of several white men's lives during the Bannock War.[2]

Sarah told one reporter: "I have just been thinking how it would do for me to lecture upon the Bannock War. I might get the California Theatre, and perhaps I could make my expenses. I would be the first Indian woman who ever spoke before white people," she explained, "and they don't know what the Indians have got to stand sometimes."[3]

The *San Francisco Chronicle* reported:

Sarah has undergone hardships and dared dangers that few men would be willing to face, but she has not lost her womanly qualities, and succeeded during her visit in coaxing into her lap two little timid "pale-faced" children, usually shy of strangers, who soon lost their fear of her dark skin, won by her warm and genial ways. She speaks with force and decision, and talks eloquently of her people. Her mission, undertaken at the request of Chief Winnemucca, is to have her tribe gathered together again at their old home in Nevada, where they can follow peaceable pursuits and improve themselves.[4]

All was not accolades for Sarah, however. The *Chronicle* reporter also described her as having "an extensive and diversified matrimonial experience, the number of her white husbands being variously estimated at from three to seven."[5] When Sarah read that report, she hastily granted an interview to a reporter on the *San Francisco Call* to refute it. In the *Call* interview she mentioned her marriage to Bartlett and subsequent divorce and a second marriage to an Indian, who grossly mistreated her.[6] Aspersions on her personal life infuriated her.

Agent Rinehart learned of Sarah's popularity in San Francisco and countered by writing to the Indian Department that she was a "low, unprincipled Indian woman of questionable virtue and veracity as well, who was formerly Interpreter at the Agency and who was discharged for untruthfulness, gambling and other bad conduct."[7] Rinehart knew that General Howard had little regard for him, and he told the commissioner of Indian affairs that Sarah had prejudiced the commanding general against him.

Sarah was encouraged by friends and army officers to lecture in San Francisco, and she spoke several times in Platt's Hall on Montgomery Street between Bush and Pine Streets. Her experience in the theater fifteen years before helped her in the dramatic performances that she presented, often to capacity audiences. A San Francisco columnist, moved by a lecture that she gave in late November, wrote:

San Francisco was treated to the most novel entertainment it has ever known, last evening, in the shape of the address by Sarah, daughter of Chief Winnemucca, delivered in Platt's Hall. The Princess wore a short buckskin dress, the skirt bordered with fringe and embroidery, short sleeves, disclosing beautifully-rounded brown arms, and scarlet leggins, with trimmings of fringe. On her head she wore a proud head dress of eagle's feathers, set in a scarlet crown, contrasting well with her flowing black locks. The lecture was unlike anything ever before heard in the civilized world—eloquent, pathetic, tragical at times; at others her quaint anecdotes, sarcasms and wonderful mimicry surprised the audience again and again into bursts of laughter and rounds of applause. There was no set lecture from written manuscript, but a spontaneous flow of eloquence. Nature's child spoke in natural, unconstrained language, accompanied by gestures that were scarcely ever surpassed by any actress on the stage. The constraint which was naturally expected by the audience in one unused to faceing the public, was nowhere visible as the Indian girl walked upon the stage in an easy, unembarrassed manner, and entered at once upon the story of her race.[8]

Sarah felt that her audiences should know something of the history of her people and their way of life. She spoke of their first contacts with whites and how they had so often been mistreated. She concluded: "Then the Indians go and harm some innocent white people in their vengeance. I do not excuse my people. But I say you cannot hold them from it unless you change your treatment of them."[9] On one occasion she observed after the war, "they told us to go on the reservation and the government would give us provisions every day. Did they do it? No—they didn't. The agents robbed us."[10]

Sarah's thoughts returned to Malheur, where her superiors had so often forced her to influence the Numa against their own best interests. She wanted her audiences, who sat in the luxury of a comfortable auditorium, to understand her position and help her people. She spoke of Rinehart, his treatment of his charges when they were on the reservation, and how, even though no Paiute had set foot at Malheur for over a year, he had a large store of supplies.

Sarah brought down the house when she spoke of how the Christian Rinehart beckoned the Paiutes to be kind and good and honest with one hand while he was busy grabbing with the other behind their backs:[11] "Mr. Rinehart is a good man probably. I think he is a good man. The biggest thief, whether a man or a woman, is good if wealthy. With the jingle in his pocket and plenty in his hand, he lives away up."[12] The audience responded sympathetically to Sarah's emotions when, in her pleadings for the return of Leggins's band, the tears streamed down her face.

After one of Sarah's lectures, J. W. Scott, the beef contractor

Sarah Winnemucca as she appeared in stage attire of her own design. (Courtesy of Nevada Historical Society.)

at the Malheur Reservation, came to her and said, "Sarah, I would like to have you help me get some of your people to go with me to the Malheur Agency." He offered her thirty dollars. Sarah thought, "The white people believe they are better than I am. They make money any way and every way they can. Why not I? I have not any. I will take it." She accepted the money, but later wrote that she regretted many times that she had done so.[13]

Natchez informed Sarah that Scott had held a council with the leading Paiutes at the Winnemucca courthouse, where Natchez, Old Winnemucca, and all the leaders had again refused to go to the reservation unless Leggins was allowed to return. Natchez had said:

> You take my people to Malheur to starve them. While scouting. . . . I saw Oitz take your hair in his hand when water ran out of your eyes. I saved your life, but you would not help me. I heard you read paper two ways and we cannot trust you. You told me you are a high officer. Now, when white men who are my friends hear you, you deny it. You take my word for it, my people will not go with you. . . . They live in peace here. You come to my camp and I'll board you for nothing.[14]

Although Sarah and Natchez both believed that the Paiutes should not give up the Malheur Reservation, which abounded in fish, game, and timber, they would not claim it as long as Rinehart was there.

While she was in San Francisco, Sarah wrote and circulated a petition to the Interior Department, asking on behalf of the Paiutes that the former Malheur agent, Sam Parrish, be reinstated, or, if that was not possible, that some other honest and humane civilian or military officer be appointed as agent. This document also requested that the Paiutes who had been sent to Yakima be permitted to return to the Malheur agency, and it affirmed their innocence in the conduct of the Bannock War.[15]

For her last lecture in San Francisco, on Christmas Eve, 1879, Sarah was billed as going to Washington with an imaginary string of Indian agents' scalps:

> [In the East, where people are not used] to English lectures by an Indian woman, her appearance will be likely to draw, from sheer novelty, and please by the picturesqueness of her costume, and a certain gracefulness and dramatic effect of her gestures as well as her sententious sentences, which frequently bear a striking similarity [to] the poetry of Holy Writ.

As Sarah claims to be a Methodist, this coincidence may, perhaps, be referred to her reading of the Old Testament."[16]

As she stood before her last audience, Sarah implored:

I am appealing to you to help my people, to send teachers and books among us. Educate us. Every one shuns me, and turns a back on me with contempt. Some say I am a half breed. My father and mother were pure Indians. I would be ashamed to acknowledge there was white blood in me. . . . I want homes for my people but no one will help us. I call upon white people in their private houses. They will not touch my fingers for fear of getting soiled. That's the Christianity of white people."[17]

Sarah had been rebuffed in her attempts to get help and was especially critical of her own denomination, the Methodists, whom she felt had not supported her:

You take all the natives of the earth in your bosom but the poor Indian, who is born of the soil of your land and who has lived for generations on the land which the good God has given to them, and you say he must be exterminated. (Thrice repeated, with deep passion, and received with tremendous applause.)

The proverb says the big fish eat up the little fishes and we Indians are the little fish and you eat us all up and drive us from home. (The audience reacted with sympathetic cheers to this statement.)

Where can we poor Indians go, if the government will not help us? If your people will help us, and you have good hearts, and can if you will, I will promise to educate my people and make them law-abiding citizens of the United States. (Loud applause.) It can be done—it can be done. (Cheers.)[18]

The acclaim that Sarah received in San Francisco was noticed in Washington, and, when she arrived with Natchez in Lovelock, Nevada, they discovered that a special agent from the Interior Department, J. M. Haworth, had been sent to check on the "unrest" of the Paiutes.[19] When they met with Haworth in Winnemucca, Sarah acted as interpreter for the Paiute spokesmen. Natchez was the first to speak:

The reason we do not want to go to Malheur is, that the man who is there now forced our people, by ill treatment, to go on the war path. . . . Rinehart gave me money to take my people to Malheur but I would not do it for This is the country we were born in, and I think the whites will not injure us. . . . We have no homes, and if the Government does not feel disposed to give us homes, leave us as we are, and not make promises to be fulfilled after we are dead. We do not say the Great Father does not want to give us supplies, but we know we never get any. . . . The Agent now at Truckee, Mr. Spencer, gives us some rations, and does better than all the Agents who were there before him. Now, my friend from the Great Father, I am glad to hear you talk and not make promises. If you came like Indian Agents, I would fly to the mountains, where I could not be found.[20]

Old Winnemucca had spent more time than usual within the previous year in the environs of the town of Winnemucca. In August he had attended a fandango, at which he had marched with two hundred members of the tribe from their campground to the train depot. Dressed in a breechclout and a few feathers, he had painted his arms, legs and face with yellow, red, and black. At the depot the passengers on the train from the east had been astonished at the sight of the chief, who was purportedly in his late eighties, carrying the Stars and Stripes at the head of the column, while another leader bore a white flag alongside. The Indians marched straight for the tracks, but then wheeled abruptly and returned to their camp, where they had danced the remainder of the night.[21]

Winnemucca had appeared again at the station in October, this time wearing his usual epaulets, brass buttons, and feathered top hat. The passengers who had never seen an Indian crowded around him and insisted on shaking hands. He gallantly extended his hand to the ladies, but asked the gentlemen for a cigar "for the privilege."[22]

Now, in December, Winnemucca spoke to Haworth with Sarah as his interpreter:

We say, one and all, we will have a home near McDermit, or anywhere on the Humboldt river, where we were born. Look at us. Do we appear like wild animals? My people are as capable of learning as other races. You, my brother, who has come so far to see us, I think my people can tell you in English what they think, and I hope to live to see the day when they will be educated.

There have been agents after agents, but none of them gave us land, or anything to dig up the roots of the sagebrush . . . Here I stand old, ready to go into my grave; but I have never been guilty of striking any of you down, and I know my white brothers will not strike me down . . .

There will be no trouble between the Indians and whites here, they will testify to the truth of what we tell you.

He turned to Haworth and said emphatically,

We are tired of promises. When you go home tell Washington we live here and beg bread for our children when we have no other means of getting it.

Those Indians [who] were taken without cause to Yakima, we want them sent back here, to their own country. The man who killed Buffalo Horn, the Bannock Chief [Piute Joe], is now an exile from his own country. . . . We beg of you to ask permission to have them returned; but those hostile Indians, who were on the war path, you can deal with according to your own laws.[23]

The old chief sat down and closed his eyes while Sarah finished her interpretation, but he was not asleep.

After other Paiute leaders had spoken, Natchez rose again and said:

We will talk to the point. First bring Leggin and his band to Malheur. I will then go there myself and see how things are conducted, and if these Indians want to go all right. . . . If you attempt to force us there without cause you cannot do it. This driving talk is not right, we are all human beings. Have the whites no hearts? . . . We were told the Indians would be brought back from Yakima, would meet us at Malheur in three weeks. This was six months ago and they have not come there yet. We want our liberty to go when we feel like it on the same terms as white men.

At that the other Paiutes concurred with nods of approval, and Natchez concluded by saying to Haworth: "I want you to help me. We want to hear the President talk, myself, Sarah, Father Winnemucca and Jerry Long want to go to Washington. . . . When I return I will go to Ochoho's at Bidwell and try to get him to go first to the reservation, if we are treated fairly."[24]

Agent Haworth's reply was to say that he was very glad to hear that Chief Winnemucca and the others valued an education for their people. He complimented Sarah on her efficiency as an interpreter and remarked that there were other Paiute women who were as smart as she and only lacked an education to make them her equal in every respect. Natchez chuckled and said, "My wife is smarter than Sarah."

The Winnemucca family: Sarah, Chief Winnemucca, Natchez, Captain Jim, and an unidentified boy. This photograph probably was taken in Washington, D.C., in 1880. (Courtesy of Nevada Historical Society.)

Haworth promised, "I will write to Washington to make arrangements to have Chief Winnemucca, Sarah, Natchez and Jerry Long taken there to talk to the Great Father and we will arrange to have a number of tents sent here for wickiups."[25] As the long-awaited trip finally began to materialize, Sarah felt some hope that influential people with good hearts would yet come to the aid of her people.

Before leaving for Washington, Sarah lectured in Centennial Hall at Winnemucca to a fair-sized audience and exhibited pieces of tapestry that she said she had made when she had gone to school in California. She spoke of the spiritual beliefs of the Paiutes and the importance of shamans, or medicine men, to the tribe, saying, "They are venerated more than the war chiefs." She frankly admitted that she did not know whether the Paiute or the Christian religion was the better.

A local reporter criticized Sarah's lecture, writing that she jumped too much from one subject to another and that the Paiute Princess was said to have become gloriously drunk afterward: "The Princess lived here some four or five years ago, and was in the habit of getting full every night. Probably she found some of her old acquaintances Saturday night and could not resist the temptation to indulge in her old habits. In this respect she differs from her brother Naches, who is an exemplary Indian and never drinks fire-water."[26]

Sarah did not have an opportunity to defend her reputation against this journalistic attack until after her return from Washington. After several disappointing delays she finally boarded the Central Pacific Railroad on January 13, 1880.[27] She was accompanied by Natchez, Chief Winnemucca, and Captain Jim, who replaced Jerry Long for the Paiute debut in the nation's capital. They rode a week before they arrived in Washington City. Once there, Sarah was to be confronted with a concerted effort to destroy her usefulness as a witness against the reservation system and the men who benefited from its bungling procedures.

16

Washington City

When Sarah arrived in Washington City, D.C., in January, 1880, she discovered that she and the Paiute delegation were confined by a strict schedule, which allowed them appearances only before government officials and a great amount of sightseeing. On the second day after her arrival she had an appointment with Secretary of the Interior Carl Schurz. An underling in the secretary's anteroom made fun of her tears when she pleaded with him for the return of the Paiutes from Yakima. He accused her of lecturing only for money. Secretary Schurz listened sympathetically to her presentation, or so it appeared. Then he instructed Mr. Haworth, who was with the Paiutes every minute when they were not in the Tremont Hotel, to take them around by carriage to places of particular interest in the city. When reporters wished to interview Sarah or find out where she was lecturing, she was whisked away by Mr. Haworth.[1]

Sarah was not aware that Agent Rinehart had sent affidavits to Washington, signed by nine gentlemen of Canyon City, which stated in part:

> We have seen with amazement the charges brought against him [Rinehart] by an Indian woman calling herself Sarah Winnemucca; not that anything this woman can say or do amazed us, but that an intelligent public and high officials should give any credence to the statements of

such a person is startling to us. . . . That her influence with the Indians has always been to render them licentious, contumacious and profligate. That this woman has been several times married, but that by reason of her adulterous and drunken habits, neither squawmen nor Indians would long live with her; that in addition to her character of Harlot and drunkard, she merits and possesses that of a notorious liar and malicious schemer.[2]

Among the signatures on the affidavits was that of D. G. Overholt, who had been in partnership with Rinehart in the merchandising business in Canyon City.

Rinehart had also obtained three affidavits at Camp Harney, sworn and subscribed to him on January 13: one by William Currey, a stock raiser; one by Thomas O'Keefe, a discharged soldier; and one from his former blacksmith at Malheur, W. W. Johnson. In an introductory letter accompanying them, Rinehart apologized for the necessity of sending the affidavits:

It has not been deemed necessary to resort to actual proof of her true standing in this community until the present, when it seems likely that the Depart. may be called upon to consider hers in connection with my own character. . . . Comment upon these affidavits is deemed unnecessary, further than to say I believe them to be true; and, so notorious is her ill-fame, that I feel assured I could obtain the evidence of scores of the best men in this country, as to her general bad character.[3]

William Currey and W. W. Johnson wrote that Sarah was untruthful and "generally regarded by those who know her as a common prostitute and thoroughly addicted to the habits of drunkenness and gambling."[4] Thomas O'Keefe stated that Sarah could be bought for a bottle of whiskey.[5]

The Indian Department's intrigue to keep Sarah from reporters and other interested parties was merely an attempt to allay the criticisms that she would make of them and their department. It is doubtful that the affidavits reached the capital before Sarah's departure in early February, and, since she knew nothing of Rinehart's nefarious schemes, she did not defend herself.

Sarah did gain a short interview with a reporter from the *Washington National Republican*. He wrote, "Dashing Sarah . . . in intellect, grace and knowledge of the world, will compare favorably with many belles of Pennsylvania avenue."[6] She told him that she still planned to lecture. Consequently Secretary Schurz called her immediately to his office and confronted her, saying, "Sarah, so you are bound to lecture."

"People want me to," she replied.

Then he said, "I don't think it will be right for you to lecture here after the government has sent for you, and your father and brother, and paid your way here. The government is going to do right by your people now. Don't lecture now; go home and get your people on the reservation; get them located properly; and then, if you want to come back, . . . we will pay your way here and back again."[7]

Schurz told Sarah that his department had granted all that she had wished and presented her with a letter with his signature that confirmed his statement. Sarah was delighted by its contents:

Department of the Interior
Washington D.C.
[January 24], 1880

The Pi-Utes, heretofore entitled to live on the Malheur Reservation, their primeval home, are to have lands allotted to them in severalty, at the rate of one hundred and sixty acres to each head of a family, and each adult male. Such lands they are to cultivate for their own benefit. The allotment will be made under instructions of their agent. As soon as enabled by law to do so, this department is to give to the Indians patents for each tract of land conveying to each occupant the fee-simple in the lot he occupies.

Those of the Pi-Utes, who in consequence of the Bannock war, went to the Yakima Reservation, and whoever may desire to rejoin their relatives, are at liberty to do so, without expense to the government for transportation. Those who desire to stay upon the Yakima Reservation and become permanently settled there will not be disturbed.

None of the Pi-Utes now living among the whites, and earning wages by their own work will be compelled to go to the Malheur Reservation. They are at perfect liberty to continue working for wages for their own benefit, as they are now doing.

It is well understood that those who settle on the Malheur Reservation will not be supported by the government in idleness. They will be aided in starting their farms and promoting their civilization, but the support given them by the government will, according to law, depend upon their intelligence and efficiency in working for themselves.

C. Schurz
Secretary of the Interior[8]

The secretary also promised Sarah that, when the Paiutes returned to Lovelock, they would be sent 100 canvas tents for their use. Sarah was to issue the tents and send the department the name of each head of family who required one.

The important day came when the Paiute representatives were to talk with the Great White Father. They were first shown through the White House, where many women had congregated to see Sarah.[9] They found her fashionably dressed, in a neat black suit with satin trimmings, and thoroughly composed. Eventually President Hayes walked in and shook hands with the Paiute delegation.

"Did you get all you want for your people?" the president asked Sarah.

"Yes, sir," Sarah replied, "as far as I know."

"That is well," he answered and went out again. It was quite a short affair, seeing President Hayes, and therefore rather a letdown for the Paiutes. It was especially disappointing to Sarah, who had imagined he would take a personal interest in her people.

When the Winnemuccas arrived home in Nevada and stopped off at Lovelock, Paiutes came from all directions to hear their report of their trip and to find out if they had been successful in settling matters. As the days passed, Natchez did not have enough food at Big Meadows to feed the throng, and they almost starved while waiting for the tents to arrive from Washington. Old Winnemucca had been treated to a new suit of clothes by Washington officials. He gave it away when he was back home, saying to Sarah: "This is all I got from the Big Father in Washington. I am the only one who got anything; I don't care for them."[10]

The longer they waited the hungrier the people became. At last Winnemucca told his people: "My dear children, every word we have told you was said to us. They have given us a paper which your mother will read to you." Sarah read the letter from Schurz slowly, so that Natchez could translate. When they had finished, Buena Vista John rose and said:

I have lived many years with white people. Yes, it is over thirty years, and I know a great many of them. I have never known one of them do what they promised. I think they mean it just at the time, but I tell you they are very forgetful. It seems to me, sometimes, that their memory is not good and since I have understood them, if they say they will do so and so for me, I would say to them now or never, and if they don't, why it is because they never meant to do, but only to say so. These are your white brothers' ways, and they are a weak people."[11]

Still the tents did not arrive, and Sarah telegraphed a reminder to Secretary Schurz, saying "Send us something to eat." The secretary wrote in reply that she should take her people to the Malheur Reservation. She would not think of taking the people, who were already starving, three hundred miles through waist-deep snow. She told the Paiutes what the letter contained. They all laughed and said: "We are not disappointed. We always said that the Big Father was just like all the white people."[12] The large number of Numa scattered to wherever they could scavenge food.

During that winter and early spring Agent John Howe of the Duck Valley Reservation, which had been set aside for the Shoshonis, noted an unusual migration of as many as 500 Paiutes who had never been on his reservation before. They called the Shoshoni chief Captain Sam their leader, and claimed to be half-blood Shoshonis. They appeared to be from Natchez's band in the vicinity of Paradise Valley, but they would not claim Natchez or Winnemucca as their leader. They said that they did not like them and that they would not go to Malheur. Captain Sam accepted them as his own, and so Howe apportioned garden tracts to the newcomers. He had to use his seed potatoes and seed wheat in order to feed the unexpected visitors.[13]

In the spring a new chief of the Paiutes was elected: Dave Numana, who was a brother of Buena Vista John and a relative of Sarah's. Natchez no longer claimed the chieftainship because he did not wish to live at Pyramid Lake, which seemed to be a new requirement.[14] There was no doubt that Natchez and Old Winnemucca had lost ground with the Paiutes when they returned from the prestigious trip to the Great White Father in Washington with nothing in their hands. Then, too, their urging of tribal members to move to the Malheur did not set well. Old Winnemucca himself, after all his crediting of white friendship and brotherhood, was as destitute as anyone. He was described as "heap-a-hungry" in Virginia City.[15]

In the meantime Sarah had a clash with the editor of the *Winnemucca Silver State* who had printed the article intimating that she was drunk before her trip to Washington. In a rage she sent a telegram from Lovelock threatening the writer.[16] Now she was arrested for sending the missive and taken before Justice Charles S. Osborn of Winnemucca. She explained that she had sent the telegram because the New York pictorial newspapers had picked up the Nevada story and had claimed that she had been drunk and brandishing a knife. The *Silver State* reported, "This falsehood aroused her anger and caused her to threaten to have the editor's blood."[17] The case was dismissed, but other newspapers also carried the article and embroidered on it.[18]

Agent Rinehart was thrown into paroxysms of indignation by a letter from the Indian commissioner appointing Sarah, the "infamous" woman, to be interpreter once again for the Malheur Reservation.[19] He quickly reminded the department of "her notoriety as an untruthful, drunken prostitute." In the same letter he wrote the commissioner:

> It was publicly known, then as now, that her last occupation before coming to this Agency as Interpreter for Agent Parrish, was in a public house of ill-fame at the town of Winnemucca Nevada. . . . Among the "other sufficient causes", alluded to in my report to General Howard's Headquarters for which she was discharged from the position of Interpreter, was that one of my white employees says he saw her in bed with an Indian man in the mess-house. In view of such facts knowing as I do that this is only part of her infamous history, I am induced to venture the opinion that she is not a proper person to serve in any capacity at this or any other Indian Agency.[20]

Sarah had received notice of her appointment as interpreter at Malheur while she was still in Washington, but the minimal salary of $420 a year was certainly not attractive when she had to pay board. Yet, in spite of that and in spite of Rinehart, she had made up her mind to take the position. While staying with her brother Tom at Pyramid Lake in April, she contacted Rinehart concerning the appointment.[21] She, of course, did not know of the affidavits that Rinehart had collected against her. When he wrote back that, since "none of your people are now at this Agency, your services as Interpreter are not required: and I have so informed the Indian Office,"[22] he failed to add that he had also written the department requesting that she be discharged.[23]

Sarah, recognizing that the Paiutes would only return to Malheur along with Leggins and his people, decided to visit Yakima and bring him and the others back. Armed only with the letter that she had received from Schurz in Washington and accompanied by a sister-in-law (probably a wife of Lee Winnemucca), she set off on horseback in April from Pyramid Lake, traveling northward through desolate, uninhabited country. In her autobiography Sarah emphasizes the two women's worries traveling alone.[24]

On the evening of the fourth day they approached a house where Sarah's cousin Joe Winnemucca was working as a ranch hand. Joe welcomed the women and introduced them to the white rancher, who was a friend of Chief Winnemucca. The two men could hardly believe that the women had traveled alone through such formidable conditions. Sarah told her cousin of the urgency of her trip—how she was going to bring the people back to Malheur—and read him Schurz's letter. Joe was very glad, because his brother Frank was detained at Yakima.[25]

Joe offered to go with the women to the next ranch because he feared for their safety there. Upon their arrival at the place Sarah was much relieved to find a friend who said, "Why, Sarah, what in the world are you doing away out here at this time of the year?" He helped her from her horse, and they were well treated. When Sarah offered to pay for meals and the night's lodging, the ranch owner would not hear of it. In the morning Joe rode on with them a way and turned back, thinking all was well. The women had ridden only ten miles before they discovered three horsemen traveling rapidly in pursuit. They were Spanish vaqueros who worked on the ranch and had spotted them. Sarah and her sister-in-law rode for their lives, but at last they had to rest because their horses were exhausted. They planned how they would save each other if they were attacked. Luckily, their pursuers had lost heart by this time; only one came up, and he spoke politely to them. They were able to ride on without further trouble.

At the south end of Steens Mountain they stayed several days with a cousin of Sarah's who was married to a white man. Then they rode in the wagon of an acquaintance to their next lodging. There a Mr. Anderson, a United States mail contractor, was very kind to them, reading their letter and encouraging them in their efforts. After supper, however, Sarah felt like crying. There were eight cowboys in the ranchhouse, and there was no private room in which the women could sleep. At last Anderson said to the stage driver, "You and I must give up our bed to Miss Winnemucca tonight and go sleep with the boys."

At last the women lay down, but they could not sleep from fear. Sarah's description of the night and her feelings conveys some of the anxieties of unprotected females on the rough frontier. Sarah felt a hand on her in the darkness, and someone said, "Sarah."

She jumped up quickly and hit the intruder in the face with her fist, crying, "Go away or I will cut you to pieces." The man ran out of the house, leaving a trail of blood.

Mr. Anderson got up and lighted a candle. "Oh, Sarah, what have you done?" he said when he saw the blood. "Did you cut him?"

"No, I did not cut him; I wish I had," she answered. "I only struck him with my hand."

They looked outside, but the man was gone and had taken his horse. "The big fool," the rancher commented. A candle burned by the bed the remainder of the night.

Mr. Anderson got up at four and rustled some breakfast for the women, as they had to make Camp Harney that day, over sixty miles.[26]

At Camp Harney, Sarah and her sister-in-law found only three women, the wives of soldiers. They were very hospitable to the two Paiute women while the latter waited ten days for the deep snows to melt on the Blue Mountains. As Sarah had no money, she tried to sell her lame horse, but without success. Her last hope was that Mr. Stevens, the storekeeper at the camp, would loan her money. She went to him with her letter of appointment as interpreter at Malheur and, thinking that she would be paid in that position, the storekeeper lent her $100. Sarah, of course, assumed that the position would be hers when she returned with the Paiutes from Yakima.

Captain Drury at Camp Harney lent them a horse. Sarah and her sister-in-law spent two difficult days riding through the drifts of snow. Once they had to swim a river with their horses. At last they arrived in Canyon City, nearly frozen. While waiting in town for the stage to The Dalles, they had an opportunity to see Sarah's former attorney, Charles Parrish, who was saddened to hear of the deaths of his wife's students at Yakima.[27]

The stage to The Dalles was only a two-seated buckboard. When the two women reached the town, they were relieved to find Lee waiting for them; Sarah had written ahead, and he had hired horses from the Yakimas. Now they were on the last leg of the journey to the reservation. When they arrived, however, Sarah did not present her letter to Agent Wilbur for several days. She explains in *Life Among the Piutes* that she had to gather her courage before going to the agent's office. Meanwhile she told Lee of the letter's contents, and rumors circulated among the people.

When she did go to Wilbur, she asked him, "Did you get a letter from Washington?"

"No," he replied.

"Well, that is strange—they told me they would write."

"Who?"

"The Secretary of the Interior, Secretary Schurz."

"Why, what makes you think they would write to me?"

"Father, they told me they would write right off while I was there. It was about my people."

"We have not heard from them."

"Father, I have a letter here, which Secretary Schurz gave me." She showed the letter to Wilbur, who after reading it appeared to be angry.

"Sarah," he told her, "your people are doing well here, and I don't want you to tell them of this paper or to read it to them. They are the best workers I ever saw. If you will not tell them, I will give you fifty dollars, and I will write to Washington, and see if they will keep you here as interpreter."

Sarah replied, "How is it that I am not paid for interpreting here so long? Was I not turned over to you as an interpreter for my people? I have worked at everything while I was here. I helped in the school-house, and . . . interpreted sermons." She told him that she ought to be paid for what she had already done.

He told her that he would do so if she did not make the Paiutes discontented with their lot, as they were progressing nicely. Sarah did not promise, but neither did she tell the Paiutes about the paper, though they knew that she had an important message. They began to doubt her motives. At last Leggins called a council and demanded that Sarah and Lee come.

Sarah stood and, holding the paper over her head, she made the following speech:

> My dear children, may the Great Father in the Spiritland will it so that you may see your husbands, and your children, and your daughters. I have said everything I could in your behalf, so did father and brother. I have suffered everything but death to come here with this paper. I don't know whether it speaks truth or not. You can say what you like about me. You have a right to say I have sold you. It looks so. I have told you many things which are not my own words, but the words of the agents and the soldiers. I know I have told you more lies than I have hair on my head. I tell you, my dear children, I have never told you my own words; they were the words of the white people, not mine. Of course, you don't know, and I don't blame you for thinking as you do. You will never know until you go to the Spirit-land. This which I hold in my hand is our only hope. . . . If it is truth we will see our people in fifty days. . . . I will read it just as it is, so that you can all judge for yourselves.[28]

After the reading the people reacted with joyous shouts. Leggins said, "Now, you have heard what our mother has told us, we will get ready to go at once."

While all the others were dancing and singing and coming to thank Sarah, Oytes sat quietly in a corner with his hands over his face. Anguish was in his eyes when he raised them to Leggins. He said, "Oh, brother, ask me to go with you to our dear Mother Earth, where we can lie alongside our father's bones. Just say, 'Come,' I will be glad to go with you."

Sarah felt pity for him. She said, "This paper says all that want to go can go. I say for one, Oytes, come, go with us."

Leggins agreed. "Oytes, I have no right to say to you, 'You have done wrong and you can't go to your own country.' No, I am only too glad to hear you talk as you do. We will all go back and be happy once more in our native land."[29]

Sarah wrote a letter to Natchez, which was signed by the other Paiute leaders, outlining their plans to leave Fort Simcoe on July 3, 1880. She described the Yakima Paiutes' condition: "We don't know what time we will get to the Dalles and a good many of us will have to walk. . . . We are poorer than when we came. Poorer in clothes. Poorer in horses. Poorer in victuals; in everything. Our sick have been poorly cared for and many have died of want of something to eat." It was signed by Sarah, Lee, and Frank Winnemucca; Chief Leggins; Paddy Two Chief; and Piute Joe.[30]

Father Wilbur was the roadblock to their plans. He refused to talk to the Paiute leaders, who wished him to call a military escort to keep the settlers from attacking them on their way back to Malheur. This elderly fire-and-brimstone preacher had the previous year commended Sarah to the Indian Department for her "noble work in the school room, out of the school, instructing the Piute women and girls how to cut and make garments for the children of the Piute School, and themselves, and doing the essential service as interpreter."[31] He now told her: "I am sorry you are putting the devil into your people's heads; they were all doing so well while you were away, and I was so pleased with them. You are talking against me all the time, and if you don't look out I will have you put in irons and in prison."[32]

"I don't care how soon you have it done," she replied. "My people are saying I have sold them to you, and get money from you to keep them here. I am abused by you and by my own people, too. You never were the man to give me anything for my work, and I have to pay for everything I have to eat. Mr. Wilbur, you will not get off as easily as you think you will. I will go to Yakima City and lecture. I will tell them all how you are selling my people the clothes which were sent here for them."[33]

After this argument Sarah never saw Wilbur again. Subsequently he sent for Lee and tried to urge him to stay. When Lee returned after a session with the agent, he said, "Oh, sister, I am rich. I am going to have some land, and I am going to have a wagon, and I am going to have my own time to pay for it. It will only take one hundred and twenty-five years for me to pay for my wagon," he laughed bitterly. "He wants me to stay here, not to go away. Yes, I see myself staying here."[34]

Sarah and Lee went to Yakima City and talked to the newspaper editor there. They told him that fifty-eight Paiutes, thirty of whom were children, had died in the year that they had lived at Yakima; that so many deaths had occurred that the Paiutes were no longer permitted to bury their dead in the graveyard, and the bodies were thrown in the watercourses. The Winnemuccas told the editor that they had resolved to leave Yakima for Malheur, whether Agent Wilbur provided an escort for them or not, and asked him to tell the people of eastern Oregon through the columns of his newspaper that they would harm nothing of any white man as they passed through the country. Sarah pledged her own life for the peaceful intentions and good conduct of her people.[35] The editor wrote, "As Sarah has always been the firm friend of the whites on more than one trying occasion, we hope for the credit of the white race that the people of Eastern Oregon and Nevada will treat these Indians with friendliness."[36]

Sarah then traveled to The Dalles, where she awaited the Paiutes on the first step of their long journey back to their homeland. Meanwhile, however, Agent Wilbur had telegraphed the Indian Department in an attempt to get a reversal of the permission that Sarah had received from Secretary Schurz. He wrote the department in a follow-up letter:

Till Sarah Winnemucca returned from Washington, with the unfortunate permits obtained from the Honorable Secretary of the Interior, doubtless through misrepresentations—the Paiutes were contented, and expressed themselves as well satisfied to remain here. So far as I know only one or two cherished the expectation of returning to the Malheur—the rest seemed interested in my plans for their future, and were anxious to send their children to school—Sarah represented to them that it was the wish of the *President* for them to return, that numberless and indefinite benefits were to be bestowed on them, and that the Agent at Yakama [*sic*] was stealing their money, which the Department had placed in his hands for their benefit. . . . I am satisfied that her anxiety to leave this Reservation is due—not to any desire to benefit her people—but that she may be able to carry out schemes for her personal aggrandizement through a connection not at all to her credit.

I have done all in my power to benefit Sarah Winnemucca. I have concealed my knowledge of her disreputable intrigues, and on her solemn promises of amendment condoned her offenses, and bestowed every favor on her in my power, and if I have a right to look for gratitude and kind feelings from anyone, I certainly have the right to look for it from her, but am forced—in sorrow not in anger—to the conclusion that she is utterly unreliable, and that no dependence whatever can be placed on her character or word.[37]

This agent had, at the end of the year in which he had received the destitute Paiutes and had let them starve, returned $8,214.59 to the United States Treasury as the unspent balance of his budget.[38] When the belated answer to his telegram arrived, Wilbur read it with satisfaction: he was instructed to hold

Sarah's autographed picture sent to Natchez. It is inscribed, "Your loving sister Sarah Winnemucca." (Courtesy of Nevada Historical Society.)

the Paiutes at Yakima. While waiting at The Dalles, Sarah also received a telegram from the acting commissioner of Indian affairs: "We have reports from General Howard, Agent Wilbur and parties living near Malheur showing that if the Piutes attempt to march across the country from Yakima to Malheur it will be attended with great risk of life on the way. Consequently, the Secretary advised that your people remain at Yakama [*sic*] for the present."[39] Agent Wilbur had won.

It is unlikely that General Howard ever was moved by Sarah's appeals to him for the Numa's return to Malheur. In August, 1878, at the close of the Bannock War, Howard had even considered the feasibility of sending the Paiute prisoners to Indian Territory, or, if not there, to the Lummí Reservation on Puget Sound. He had written, "It will not do to reestablish the Malheur Agency."[40] A few months later he wrote again: "Sarah Winnemucca said to me that great complaint was kept up among the Malheurs on account of shortness of supplies, complaint never made under former agent. I think news of taking horses from Bannocks, dissatisfaction with their own change of Agent, a knowledge of the general conspiracy against whites, including Columbia Indians influenced Malheurs more than want of rations at time of outbreak."[41]

Howard never acknowledged that Egan and his band were forced into the war. In *My Life and Personal Experiences Among Our Hostile Indians,* published in 1907, two years before his death, he speaks of Egan as his chief adversary in the Bannock War. Perhaps Agent Rinehart had an inkling of the general's difficulty in distinguishing between the Paiutes who had remained staunch friends of the whites and the hostiles. Rinehart wrote to the commissioner of Indian affairs:

> From the evidence I have, which is partly the reports of interested parties, I am led to conclude that the effort to establish Leggin's complicity in the recent hostilities has grown out of and is incident to the payment of the bill of expenses incurred in their removal from Harney to Yakima, which is no inconsiderable amount. If their removal was unauthorized the expenditure for their removal would necessarily be unauthorized; hence the effort to bring these people within the purview of the Department order which authorized the transfer of all the hostiles by implicating Leggins also in the hostile outbreak.[42]

17
Mrs. Hopkins

Sarah's grand hope that she could help her people at Yakima was shattered. The letter from Secretary Schurz, now folded and worn after the hard riding and perils of the journey to Yakima, seemed like a taunt to her old belief that there were white men of good will to whom her people could appeal for understanding and fairness. She herself was in a desperate situation. There was no chance that she could return with her people to the Malheur Reservation. She was out of money and in debt, with no possibility of a position as interpreter at Malheur, and she was banned from the Yakima Reservation with no means to return to Nevada. Could she appeal once more to a white man for the means to survive? General Howard was stationed sixty miles down the Columbia River from The Dalles at Vancouver Barracks. She wrote him, and he did not fail her. He sent for her to work as a teacher and interpreter among Bannock Indian prisoners.

The Indians at Vancouver Barracks were Sheepeaters and Weisers captured during the war, and Sarah found the twelve girls and six boys among them apt pupils. She wrote the secretary of the interior on behalf of the fifty-three prisoners at Vancouver to ask that they be given land so that they could commence farming, and that a special dispensation be made for the women and children who had not been issued clothing.[1] There was no reply to Sarah's letter from the secretary; possibly she did not expect one.

General Howard was pleased with Sarah's work at Vancouver Barracks and termed her service to the prisoners "invaluable." He wrote a general letter of recommendation for her, saying: "[she] gave abundant satisfaction to all who were interested in Indian children. She always appeared to me to be a true friend to her own people, doing what she could for them."[2]

In the fall of 1880, Sarah wrote to Natchez from Vancouver.

Dear Brother,

I received your letter on September 7 and am very glad to hear from you. I am glad you are all well down there. That is more than I can say of myself, as I have been very sick for three weeks. I had a fever and thought I was going to die, but no such good luck befell me. I am well again and doing duty. I do hope you will all go to the Malheur. I have not heard from Lee Winnemucca for a long time and I do not know how they are getting along at Yakima. Last time he wrote he said 15 Piutes had died since I had left there. You say you will send me some Indian sugar—our pe-ha-ve. I would like to have some but I am afraid it will cost too much to have it sent here, if it does not, send me some right away. The Indians here are most all sick. Seven are out scouting, but will soon be back if they do not run away.[3]

While Sarah was working with the children in the Indian camp, she again met the president of the United States. Sarah did not allow this second opportunity to speak with President Hayes to pass without expressing her concerns in a forceful way. While touring Vancouver Barracks, the president visited Sarah's class and shook hands with the Bannock Indian children. She followed him to his carriage and "made petition for her poor people in a trembling voice and tender manner," so that the ladies present, including Mrs. Hayes, were moved to tears. Hayes replied that he could make no promises, but that he would remember her request, which was to have her people gathered at some one place where they could live permanently and be cared for and instructed.[4] "You are a husband and father," she told him, "and you know how you would suffer to be separated from your wife and children by force, as my people still are, husbands from wives, parents from children, notwithstanding Secretary Schurz's order."[5]

This impromptu interview with the president made no change

in the conditions of the Paiutes at Yakima, nor did it hasten their removal to the Malheur. Sarah's half brother Lee was permitted to return to Oregon, accompanying Agent Wilbur, who had come with some teams of horses to remove all of the usable material and Indian goods from the Oregon reservation. The Malheur Reservation's status was still undetermined, but Rinehart now had the title "farmer in charge" and was expected to resign at an early date. On behalf of Lee Winnemucca, Rinehart wrote a letter to the commissioner of Indian affairs in which he begged for justice for Leggins's band and the others who were forceably detained at Yakima. He may have had the Paiutes' welfare at heart, but his letter can also be interpreted as a last-ditch effort to keep the Malheur agency.

When he had learned of Lee's imminent departure, Leggins had become so frenzied with the desire to return to his own country that he made a noisy protest, and Agent Wilbur had had him arrested. Rinehart wrote:

> He [Leggins] has trusted and waited now for two years and a half and still they are held at Yakama. It cost the government plenty of money to break its promise and do wrong in sending them to Yakama, but it is unwilling to spend a dollar to undo that wrong or to assist and protect them on their journey back to their friends and kindred. . . . No one subject—no single matter of official duty has so profoundly engrossed my thoughts as the unwarranted removal and unjust detention of Leggins and his people in their present galling and grievous exile against their expressed will and repeated protest.[6]

When Lee returned to the settlements along the railroad in Nevada and rejoined his people in late July, he told them of the frustrations of the Paiutes who were attempting to go back to Nevada on their own. Ferriage across the Columbia River cost at least $150, which they did not have. Then they had to pass five hundred miles through settlements where no unarmed and unprotected Indian was safe. So many of their horses were stolen from them that they had not enough to carry them back. By this time Leggins had become an old man, almost blind, who had nearly given up hope.[7]

Father Wilbur held a different view of the Paiutes' adaptation to his reservation. He told the Indian Department that many had declared their intention to remain under any circumstances and that the others were only anxious to leave from a desire for change, which he said was "inherent in all savage natures." He had found most of the Paiutes to be steady workers. He had given them camas irons so that they could forage for the camas root, and he planned to take them off rations entirely except for the old and infirm and those women and children who had no able-bodied male friend to depend on. He wrote:

> With feelings of profound gratitude to the Providence, that has permitted me to witness the gradual progress of the people committed to my charge, from a state of degraded barbarism to comparative civilization, from the gross blackness of heathen corruption, to the glorious light and liberty of the Gospel of the Son of God, I can realize that from month to month, and from year to year, solid progress and improvement is being made.[8]

Arthur Chapman, an experienced interpreter for the army, was sent to Yakima by General McDowell and General Miles to observe the condition of the Paiutes. His arrival was greeted with suspicion by Agent Wilbur, especially when he found that Chapman was encouraging the Paiutes to leave, meeting with the leaders in secret council, and telling them that he would have transportation ready with an escort for them at the Columbia River. In the meantime Wilbur wired the Indian Department and demanded a fixed policy toward the Paiutes: Were they to go or stay? On October 31 he received a reply: Yakima was to remain the home of the Paiutes, as the Malheur Reservation had been abandoned.[9]

When Agent Wilbur showed Chapman the telegram from the Indian Department, the interpreter was much disconcerted. He returned for another conference with the Paiutes, in which he told them that, because of the lateness of the season, the departure would be postponed until spring, when he would return for them. Wilbur was rankled that Sarah Winnemucca and Chapman were making promises to the Indians that kept them from taking any interest in working the land or sending their children to his school. He termed their actions "outside interference" in his tightly run reservation. He wrote to the Indian commissioner, "To be rid of them [the Paiutes] would be an inexpressible relief to me; yet notwithstanding the trouble, labor and anxiety they have caused me, I have faithfully tried to carry out what I understood to be the wishes of the Department."[10] Wilbur was soon to retire. It rankled him that the Paiutes had not submitted to his ordered intentions and that they were leaving his accounts not entirely on the plus side of the ledger as he would have liked.

Interpreter Chapman had been appalled at the condition in which he found the Paiutes under Wilbur's care. He had never seen people in such destitution. There was no food, not even stored in baskets in their tents. The leaders told him that sometimes they had nothing for four or five days, contrary to the statements of Father Wilbur, who said that they had plenty to eat. Sarah claims that Chapman found the clothes on their backs in rags.[11]

During the long, despairing wait for the return of Leggins's people Sarah received $500 from the army as her reward for bringing Winnemucca's band to safety during the Bannock War. When the Sheepeaters and Weiser Bannocks were ordered to return to Fort Hall, Sarah accompanied them with an army officer, a Lieutenant Mills. She took this opportunity to visit her sister Elma at Henry's Lake, Idaho. They were reunited for the first time since girlhood. Elma's husband, John Smith, was a lumberman, and, though Elma lived in a typically modest frontier cabin, she made her home comfortable and attractive. Sarah envied the peace and contentment of her sister's uneventful life, but she knew it was not for her.

Elma, who had been isolated for so long in the Yellowstone country, was excited by the prospect of a trip to Nevada for a reunion with relatives. The two sisters arrived in Winnemucca on the Central Pacific in a palace car, dressed in fashionable attire.[12] They probably visited Natchez at his home in the Big Meadows near Lovelock, where he was farming and raising his large family. Their conversations may have dealt with the disappointment of the Paiutes' loss of the Malheur Reservation and the seeming impossibility of returning the Yakima Paiutes.

Then Lee brought news that after traveling for months, Frank Winnemucca, Piute Joe, and several other Yakima Paiutes, had arrived with their families at Fort McDermit. They had made their way back through great hardship and danger to their old hunting grounds. Others also had escaped and had stopped at the Warm Springs Reservation in northern Oregon, where members of their families had been held prisoners.[13] The majority of

Leggins's band and the old chief himself were still captives at Yakima.

Sarah was now about thirty-seven years of age. She was an integrated, but complicated, person who understood the realities of her situation as well as anyone and yet had a romantic attitude toward life. She wanted to believe in the wisdom and sincerity of the whites and to have their respect. She also wanted to believe in the natural, intuitive wisdom and goodness of her people and to continue to command the Paiutes' respect.

We must understand that she walked a tightrope between two worlds. She always had the view of the precipice around her, yet she believed that she would in the end take the right steps to achieve recognition for herself as her people's savior. Morals were important to her, but the differences between the Indian and white cultures often made her behavior appear suspect. Methodism, for example, was naturally appealing to her because it supported the traditional strict moral code for relations between the sexes that her own people followed. The Paiutes' marriage vows were less formal, and polygamy was accepted among them because many female hands were needed to find and prepare food in the sparse desert environment. Sarah's brother Natchez had two or three wives and was considered a congenial husband and father. Similarly, there is no doubt that Sarah gambled, but gambling was a highly regarded pastime among her people. Her father was said to have lost (and won) many ponies playing the hand game.

Sarah certainly drank on occasion, though she deplored the effects of alcohol on her people.[14] Whether she was intoxicated from time to time cannot be proved or disproved. It is irrelevant except when the question exposed her to criticism by her contemporaries. White critics were always seizing opportunities to play down her positive attributes.

As we have seen, Sarah grew to understand power in the white men's terms, and she became adept, in collaboration with Natchez, in using it to her advantage. She was a determined woman with strong opinions, ready to defend her honor with action and words. Yet she was also high-strung and emotional, needing companionship, love, and understanding.

It is likely that it was this combination of personal qualities that led Sarah abruptly to marry again on December 5, 1881.[15] The man, Lewis H. Hopkins of Virginia, was five years her junior. He wore his light brown hair parted down the middle, sported a handlebar mustache, and was a bit of a dandy. His background and where he met Sarah are open to conjecture. Some say that they met in Montana while Sarah visited Elma.[16] Others associate Hopkins with the Indian Department and the feeding of Indians during the Bannock War, which would mean that he and Sarah were acquaintances of several years' standing.[17] Although it is unfortunate that we know few of the particulars about Hopkins's past, at least we can draw some conclusions about his character from his behavior following the marriage.

Sarah and Lewis were married at the Russ House in San Francisco by a justice of the peace, and soon after the ceremony it was announced that the couple would leave for the East on a speaking engagement.[18] Sarah was to give lectures on "The Indian Agencies" and "The Indian Question as Viewed from an Indian Standpoint." She had expanded her interests to include the conditions of all Indians and their status under the agents and the "ring" in the Indian Department. She told a San Francisco reporter that the agent at Pyramid Lake was treating her people high-handedly: "We want no more of these white hypocrites, who are not content to steal half the Government allowance, but take it all." She suggested that a head chief of each tribe act as agent on the reservations and distribute the goods and annuities.[19]

Sarah and her new husband did not go east at once. Lewis Hopkins was another white husband with habits that caused problems for Sarah. While they were yet in San Francisco, he gambled away $500. This was money that she had earned teaching at Vancouver Barracks plus some of the reward that she had acquired for her arduous efforts to save her father's band at the onset of the Bannock War.

The couple traveled to Pyramid Reservation and stayed with Sarah's brother Tom until they obtained the means to make the long trip east. Apparently Hopkins had no money of his own, nor was he interested in working. Gambling was still one of the chief pastimes on the reservation, and Lewis played poker with some of his new relatives by marriage. Once, after losing a small amount of money, he gave his place to Sarah, who lost a few

Lieutenant Lewis H. Hopkins, Sarah Winnemucca's last husband. (Courtesy of Nevada Historical Society.)

dollars as well. Lewis was quite angry with her, and according to one account, when she reminded him of the losses that she had incurred from his playing in San Francisco, he walked off threatening to leave her. Sarah drank herself into a state of forgetful sleep. When she awoke, her new husband had returned, and all was forgiven.[20]

While at the reservation Sarah observed firsthand the policies and relations with the Paiutes of the new agent, who had succeeded the well-liked James E. Spencer. His name was Joseph McMaster. When the young son of a family living near Tom's place died on New Year's Eve, the relatives wailed and mourned in their customary way. Three of the agent's men—the doctor, the carpenter, and the blacksmith—and one of their friends came to the grass hut, or *karnee,* imitating the sounds of Paiute mourning in a mocking manner. They handed Lewis a bottle of whiskey, suggesting that he pass it around to his relatives. He said, "Pass it round yourselves."

They replied, "Give some to your brother-in-law."

Lewis answered, "Give it to him yourself."[21]

This interchange, of course, showed the whites' disdain for the Paiutes' customs and feelings. They were putting Hopkins down for having as a brother-in-law an Indian to whom he could not legally give whiskey. Sarah wrote in her autobiography, "This is the kind of people, dear reader, that the government sends to teach us at Pyramid Lake Reservation."[22]

Sarah found that at Pyramid Lake the Paiutes with crops, who had planted their own seed on their own farms, were expected to give every third sack of grain and every third load of hay to the agent. If they did not, their wagons were taken from them, or they were told to leave the reservation.[23] The beef contractor for the reservation ran nothing more than a butcher shop: "Those that have money can come up and buy. Those that have none stand back and cry, often with hunger."[24]

McMaster appointed Sarah's cousin, Dave Numana, as police chief, and she wrote that he was used as a front for the agent's activities.

Sarah and Lewis Hopkins left Nevada in late February, 1882, for Elma's home at Henry's Lake. They planned to move east that spring, but it was more than a year before Sarah actually arrived in Boston.[25] W. V. Rinehart also moved at this time—to Canyon

City. The Malheur Reservation, its improvements, and animals had been sold. The land was disposed of at public auction. Rinehart was an embittered man, particularly hostile toward General O. O. Howard, who, he claimed, had never officially requisitioned to replace the Indian supplies that were taken by the army at Malheur during the Bannock War. The former agent protested that he was left with a suspension of his property accounts for $18,000.[26]

Meanwhile, Leggins's band of forty-three lodges, spurred by Arthur Chapman's promise that he would return in the spring to accompany them to their old home, made plans to escape from Yakima even if no help arrived. About three hundred Paiutes wished to return with Chapman. When the army interpreter had not arrived by late July, they asked for a permit from Father Wilbur to fish at Tumwater, Washington, on the Columbia River and made their escape attempt. They sold some horses to pay their fare, crossed the river by ferry, and then started south, hoping to live on roots, game, and fish on their journey home.

Father Wilbur sent Yakima Indian policemen after them, and they were forced back. Three of the leaders were subsequently held as prisoners at The Dalles.[27] Wilbur denied Chapman's account of the Paiutes' condition at Yakima. He admitted that he had not given them full rations and that they had no houses, but countered that they had subsistence of their own. He also stated that the Yakima Indians had cheerfully agreed to cede their land for wheat and had voluntarily given Christmas presents to the Paiutes. He blamed much of the Paiute dissatisfaction on Sarah: "Since Sarah Winnemucca had excited their hopes of a return to their old country, their feeling was such, that *should Mr. Chapman tell them he had come to escort them back*, it would require a military force to keep them."[28]

Howard was very defensive when Wilbur accused him of making false promises to the Paiutes, saying: "The return of Leggins or indeed of any of the Piutes to the Malheur reservation would have, inevitably resulted in war. Whenever I had occasion to talk with Sarah Winnemucca, or any of her people on this subject, I always urged the necessity of their abandoning all thought of returning to Malheur and of their making themselves contended (*sic*) where they were."[29]

18
Old Winnemucca

Widowed for many years, Winnemucca was married again in July, 1882, to a widow with a young child.[1] A month later reports arrived in Nevada from Camp Bidwell, California, indicating that the old chief was dying. With him were his new wife, his son Lee, and his two elderly sisters, all of whom had been traveling with him to Surprise Valley, near Camp Bidwell, to visit Chief Ocheo.[2]

Winnemucca was now over ninety years of age. He had fallen ill near Coppersmith Ranch, before his small band reached Ocheo's territory.[3] A runner was sent ahead to Ocheo, who immediately came to the aid of his friend by traveling to the place of sickness and ordering a doctoring *karnee* built. After sundown a shaman began working on the old chief, while the people sat about the fire repeating the shaman's song of power. Old Winnemucca was expected to improve after the all-night performance of the doctor. Instead he settled into a coma, from which he sometimes woke and spoke to those about him. He said that he had dreamed that his wife had poisoned him.[4] By this he did not mean literally that she had given him poison, but that she had caused an evil power to enter him.

The old man lay by the fire, wrapped in a rabbit-skin robe, his feet buried in the warm ashes. As his relatives stayed by his side, their eyes often moved to his young wife, who huddled in a corner, increasingly frightened. In the minds of the assembled Paiutes the woman was guilty of her husband's illness.

We do not know the particulars of all that occurred in the next few weeks before Chief Winnemucca's death, but anthropological studies of Paiute shamanism and sorcery help us to understand the drastic measures that were taken by the Numa to ensure the extinction of the supposed evil powers.[5]

The woman was taken to a spring by some of the other Paiutes who were assembled. While they were not looking, the alleged sorceress found a rope and attempted to hang herself from a post.[6] The band had been confident that she was guilty of causing Winnemucca's illness because she had not atoned for her dark sorcery by bathing. Now the attempted suicide proved her guilt in their eyes.[7] A council was held, and Ocheo's band agreed that the woman should be stoned, which was the customary practice against evil-intentioned shamans. Her child must die also, because it was believed that her offspring would perpetuate her dark powers.[8]

The doomed woman was taken again to the spring, where she was stripped, forced to bathe, and then sprinkled with ashes. When night fell, a circle of fires was lit on a nearby hill. The woman was brought and tied by one leg to a stump, while the Paiutes joined hands and began a monotonous chant, circling their victim. One of them stepped near the fire and began to harangue in a loud voice, while the trembling woman kneeled over her child in a protective manner, crying for mercy. The speaker finally sprang forward and tore the child from her arms, swung it around several times, and dashed its head against a pile of rocks, where it was killed instantly.[9]

The dance and chanting continued. At last the leader stopped near the woman, picked up a large rock, and hit her full force with it on the back. She shrieked and fell forward. A small trickle of blood flowed from a long gash in her side. More rocks followed, and after a few agonizing moments a large rock was brought down upon her head. Her dead body and belongings and those of her child were laid on a fire. A few of the Paiutes remained to see that all was consumed.[10]

The Numa believed that Chief Winnemucca's health would now be restored. Instead, the old man continued to lie semicon-

Chief Winnemucca, whose request to the United States government for land for his band was never realized during his lifetime. (Courtesy of Oregon Historical Society.)

scious, refusing to eat or to take healing concoctions of herbs. He was bled several times, but, as the weeks passed, his body did not respond to the age-old treatment and he became skeleton-thin. At last, on October 21, 1882,[11] Chief Winnemucca died. According to Paiute belief his spirit ascended the Milky Way, and he entered an afterlife. There he would meet his ancestors in a world where there were many animals to hunt and much bountiful land that was possessed by no one and used and respected by all.

Sarah would, of course, grieve at the loss of her father. Adding to her sense of loss was her great regret that she had not been able to help him fulfill his modest desire to acquire land for his people in a place of their own choosing. After her marriage to Lewis Hopkins, she was not able to help him monetarily or even able to be present at his deathbed. It appears that she and her new husband were in residence at Henry's Lake at the time of his death.

Sarah surely deplored the death of Winnemucca's wife, though execution by stoning was a traditional means of ridding the band of a member who had not conformed—such as a woman found in intercourse out of marriage or a shaman suspected of poisoning or harming his patients. Sarah was hardpressed to explain such a group-willed and executed fate to "civilized" society. In an article published before her father's death she was critical of the Numa: "Virtue was a quality whose absence was punished by death—either by burning alive or stoning to death. The ceremony of marriage is not so strictly carried out as in olden times. They take a woman now without much ado, as white people do, and leave them oftener than of old."[12] This article of several pages in *The Californian*, plus the recent publication of Helen Hunt Jackson's popular *A Century of Dishonor*, in which Sarah's letter of 1870 to Major Douglass appears, caused renewed interest in the East concerning this literate Indian woman. Thus, when Sarah and her husband arrived in Boston in the spring of 1883, they found many earnest sympathizers and a public that was anxious to receive her.[13]

19

A Trip to the East

Two influential Boston sisters were to be Sarah's mainstays for several years to come. First was Elizabeth Palmer Peabody, who, from the time when she first met Sarah and heard her impassioned plea for the Paiutes and other American Indians, continued faithfully to support her cause.

Outwardly Elizabeth was a chunky spinster, always dressed in the same black silk, but she had created an illustrious aura about herself from her associations with the Concord Transcendentalists, whose books she published. Her own learned lectures and writings on world history, plus her dynamic enthusiasm and support for the establishment of German kindergartens in the United States, added to her stature.

Elizabeth's sister, Mary Mann, was the widow of Horace Mann. Though not so dynamic as her impulsive, talkative sister, she was accomplished as a writer and was instrumental in organizing and supporting Elizabeth's many ventures into humanitarian causes. A third sister, Sophia Peabody, had married Nathanial Hawthorne, but she was deceased before Sarah and Lewis reached Boston in the spring of 1883.

When Sarah arrived in Boston, Elizabeth was seventy-nine years old and had suffered a slight stroke but she soon began working assiduously for the cause of the "Princess" Sarah Winnemucca. She proposed that Sarah give a series of lectures, so that subscribers would learn the history and culture of the Paiutes as well as their present circumstances. When Sarah found that she could cover only a few points in each lecture, she became determined to write about her people at length.[1] Elizabeth was willing to see that the book was published. It would be a means of introducing Sarah and her cause and also would bring in revenue.

Thus Sarah gained innumerable speaking engagements up and down the East Coast before large church gatherings and Indian Association groups. She brought a new awareness to her audiences of the plight of the American Indian: their lack of land, sustenance, citizenship, and the rights that go with citizenship. She reminded her audiences that the Indians had no representation in the United States government.

Sarah lectured in New York, Connecticut, Rhode Island, Maryland, Massachusetts, and Pennsylvania within the first few months of her stay in the East. She enjoyed creating a dramatic impression, dressed in fringed buckskin and beads, with armlets and bracelets adorning her arms and wrists. She even included the affectation of a gold crown on her head and a wampum bag of velvet, decorated with an embroidered cupid, hanging from her waist.[2]

The first lecture in Boston, where she spoke on the shortcomings of Father Wilbur, offended an influential Methodist woman, who had expected Sarah to tone down her criticisms in return for support and hospitality. Sarah did not bow to such pressure. As a result opposition started against her, including the Women's Association of the Methodist church.[3]

Sarah, however, was moving in select circles, thanks to Elizabeth Peabody and Mary Mann. John Greenleaf Whittier, Ralph Waldo Emerson, and Justice Oliver Wendell Holmes were made aware of her cause through Elizabeth, who knew everybody of consequence in New England. She was a guest of Mrs. Ole Bull, the wife of the famous musician, and spoke to the students of Vassar College by invitation of their president.[4]

One early lecture in Boston was intended for women only. Sarah spoke of the domestic education given by Paiute grandmothers to the youth of both sexes concerning their relations with each other before and after marriage. It was "a lecture which

The "Princess" Sarah, as she appeared in Boston and other cities on the East Coast. (Courtesy of Nevada Historical Society.)

never failed to excite the moral enthusiasm of every woman that heard it," according to Elizabeth.[5] The elderly woman was convinced by Sarah that the Paiutes' education of their young was based on "natural religion and family moralities."[6]

As well as lecturing, Sarah found time to write *Life Among the Piutes: Their Wrongs and Claims,* the story of her own life arranged in eight chapters. In the book she made the Paiute woman's position in councils and family life sound somewhat liberated: "The women know as much as the men do, and their advice is often asked. We have a republic as well as you. The council-tent is our Congress, and anybody can speak who has anything to say, women and all." She described how women were quite willing to go into battle alongside their husbands, if need be.[7]

Mary offered to edit Sarah's manuscript and found it difficult work. She wrote a friend:

> I wish you could see her manuscript as a matter of curiosity. I don't think the English language ever got such a treatment before. I have to recur to her sometimes to know what a word is, as spelling is an unknown quantity to her, as you mathematicians would express it. She often takes syllables off of words & adds them or rather prefixes them to other words, but the story is heart-breaking, and told with a simplicity & eloquence that cannot be described, for it is not high-faluting eloquence, tho' sometimes it lapses into verse (and quite poetical verse too). I was always considered fanatical about Indians, but I have a wholly new conception of them now, and we civilized people may well stand abashed before their purity of life & their truthfulness.[8]

Doubtless, Sarah's purpose in writing and lecturing at this hard pace was partly to provide much-needed financial support for her and Lewis. Mary Mann understood, however, that her principal motive was "to influence the public mind by the details of the Indian wrongs she can give so as to induce Congress to give them their farms in severalty and give them rights to defend them in the courts." There was also an effort underway to form an association to aid Sarah's educational plans.[9]

Sarah trod on dangerous ground in most of her speeches. She said: "I have asked the agents why they did these wrong things. They have told me it is necessary for them to do so in order to get money enough to send to the great white Father at Washington to keep their position. I assure you that there is an Indian ring; that it is a corrupt ring, and that it has its head and shoulders in the treasury at Washington."[10]

The Council Fire and Arbitrator, a monthly journal purportedly devoted to the "civilization" and rights of American Indians, called Sarah "an Amazonian champion of the Army [who] was being used as a tool of the army officers to create public sentiment in favor of the transfer of the Indian Bureau to the War Department." *The Council Fire* publicized the Indian Bureau files on Sarah and the affidavits that Rinehart had sent to prejudice officials against her on her first trip to Washington: "She is so notorious for her untruthfulness as to be wholly unreliable. She is known . . . to have been a common camp follower, consorting with common soldiers. It is a great outrage on the respectable people of Boston for General Howard or any other officer of the army to foist such a woman of any race upon them."[11]

In Nevada the *Winnemucca Silver State,* which was not always kind to Sarah, came to her defense this time:

> Now, because she states, before an audience in Boston, what the whites in Nevada and on the frontier generally know to be facts, the "Council Fire," the Washington organ of the Indian Bureau, roundly abuses her. . . . Without attempting to refute or dispute her assertions, which it undoubtedly knows would be futile, it endeavors to break their force by attacking her character. It adopts the tactics of the ring organs generally, and instead of showing wherein she has misrepresented the Indian agents, it contents itself with slandering her, ignoring the fact that it is the Indian Bureau System not Sarah Winnemucca's character, that the people are interested in and that is under discussion."[12]

Elizabeth Peabody and Mary Mann decided that they should add an appendix to Sarah's book with letters of recommendation and affirmation in defense of her character. M. S. Bonnifield, the Winnemucca attorney, who had transmitted the *Council Fire* article to the editor of the *Silver State,* wrote the following: "I take pleasure in saying that I have known you personally and by reputation ever since 1869. Your conduct has always been exemplary, so far as I know. I have never heard your veracity or chastity questioned in this community." It must have been a moment of regret for Sarah and her defenders when a letter was received from General Howard with the request that it not be published.

Howard had led many battles for the Union during the Civil War, losing his right arm at Fair Oaks, Virginia, in 1862. He had ridden unarmed into an Apache stronghold in 1872 to treat with Cochise. Devoted to the betterment of the Negro, he was named head of the Freedman's Bureau after the Civil War and was president of Howard University between 1869 and 1873. Now his courage left him. His reason was:

> My feeling towards Mrs. Hopkins is like yours, but for reasons which are imperative with me, I cannot publish a letter in defence of her character. I will say to you that when with me, or near me, her behavior was above reproach. I think her ardent love for her people, and her profound sympathy for them, has led her into several errors with regard to them, and her desires, in this respect, are positively against my own views or recommendations [referring to the removal of Leggin's band from Yakima], but this, in no way, affects the question of Sarah's moral character. . . . Should I write I would lay myself open to be assailed by the same bad man, who is thoroughly wicked, and unscrupulous. . . . You may show this to any of your friends, but do not publish it.[13]

Upon reading this letter Elizabeth Peabody wrote in the margin in her distinctive handwriting the name unstated by Howard, "Agent Rhinehart."

If a general of the army was wary of Rinehart's wrath, one can understand Sarah's predicament. An earlier letter of General Howard's was, however, printed in the appendix of *Life Among the Piutes*, along with many statements of high regard by army officers who had worked with Sarah during the Bannock War. The commander of the Military Division of the Pacific at the Presidio in San Francisco, Major General Irvin McDowell, pointedly made it his last act before his retirement on October 15, 1882, to offer a military escort to Leggins's band back to their home near Camp McDermit.[14] McDowell's offer was duly rejected, however, by Commissioner H. Price of the Office of Indian Affairs.[15]

The policy, instituted by President Grant in 1870, to use Christian agents, rather than military men, on Indian reservations had been termed "the Quaker policy." When Sarah spoke before the Universal Peace Union, the *Council Fire* criticized that organization for placing her on their agenda. In September, 1883, the Peace Union's president, Alfred H. Love, wrote a letter to the *Council Fire* in response:

> Sarah Winnemucca came thoroughly endorsed by prominent Boston friends of peace. She was as free as anyone else to express her views. We were gainers by hearing her. She modestly waited to be heard, and when she spoke, affirmed our resolutions.
>
> We think her reference to the army meant she preferred it to the loose, uncontrolled, and unscrupulous spectators and adventurers and recreant agents. . . .
>
> I wish the Quaker policy could be better understood. It comprehends more than opposition to military surveillance. It accepts the good wherever found. . . . In reference to this person, once the Indian girl of the West, even if the statements you make be true, would it not be kind to keep them from the public. Suppose she had been attracted by the soldiers with their gay trappings, and perhaps their promises of favors; they are called Christians, she is styled savage. What wonder if she went astray? Of whom should we expect the most? Who were more to blame?
>
> I would like to see those who dare make the personal affidavits you quote. Rather should we applaud this woman for now coming forth in all of womanly dignity and earnestness and upholding justice, virtue, and peace. The true Quaker policy is to encourage the good everywhere and in every thing.

Sarah wrote: "Everyone knows what a woman must suffer who undertakes to act against bad men. My reputation has been assailed, and it is done so cunningly that I cannot prove it to be unjust. I can only protest that it is unjust, and say that wherever I have been known, I have been believed and trusted.[16]

Every effort was made by Sarah and her Boston friends to get the autobiography printed, bound, and out to the public before the next session of Congress, when the legislators expected to consider legislation for the benefit of the Indians. Subscriptions were gotten up to help defray expenses, and the price of the book was expected to be one dollar per copy. John Greenleaf Whittier subscribed for ten dollars' worth, and Mrs. Ralph Waldo Emerson for the same amount. Elizabeth found five persons who underwrote the expenses of publication for a total of $600. Thus, when Sarah sold her 600 copies, the money that she received was free and clear and helped pay her expenses.[17]

Mary and Elizabeth had always lived frugally, and now they were in modest rented rooms at 54 Bowdoin Street in Boston.

Elizabeth had earned her own living since age sixteen, and Mary, the widow of an honest politician and liberal educator, had never experienced a surplus of funds. Yet they willingly gave their limited resources to this new cause. In her typical lengthy sentences and almost undecipherable slanting scrawl, Elizabeth also wrote letters to friends and congressmen regarding her good friend Mrs. Hopkins. The following appeal to Congressman Newton Booth was typical:

> I have been all my life a student of Indian history and character, a great uncle of mine who was a Revolutionary officer having married an Indian princess [who] brot up her family so nobly and wisely as to have been a lesson to her civilized relations by marriage, a family that yield now some of the most respected citizens of Michigan. . . . I hope you will think it worthwhile to look into her book the first book of Indian literature—I will send you the appendix to it which contains her credentials. . . . The degree of ignorant nonsense that prevails is comparable to what was upon the negro question *fifty years ago* and will seem as amazing fifty years hence as that does now. I shall send you her book when it comes out.[18]

In this time of absorbing productivity for Sarah, who often bedded and boarded with Elizabeth and Mary, where was Lewis Hopkins, her husband? He traveled with Sarah often, sometimes introducing his wife to her audiences, and helped with the autobiography by visiting the Boston Athenaeum and other institutions for background material.[19]

A typical scenario for one of Sarah's lectures occurred in Philadelphia in Christ Episcopal Church. At least an hour before the time appointed for the lecture, masses of people began to crowd into the church's front entrance. They continued to file in until the entire building, including the galleries, aisles, and chancel steps, was completely packed.

After the singing of a hymn the rector introduced Lewis Hopkins as the husband of "Princess Winnemucca." Lewis gave a brief sketch of his wife's history and stated the purpose of Sarah's visit to the East.[20] Sarah then flashed him an appreciative smile and told her story in such a way that the audience was overcome with emotion. For almost an hour she spoke very effectively. Afterwards people crowded around, wanting to touch the hand of this resplendent Indian woman wearing a gold crown and intri-

Mary Mann, widow of Horace Mann and editor of Life Among the Piutes: Their Wrongs and Claims, *by Sarah Winnemucca Hopkins.*

cately beaded buckskin dress. Sarah's dark eyes glowed with enjoyment at the attention. Elizabeth Peabody, who often sat on the rostrum with her protégé, commented that, although she had heard Sarah lecture fifty times, each speech was different, because she never spoke from notes, but from her heart.[21]

After her lectures Sarah would obligingly sign copies of *Life Among the Piutes* for those of her followers who wished to purchase the handsome volume. The book contained 268 pages, including the 20-page appendix. The title was stamped in gold on the spine of the green or red cloth cover (the color was different in various printings). In her editor's preface Mary Mann had written: "At this moment, when the United States seem waking up to their duty to the original possessors of our immense territory, it is of the first importance to hear what only an Indian and an Indian woman can tell. To tell it was her own deep impulse, and the dying charge given her by her father, the truly parental chief of his beloved tribe."

Senator Henry L. Dawes invited Sarah and Elizabeth to his home and arranged for Sarah to lecture there one evening. Aware that the senator could make some of her ideas into law, Sarah spoke with special animation, and Dawes was greatly moved by her speech. He took her into his study and had a long talk with her—promising he would bring her before the Indian committee of which he was chairman. He encouraged her to continue speaking, because it was desirable that she "stir hearts," as she had done that day, to press congress to consideration of the Indian question.[22]

Sarah lectured in Providence, Rhode Island; Hartford, Connecticut; New York City, Newburgh, and Poughkeepsie, New York; Dorset, Vermont; Boston, Salem, Cambridge, Germantown, and Pittsfield, Massachusetts; and Philadelphia. She circulated a petition, which was signed by almost five thousand people, asking that the Indians be given lands in severalty and rights of citizenship.[23] Plans were afoot for three representatives to present the legislation in the House. Thus the "princess" was happy, feeling that her efforts for the cause of her people might yet be successful. She bought a fine overcoat for Natchez, who, when he received it found it much too large and generously gave it to his half brother Lee, who was especially tall and broad-shouldered.[24]

Elizabeth Palmer Peabody, Sarah Winnemucca's staunch supporter. Sarah's Peabody Indian School was named in her honor. (Courtesy of Massachusetts Historical Society.)

Through the Christmas season Mary Mann stayed at home collecting and mending serviceable clothes to send to the Paiutes in Nevada. Though she could not afford Christmas cards for her friends, she sent a large barrel of used goods to the Paiutes. She hoped it was not as cold in Nevada as it was in Boston, where she sat frozen by the fireside.[25] Elizabeth was expected home for the holidays. Sarah and Lewis were to move to Baltimore, where a series of lectures was planned.[26]

When the bells rang in the New Year of 1884, Sarah may have kissed Lewis without hesitation, but she may also have ignored a growing discontent in the relationship. Hopkins had helped her in Washington, visiting the Library of Congress for material for her book. He had sat on the lecture platforms, and with his gentle manners he had charmed those with whom he came in contact. At the same time the joint bank account of the Hopkinses was a temptation to Lewis's gambling propensities. He and Sarah had agreed in principle that most of the money that they collected for the cause should be reserved for a school that Sarah intended to start for Paiute children in Nevada,[27] though, of course, the expenses of traveling and accommodations had to be met before banking the remainder. Six months after they had arrived in the East the *Council Fire* had accused Hopkins of squandering funds given to Sarah for the benefit of her people in "low gambling dens in Boston." The article said, "When Sarah complained of this to her husband his reply was, 'You need not say anything; if I should tell your Boston friends what I know about you, you would not hold your head so high.' "[28]

According to Elizabeth, Sarah spoke in Baltimore sixty-six times in a variety of places, including churches of various denominations and the Young Men's Christian Association. The Methodist Episcopal Church seemed to enjoy a special claim on her presence.[29] Admission was charged, from ten to twenty-five cents, and copies of *Life Among the Piutes* were sold after the lectures. The Hopkinses were dependent on Sarah for their income,[30] and her competition in Baltimore was of the highest quality, including the Shakespearian actor Edwin Booth and Henry Ward Beecher, who was heralded as the "World's greatest orator." The autobiography, personally autographed by Sarah, was also made available through the mails for one dollar. If a purchaser so wished, he could receive an autographed picture of the "princess" for another fifty cents.[31] Lewis acted as her agent, responding personally to such requests.

In the spring Sarah heard from Natchez that the bands of Leggins and Paddy Cap had escaped from Yakima and had made their way back to the Harney Valley. Her brother wrote that he had gone to see them and that they had told him they would never return to Yakima without a fight.[32] Fortunately, Father Wilbur had retired by this time, and the new agent R. H. Milroy, was more realistic than Wilbur had been. He wrote the commissioner of Indian affairs that it was best for the Paiutes to stay in their own country, for they had never been satisfied at Fort Simcoe and had been badly treated by the Yakimas.[33] Thus one of Sarah's battles with the authorities was settled off the field by the Paiute bands themselves with little fanfare.

Elizabeth Peabody now voiced her concern about Leggins's destitute condition to Congressman J. B. Long. She had celebrated her eightieth birthday on April 13, 1884,[34] but despite almost total blindness continued her correspondence for the Paiute cause, guiding her hand by the sense of feeling. She wrote that she understood Senator Dawes was going to push a bill to acquire Camp McDermit for Leggins's band, and she asked for Long's support: "I depend upon Mr. Ranney and yourself to immediately take up the subject when it comes before the House—for if there is delay they must starve. It is a matter of life and death."[35]

Over three hundred exiles had returned. McDermit seemed to be the only unsettled country still available to them, and it was the area where Old Winnemucca had often requested a reservation. Sarah was encouraged when Adjutant General J. C. Kelton and General John Pope indicated to her that McDermit could be spared as a military reserve. Pope advised the commander in chief of the army, General Philip Henry Sheridan, to give the land to the Paiutes in severalty, making them United States citizens and allowing them to govern themselves.[36]

Elizabeth told Congressman Long that Sarah's cause was supported in Washington by the best and most intelligent citizens, many of whom had tried to stir up action. She continued:

But they tell me a subtle but powerful influence from the Interior office opposed her—casting the form of unfavourable insinuations against her personally and sometimes open accusations which can all be answered as I know—who during the whole year have been investigating her life and words and find them all reliable. Lately, the enemy has changed the tactics and endeavoured to misrepresent and fabricate monstrous lies about the tribe which are pronounced fabrications and demonstrated to be absurdly false by citizens of Nevada who have been written to—and disinterested persons who have been out there—individuals who have unexpectedly risen in her audiences and endorsed her statements and declared them under-coloured rather than exaggerated.[37]

In an article on American Indians a nephew of Horace Greeley had used the stoning of Chief Winnemucca's young wife as an example to assert that the Paiutes were blood-thirsty, drunken, lawless savages undeserving of any white man's solicitude.[38] He had conveniently forgotten the burning biers that roasted human flesh during the witch hunts in Massachusetts two hundred years before.

20
Disillusionment

Sarah's petition was presented to Congress and referred to the appropriate committees in the first session of 1884. She appeared before the senate subcommittee on Indian affairs and spoke at length, answering the pointed questions of her admirer, Chairman Dawes. She pleaded that a reservation be established at Fort McDermit and land given to each head of a family, and she asked that the annuities granted by Congress to the Paiutes be administered by the military rather than the Indian Bureau.[1]

When a House bill passed giving Camp McDermit to those Paiutes who had not yet been assigned a reservation, there was a short time of rejoicing. General Sheridan, however, soon countermanded the legislative decision by claiming that the fort was still essential for the use of the Department of War.[2] As a result, a Senate bill was passed on July 6, 1884, which gave permission to Leggins's and Winnemucca's bands to return to the Pyramid Lake Reservation, where each head of a family was to be given 160 acres of land in severalty. The legislation was to be carried out under the direction of the secretary of the interior.[3]

Sarah understood immediately that all was lost. Those Paiutes had already nominally possessed Pyramid Lake Reservation since the time of Agent Frederick Dodge in 1860. There was no arable land left there to be assigned to newcomers, and white squatters had been settled on the best land along the Truckee River for decades. The whole fishery at Mud Lake, or Lake Winnemucca, was dominated by Chinese fishermen. Also there was a problem of producing crops on the small amount of usable land left to the Paiutes, because of broken dams and other irrigation difficulties. It was a preposterous solution to try to find a living for 500 more individuals on the Pyramid Lake Reservation.[4]

When she had returned to Baltimore, Sarah's personal concerns had been increased, because she had found that Lewis, for whom she had been paying a doctor and furnishing medicines[5] for several months, was not improving. It was feared that he had tuberculosis. Now she also had to acknowledge that there had been no result from her efforts in Washington except for financial aid to her immediate family and the barrels of old clothes from Boston. At least, she reminded herself, she would have the means to start her Indian school with the money in the Hopkins bank account. Then the despairing woman was notified by her bank of large drafts that Lewis had written which the precious account would not cover. Hopkins had been gambling and had even given fraudulent drafts to their acquaintances and supportive friends.[6]

Sarah wrote Elizabeth that Lewis had left and that there was little more that she could do. She begged the elderly woman to keep her position a secret, as she knew that it would only provoke further accusations against her from the Interior Department if her insolvency were known.[7] Although her heart was not in it, she would go once more to Washington to see Secretary of the Interior Henry Moore Teller, who was to carry into effect the act for Winnemucca and Leggins's bands in the Indian appropriation bill.[8] She would ask Teller if there was anything that she could do and what word she was to take back to Nevada.

After Sarah had paid her husband's medical expenses and covered his gambling debts, she had only a few hundred dollars left. Then she arrived in Washington only to discover that she could not make an appointment with Secretary Teller because he refused to see her.[9] Congress had dispersed, leaving the administration of the legislation to Teller, who planned to leave Washington to electioneer in Colorado.

Now Sarah was in real despair. She could not return to Nevada without some evidence of help for her people. It would be all too reminiscent of her previous trip to the capital, which had produced nothing but a "rag friend" from Secretary Schurz that was not worth the paper on which it was written.

There was nowhere to go but Idaho, to her sister Elma at Henry's Lake. From there she wrote Elizabeth and Mary that all was lost, for she would not be recognized as the messenger and guardian of her people.[10] Mary Mann immediately wrote to Commissioner of Indian Affairs Price, asking what Mrs. Hopkins was to do, now that an act had been passed to help the Paiutes, and what preparation was being made at Pyramid Lake for the arrival of the two bands. Commissioner Price replied that Sarah was to go out and "settle down" with these bands on the Reservation and tell them what to do, and he would "cooperate with any definite plans of Education."[11]

Adjutant General John C. Kelton wrote Sarah that General John Pope would see to it that Pyramid Lake Reservation was cleared of squatters. Finally, in August, 1884, acting under orders from Washington, Lieutenant Henry D. Huntington came onto the reservation and removed settlers, fishermen, and others, destroying their property and confiscating their boats on Pyramid Lake. The old settlers dwelling on the best lands along the Truckee River were not disturbed, however.[12]

Sarah, with much apprehension about the possible success of her mission, prepared to go to Pyramid Lake. She stopped by Lovelock to see Natchez, whose people were assembling to go into the mountains for pine nuts and game, hoping to lay aside enough for the winter. Natchez had harvested sixty acres of wheat, thirty bushels to the acre, but he had paid much of it out to other Paiutes for help in the planting and harvesting. When he had experienced a bout with pneumonia during the winter, Sarah had sent him gifts and money. Now, upon her arrival, a white neighbor made a demand on him for $195 on an unpaid bill, threatening him with imprisonment. Naturally, Sarah paid the requested amount, though her brother told her that the neighbor was lying. She did not reveal to Natchez her own financial state. When she finally returned to Wadsworth, she had only fifty dollars remaining of all that she had earned from the sale of her book and from lecturing.[13]

Joseph McMaster was still agent at Pyramid Lake when Sarah

Pine-nut harvest, Carson City, Nevada. The men have already knocked the pine nuts off the trees with their long poles. Many women, barely visible, are collecting the nuts under the trees. (Courtesy of Nevada Historical Society.)

arrived on August 29. Sarah found he and his employees were, not surprisingly, opposed to her enterprise. They swore that Winnemucca's and Leggins's bands should not come on the reservation. Furthermore, Sarah found that the fishermen and squatters removed by the military had drifted back upon the land and lake; they were ensconced as usual. It was to no purpose that money had been appropriated for the removal of the settlers, for bringing in Leggins's and Winnemucca's people and giving them lands in severalty and citizens' rights, and for providing them with tools, labor, and instruction.[14]

Sarah had no alternative but to wait and hope that something would be done. She slept in a *nobee* on the ground with a couple of blankets, having given most of her belongings and clothing to destitute friends and relatives. She returned to the old diet of pine nuts and fish.[15] The cheapest hotel in Wadsworth was fifty cents a day, and lodging in a home was five dollars a week; those were beyond her means. Mary Mann was able to raise another fifty dollars from the sale of *Life Among the Piutes*. She sent it on with the hope that it would improve Sarah's situation.[16]

Sarah found that Commissioner Price had instructed a man named Ellet to gather Leggins's band at Fort McDermit and make arrangements to bring them to the reservation. This helped her to determine to remain longer at Pyramid Lake. Late in September, when the weather suddenly turned quite cold, she became violently ill with fever and chills, and her relatives reported to Elizabeth Peabody that she was dying. Elizabeth telegraphed back that they must get Sarah into a warm room, and she promised to send not less than ten dollars a week so that she might stay and observe occurrences on the reservation.[17]

When Natchez and the other Humboldt Paiutes returned from the mountains, Sarah got up from her sickbed. With one hundred of them she and her brother went down to the reservation to see the new agent, W. D. C. Gibson. He did not invite Sarah into the agency house, though it was apparent that she was sick, and he said that he could not talk until the next day. Since it was very cold, and the wind blustery, they went down by the river and camped for the night. Again Sarah was gripped with chills. The women raked ashes out of the fire, spread sand over them, and then laid blankets down to warm her. When the bed grew cold, she got up and hovered over the fire.[18]

In the morning the agent came and said that he had had no orders respecting the bands of Winnemucca and Leggins or Sarah. Sarah was shocked at this news. When she showed him Commissioner Price's letters to Mary Mann, Gibson changed his attitude and said that the bands could come to the Pyramid reserve if they chose. Sarah told him that Leggins's band could not come unless they were sent for, as they had no money. She showed him Price's comment about cooperating in any definite plans of education. Gibson suggested to Sarah that she come and see the school on the reservation that his wife was keeping, but he did not invite Sarah to come as a teacher.[19]

Sick at heart, Sarah returned to Wadsworth. There she stayed on waiting for the special agent, Ellet, to arrive with Leggins. The position that Sarah had coveted, if she were not hired as a teacher, was that of interpreter. That was soon given again to her cousin Dave Numana, who was also chief of the Indian police. Sarah wrote Elizabeth and Mary that Gibson was similar in spirit to the old agent, McMasters, and had taken McMasters's same "gang of employees."[20] Miss Peabody complained that it seemed inconsiderate of Price to have directed Sarah to go to Pyramid Lake while not providing her with money to travel or the assurance of a salary as teacher.[21] It was difficult for Elizabeth to explain to friends why Sarah needed money for board when everyone had assumed that she, as well as her people, had been well taken care of by Congress.

Sarah waited three months before Ellet appeared at Fort McDermit to consult with Leggins's band and bring them to the Pyramid reserve. Ellet held a council with the head men at McDermit, and they protested against being taken away from the land of their birth, saying that they would herd cattle for the settlers and hunt game before coming on a reservation where they were not wanted and where there was no land for them anyway. They only asked that the government provide for them in the winter months, particularly for the old who could not work—as the military had done in the past.[22] When Commissioner Ellet arrived at Pyramid Lake to look into the preparations that had been made for the new arrivals, he was appalled to see the squatters back on the land. He recognized that, even if they were removed, there would not be enough land to support another five hundred Paiutes.[23]

When the Paiutes had lost McDermit, Sarah's cause was lost, and well she knew it. She could no longer turn to her father for comfort or use his dignified position as a rallying point for a new campaign. She was very much alone at a time when she had been put in an untenable position. Instead of the heroine's role that she had sought, she appeared to be forcing the McDermit bands to come to Pyramid so that she could acquire a salaried position. Obviously this would have been resented both by the Paiutes at Pyramid Lake and by those who had escaped from Yakima and were now at McDermit.[24]

Sarah knew that Gibson had won his lucrative position as agent through Senator Jones as a political payoff, but it was difficult to make him out as an ogre, even though he had run a gambling house in Gold Hill for six years and owned a faro bank at Virginia City. At Christmas, Gibson presented the students at the Pyramid Lake boarding school with their first Christmas tree, and he played Santa Claus, distributing candy and presents during the holidays. In the last days of December, Sarah knew that the situation was hopeless: she must move in another direction.

21
The Turning Point

Natchez was embarked on a venture of his own at the Big Meadows on the Humboldt River near the town of Lovelock, Nevada. He had lived with his family in this area since 1875. White settlers had taken most of the land, and he now felt an urgent need to acquire some of his own. In 1875 the *Humboldt Register* remarked:

The great drawback to this enterprise is that the Indians have not the means of subsistence, nor the material to work with while clearing the ranch of sagebrush and otherwise preparing the crops. Natchez is quite enthusiastic over the enterprise, and thinks that he can bring nearly all of his people, over which he has control to be steady producing civilized people, if he can receive a little encouragement from the white people. But he does not like the agency system, and will not adopt it; but if they can get a start they will select their own white man as Superintendent and Instructor—one whom they can have confidence in and trust, until they shall be able to carry the business on themselves. Natchez also wants to start a school for the education of the rising generation of his tribe, and thinks most probable that Sarah Winnemucca can be got as teacher, or that they can employ some white person as soon as they get a return from their crops. . . . The ranch is to be irrigated from the new ditch recently constructed at the Meadows, water from which will be given them on very reasonable terms. We hope they will receive from the government and our people all the assistance and encouragement requisite to make the experiment a success.[1]

Natchez went to California to interview railroad officials concerning ownership. On November 27, 1876, the *Winnemucca Silver State* announced that Natchez had received title to the land from the Central Pacific Railroad Co. He had a frame house built on a railroad section (on the east half of the southwest quarter of section 35, Township 27, north of range 31, east Mt. Diablo base and meridian)[2] , then he moved in with his two wives and large family. The *Silver State* reported the status of his wheat harvests often in the next few years, saying, for example, on August 25, 1884, "Naches had a good wheat crop of 60 acres, 30 bushels to an acre."

In early 1885, Sarah planned to lecture again, in San Francisco, in order to raise money for her school for Paiute children, which she planned to establish on Natchez's ranch. Before she could leave Wadsworth for her engagement in San Francisco, an incident occurred that gave Agent Gibson at Pyramid Lake ammunition for a continuing duel of words with Sarah.

While Sarah was staying at a Mrs. Nichols's rooming house in Wadsworth, twenty dollars was stolen from her. The landlady advised Sarah to go to the police, and she did so, but they gave her no satisfaction. Sarah suspected that a Bannock who had come to borrow money from her had taken the twenty dollars while she was at dinner. She went to two of her cousins for help, and with them she found the Indian's camp. Sarah wrote: "The man abused me grossly. In a fit of ungovernable passion I struck him. My cousins never touched him. I felled him to the ground with but one slap. We then searched the premises and found the money, with the exception of 75 cents. The man admitted the theft."[3] Sarah thought no more of the incident.

In San Francisco at the Metropolitan Theatre, Sarah was billed as the first Indian to write in the English language. The *Morning Call* reported, "In the history of the Indians she and Pocahontas will be the principal female characters, and her singular devotion to her race will no doubt be chronicled as an illustration of the better traits of the Indian character."[4] Sarah informed her audience: "General Sheridan asked me a short time ago if our reser-

Natchez Overton, Sarah's brother, late in life. (Courtesy of Nevada Historical Society.)

vation did not afford us a good living. I told him that high bleak hills that only a goat could safely climb rose out of the water all around the lake; that the only arable lands were . . . on the river. He seemed astonished at the revelation, for he feels very kindly toward my people."[5]

Sarah found that her stage talents were still with her, and, though she was now forty-one years old, she riveted her audience with her dramatic presence and her words of passionate sincerity. Her listeners were immediately introduced to the agents and their doings:

> If a conspiracy were formed by the most cunning men to desert and neglect the Indians on our reservations, it could not succeed better than the selfish policy of Bill Gibson, the agent, and his hungry relations. Not a cent of the $17,000 which was appropriated for the support of the Piutes has been spent for us. Where it has been side-tracked on its journey from Washington I do not know. . . . Every one connected with the agency is wholly devoid of conscience. They are there to get rich.[6]

On another occasion she said that, "if she possessed the wealth of several rich ladies whom she mentioned, she would place all the Indians of Nevada on ships in our harbor, take them to New York and land them there as immigrants, that they might be received with open arms, blessed with the blessings of universal suffrage, and thus placed beyond the necessity of reservation help and out of the reach of Indian agents."[7]

Reviews of Sarah's lectures reached such papers as the *New York Times*. Because of the public attention the Indian Department finally ordered Agent Gibson to give supplies to the Indians on the Humboldt River.[8] Yet, since Leggins's band refused to go to Pyramid Lake, Gibson received instructions from the department not to supply them, though it was well known that this was the most destitute group of all.[9] Sarah laid into Gibson again, saying that he and his employees drank "firewater" publicly in an ostentatious manner, so that the Paiutes were forced to wonder what was wrong with drinking themselves the exhilarating liquids that made them sing and dance.[10] The Indian Service did not let Sarah's attacks on Gibson pass without continuing their past aspersions on her character. The incident with the Bannock Indian was twisted so that according to the Indian Department's account Sarah and her cohorts had committed a rob-

Sarah Winnemucca, probably as she appeared on stage in her last performances in San Francisco. (Courtesy of Nevada Historical Society.)

bery and attempted to murder the Bannock. Sarah in turn did not allow this new accusation to go unnoticed and vented her anger against the department in an open letter:

> Under ordinary circumstances I do not notice charges made against me by the Indian ring. They are very powerful, I know, but not powerful enough to stop me from exposing their rascality. This attack is no new thing. In 1879, I charged Agent Rhinehardt [*sic*] with driving my people into the Bannock War. . . . After I went East this same man wrote letters and fake affidavits and sent them to Washington. The appendix to "Life Among the Piutes" shows how I nailed those lies; and now comes Mr. Gibson and his charges, and time will show how I will settle them. . . .
>
> For years the government has been fattening preachers, and now they have changed and are going to fatten gamblers. It is a well-known fact that this man Gibson, who charges me with gambling, etc, for years and years kept the largest gambling resort in Gold Hill, Nevada. I will do him credit of saying he is considered a square gambler. In an interview with Dr. Dan DeQuille and others in Virginia City, a few months ago, some of the gentlemen asked me what I thought of having an "old sport" for an agent. I said I was willing to try him and see what he would do, that I would rather have a gambler than a preacher with a bottle in one pocket and a Bible in the other. . . . I am only an "old squaw" and, of course, people will not believe me, but no matter: there is an "all-seeing eye" that keeps my account and I am sure Mr. Gibson's charge is not entered against me "up there." He has made a mistake if he thinks he can frighten me: I am not that stock. He can find me at any time ready to tell him to his face what he is, and on the other hand I refer to Deputy Sheriff Shields, Mrs. Nickols, and to Henry Harris, all of Wadsworth, as to the truth of my statement.[11]

On one evening, toward the end of Sarah's lecture series, Natchez appeared on the stage with her. He expressed to the audience his joy at having received 160 acres of land from the Central Pacific Railroad Company and pleaded that all of his people should receive land of their own. Probably he had received the deed from the California railroad magnate Senator Leland Stanford.[12]

Sarah later went home with Natchez to their ranch near Lovelock. His six children liked to come to her *karnee* and loved to hear her marvelous stories of her adventurous life. She began holding regular classes for them. It was her intention, supported by Elizabeth Peabody, to create a school taught by and for Indians, where they would not be separated from the Indian life-ways and languages, as they were in the government boarding schools, which were miles from their homes.[13]

Early in the spring of 1885 several members of Natchez's household contracted pneumonia. Natchez's promising eldest son Kit Carson died,[14] and Sarah was made distraught by the death. Indomitable Elizabeth Peabody ordered a new printing of *Life Among the Piutes* to encourage Sarah in her new enterprise and also raised funds to send a horse wagon, harness, and plow to Natchez. She was spending several months in Washington in the interest of her "Piute friend."[15] Under the new administration of President Cleveland, the first Democratic President in twenty-five years, she was hopeful that the federal government's Indian policy would improve and the "ring" would be removed from office.[16] Meanwhile Mary Mann suffered from dyspepsia and missed her sister. She wrote: "It seems as if the world has stopped going since Elizabeth went to Washington. Life is a perfect *rush* wherever she is. She is very much occupied there with her Indian mission. Under the new administration we feel that there is some hope for that race."[17]

When Elizabeth returned home late in May, 1885, Mary wrote a friend: "She has had much satisfaction in what she has been able to achieve for her beloved Indians (for her love for Sarah diffuses itself over the whole race). . . . I am curious to see how far E. has been battered in the strife. She declares she is well, but she is apt to believe what she wishes to." A bill before Congress to stop appropriations for the Indian schools had been beaten, and new appropriations had been made. A huge gift of seed was sent to Nevada, plus three tents and more farm equipment. Elizabeth was confident that a school building would be erected on Natchez's land and that Sarah's desire to teach would at last be fulfilled. Nevada congressmen and officials had expressed interest in such an enterprise as well.[18]

Although Sarah was a controversial figure among the Indians, as well as in the white world, she was well regarded by many Indians because of her competence in white society and as a spokesman for her people's welfare. On one occasion some Washo women saw her on the street in Carson City, where she had been lecturing, and followed her with great admiration at a respectful distance. They gathered about her hotel for another glimpse, and, as the "princess" emerged from the main entrance of the hotel, rigged out in good toggery, an exclamation of delight ran along the line of waiting women. They were well rewarded when Sarah spoke a few kind words to each; according to a local newspaper, "Their . . . faces were lighted up with joy."[19]

On another occasion, when some Paiutes were thought to have been killed by Chinese, Sarah prevailed upon the assembled Indians and prevented them from attacking the Chinatown area of Carson City.[20] She was also called upon to act as a judge in a murder case in an informal Indian court.[21] Those were isolated incidents, but they indicated a general feeling for Sarah as a leader and a spokeswoman. Unfortunately, it was still true that her dealings with Washington officials had never yielded the kinds of results that were desired by the leadership of Winnemucca's and Leggins's bands. Sarah knew that they did not understand the machinations of white politicians, and, when her word was doubted by her fellows, she could not blame them. The feeling was particularly strong among the Paiutes who had homes at Pyramid Lake that Sarah had double-dealings with them for the benefit of the McDermit bands.

In the end Sarah came to believe that she could now help her people only by teaching English to the children and giving them a basic education. She also wanted to help the children to take pride in the old attitude of concern and caring for one another and to respect the sacredness of life around them.[22] The lot of her people had not improved during the years that she had been working on their behalf. They had learned how to earn money, and they had acquired clothing and some food in payment from the whites, but they had no land of their own. The majority still lived in ragged *nobees,* which were partially covered by tin, canvas, and blankets thrown away in the refuse piles of the towns. Many did not wish for a more permanent kind of home; they preferred the easily kept, but drafty, *nobee,* and they had no desire for the objects that were so necessary in white men's homes except for an occasional table or iron kettle.

Much of the food supply was still gathered in the summer months and stored away for winter hardships. If money was acquired, it was often lost, by both the men and the women, in the excitement of the gambling games, or it was spent on liquor

Gambling at the railroad station in Reno. (Courtesy of Nevada Historical Society.)

to enchance existences that were often bleak. Some of the women, both married and single, sold their bodies to bring money into the house, but more often they worked as cleaning women and cooks in white households for a dollar a day. Sarah was upset by the seeming apathy, the docile attitude, of many of her tribe. They took what came their way; they did not strive as she had for improvement of their lot.[23]

Sarah could not contain her indignation when she considered how her people were regarded by whites as servants and low-class hangers-on instead of equal citizens and brothers. The hard circumstances in which the Paiutes lived might have been more acceptable if only the whites had paid them due respect as human beings. Thus her desire was the same as the old dreams of her father and grandfather.

Sarah's bitterness reached its zenith at the death of her oldest brother, Tom, at Pyramid Lake in May, 1885. Natchez had telegraphed her to come because Tom was very ill. She traveled in an open wagon in a rainstorm from the Wadsworth station to the reservation. There she found the sick man in a brush corral on the top of a hill, where the shaman was singing over him. Sarah had lived with her brother from time to time, but she was appalled now again at the conditions of his life. He had worked faithfully for the agents for many years, but in this last illness the agency doctor had not been called, and the white employees took no interest in his condition. Before he died, while he was still conscious, Tom dispensed his few belongings to his relatives. He left Sarah his farm and everything on it. His wife received two cows, four calves, and twelve horses. He thanked his sister for all that she had done for him over the years, saying, "I never could have made it without you."[24]

Sarah wrote:

> As to the coffin I can hardly express myself. He died about 4 P.M. An hour afterwards I sent for Mr. Gibson. He came and holding out his hand to me, said, "So Sarah, your brother is dead." Out of respect to the memory of my dead brother I choked back the thought of the injury he had done me and mine, and placing my hand in his I said, "Yes sir, and we have sent to ask you to make us a coffin for him." He then began measuring him and I noticed he only measured his length, as I said, "Mr. Gibson, my brother was a hard working, sober man, and as he would have given me a decent burial, I want to give

him one. Please make him a nice coffin and I will pay for it." He went away and the next morning the coffin came. No agent, no doctor, no anyone. . . . How shall I describe it? A rough pine box such as civilization uses for an outside coffin, the lid had to be nailed down. . . . For years and years he was worked from sun to sun. He never drank, he never gambled, he had a saving wife, and yet he was that poor, we had to wrap him up in a blanket and put him away. He was only an Indian, a pine box was good enough for him. He had none of the vices of civilization, but he was unfortunate. He was the brother of Sarah Winnemucca. This is no sentiment. On my last trip to Wadsworth during Mr. McMasters time, my brother came to the depot as usual to haul supplies. McMaster went up to him and said, Tom I do not want you to haul anything *your sister has been talking about me.* So instead of fighting me they cowardly fought him. A week or two since I went down to the agency to settle the affairs of the ranch, which was left to me, and Mr. Gibson refused to speak to me. Now I desire to say here that I have no personal feelings against Mr. Gibson, I have fought him and all other agents for the general good of my race, but as recent events have shown that they [the Numa] are not disposed to stand by me in the fight, I shall relinquish it. As they will not help themselves, no one can help them. "Those that would be free must strike the blow themselves."

I have not contended for Democrat, Republican, Protestant or Baptist for an agent. I have worked for freedom, I have laboured to give my race a voice in the affairs of the nation, but they prefer to be slaves so let it be. My efforts hereafter shall be for my brother alone, we have plenty of friends east that will help us to build a home at Lovelock, where I will teach a school.[25]

. . . My brother asks that the Paiutes be notified of this [that the chief was now Captain Dave Numana] so they can go to Dave to settle their disputes. Hereafter, they must not come to my brother with their troubles, as he will be farmer Natches and not Chief Natches.[26]

22

The Peabody Indian School

Through the summer of 1885, Sarah taught a group of twenty-six Paiute children whom she assembled from the vicinity of Lovelock. The citizens of the town noticed them walking through the streets in the early morning, often with a little food tied neatly in a rag, ready for a day's scholarship under a brush arbor. Natchez's farm was about two miles from town.

Sarah started the students with a military drill in which they learned to respond to rhythmic directions. Early on she taught them gospel hymns, which she interpreted to them in Paiute. She began teaching them English by asking each one to say something in Paiute. Then she would tell them how to say it in English, writing the works in chalk on the blackboard so that they could copy them and find them in their books. Sarah told Elizabeth that her students never forgot those words, but wrote them all over fences in Lovelock and told their meanings in Paiute to their proud parents. She also taught her students to draw and cipher.[1] Sarah sent examples of the children's work to Elizabeth and Mary, who were deeply interested in the advancement of each of the students.

This school that Natchez and Sarah had started fired the interest of many citizens in Nevada and on the East Coast, because it was an Indian-initiated project in contrast to the reservation farms and schools. There was great pressure on the brother-and-sister team to succeed, particularly considering the formidable obstacles that confronted them from the outset. One of the more serious problems was that Sarah was not well. She had been plagued by chills and fever every other day since her illness on the Pyramid Lake Reservation, and for the past two years she had suffered from chronic rheumatism, which caused her continual pain and half paralyzed her.[2] Elizabeth dreaded the coming winter without proper shelter for her. One of the first of the Winnemuccas' enterprises was to make adobe bricks to build a large and comfortable house.[3] They had inherited some chickens and a few steers from Tom Winnemucca, and Natchez purchased a fine span of work horses with money from Boston.[4] Through the summer he prepared the land for future crops.

When Natchez spoke with their old friend M. S. Bonnifield of Winnemucca, the lawyer told him that "it was probable that Senator Leland Stanford of California would stop and see what he had done on his way to Washington next November," which greatly elated Natchez. Bonnifield also told him that, if he and Sarah showed by their works that they were capable and worthy, the president probably would make them the agents of their people, and in a few years any Indian who was industrious would be given all the land that he could till and have all the rights and privileges of white citizens. Bonnifield wrote Elizabeth, "If they make the industrial showing on their farm which I anticipate I will try and get Senator Stanford to call and see them."[5]

Miss Peabody and her friends sent $1,000 worth of goods, equipment, and money through the summer, including funds to start building the house, which was to contain the school and a room for a white teacher whom they hoped to bring from the East. The building would also serve for cooking, eating, council rooms, and a worship center.[6] Sarah kept receipts for the workmen's wages and the cost of materials and sent them to Elizabeth, so that there would be no question about how the donations were used.[7] When Natchez generously set aside six ten-acre farms from his own lands to give to landless Paiute families, Elizabeth was delighted with his action. She felt that it showed "his appreciation for the principle of individual property."[8] She was confident that the Winnemucca's small experiment would be successful, accomplishing in a small way what the government should have been doing on a large scale.

Because of Elizabeth's prodding, a special agent, Paris H. Folsom, was sent to Nevada in midsummer to investigate the Paiutes' situation. He went directly to the Indians to hear their viewpoint and stayed a week at Fort McDermit talking to Leggins and Paddy Cap. He also consulted with Sarah at Lovelock on affairs pertaining to the welfare of the Fort McDermit bands.[9] Gibson was finally required to send blankets and other supplies to those long-suffering Paiutes.[10]

Although Sarah's school progressed, and the children learned surprisingly rapidly, there were problems of almost insurmountable magnitude. Elizabeth had exhausted her sources of money, and still the water problem on Natchez's arid farm had not been solved. An irrigation ditch ran right through the property, but he was not eligible to use it because he could not make payments. Elizabeth, who was kept abreast of events by frequent letters from Sarah, surmised that the Winnemuccas' neighbors were taking advantage of the situation, trying to force them from the property.[11] Since there was no other source of water, the only recourse was to dig a well and erect a windmill—an impossible task without more funds.

The house had not been finished, nor the windmill erected, by late October.[12] Elizabeth was increasingly concerned. Then Miss Alice Chapin, an experienced kindergarten teacher who they had hoped would come to Nevada in the spring, declined the invitation. Miss Chapin had met Sarah in the East in 1883 and had become at once a convert to her cause. "How Sarah's great solemn face looms up before me," she wrote Elizabeth. "Were I rich, very rich, I would go to Sarah and see if some way could not be followed to make things right. But I have a fancy that when my purse was empty I should flee. Misery one can not alleviate is unendurable."[13]

Elizabeth Powell Bond, an associate of Elizabeth's in the promotion of kindergartens, had acquired an interest in the Paiutes. After she spoke of Sarah's school to the Philadelphia Human Rights Association, she was taken aside by the president of Smith College, Laurenus Clark Seelye, who told her, "Mr. Welsh [the secretary of the Indian Rights Association] wished me to put you on your guard against the woman you spoke of yesterday. He says Professor [C. C.] Painter [the Washington agent of the association] has had evidence of the most indisputable character, that she has been engaged in transactions disreputable, and is unworthy of trust. He will give you further particulars if desired."[14]

Miss Peabody despaired of correcting the unjust sabotage of the Indian Department, but immediately wrote Professor Painter of her own knowledge of Sarah Winnemucca: that she was a wise and extraordinary woman. She told him that she had letters of commendation of Sarah's character from good citizens of Nevada who knew her well. In the meantime Indian Commissioner Price told Mr. Welch that "if any of 100 affidavits in his office were trustworthy, Sarah Winnemucca was not a proper person to associate with good people."[15] The Bureau of Indian Affairs file on Sarah Winnemucca contains only four such affidavits, written at the time of Rinehart's attempt to discredit her, by persons associated with his interests. The allegations of such high officials, however, put a check upon public appeals for money. Even a friend who felt strongly that Sarah was not at fault wrote, "As I think Mr. Hopkins behaved so badly here it would be unwise to make any extended appeal for aid in her behalf."[16]

Devoted persons like Mary Bean were a heart-warming mainstay for Sarah and Elizabeth. This elderly, fragile woman wrote Miss Peabody:

> Yours of yesterday 28inst. came about five minutes since. It is a great relief to me, for two reasons. First it gives me some facts, that I can use at discretion to answer slanders with which I am so often met, when I try to advocate the cause of the Piutes and of Sarah. . . . I shall give your letter a thorough, careful reading and trust to use with discretion what you have written, including the addresses of some persons if I should need information. . . . I am not sanguine nor in anyway strong but I am patient and persevering, and I have a little faith that after the holy-days I may be able to add a mite to your bank of mercy and justice and truth.[17]

Happily, the house on the ranch was finished before Christmas. Sarah's school was now in more comfortable quarters, though it was without school desks or the other helpful conveniences of the government boarding school at Pyramid Lake run by Agent Gibson. In February, 1886, Elizabeth received encouraging news from a group of prominent citizens of Lovelock. Miss Peabody sent it immediately to the *Boston Transcript:*

Miss Peabody—A few of the principal residents of Lovelocks, having heard so frequently of the Piute school and the aspirations of the Princess, concluded, after very little cogitation, to verify in person the truth of these prodigious reports [concerning her school].

When we neared the school, shouts of merry laughter rang upon our ears, and little dark and sunburnt faces smiled a dim approval of our visitation. . . .

Speaking in her native tongue, the Princess requested the children to name all the visible objects, repeat the days of the week and months of the year, and calculate to thousands, which they did in a most exemplary manner. Then she asked them to give a manifestation of their knowledge upon the blackboard, each in turn printing his name and spelling aloud. It is needless to say, Miss Peabody, that we were spellbound at the disclosure. Nothing but the most assiduous labor could have accomplished this work. But most amazingly did I rudely stare . . . when these seemingly ragged and untutored beings began singing *gospel hymns* with precise melody, accurate time, and distinct pronunciation. The blending of their voices in unison was grand, and an exceedingly sweet treat. We look upon it as a marvelous progression; and so gratified were we that we concluded to send this testimonial containing the names of those present, in order that you may know of the good work the Princess is trying to consummate. . . . We feel that any further assistance would be well deserved and profitably expended by Sarah.[18]

By the middle of March, Natchez's ranch had been surveyed and partially fenced. Sarah wrote to a friend in New York that her brother was busy plowing and "trusting to his friends and Providence" to supply the seed for his harvest.[19] By April the money for the seeds had arrived, and the same donor, Mr. Warren Delano of New York, sent a large barrel of dress goods, clothes, sewing notions, and vegetable seeds.[20]

Sarah wrote Elizabeth of her illness. The chills and fever would not abate and were coupled with a worsening arthritic condition.[21] It would have been a great help if Alice Chapin would have come to support her.

Sarah was disturbed because the time was near when the parents of her students would take their children into the mountains on their annual hunt for winter stores. She told Elizabeth that already some of her best scholars had gone. As she still had hopes that Senator Stanford might stop to see the school when he re-

Northern Paiute women gathering pine nuts near Lovelock, Nevada. (Courtesy of Nevada Historical Society.)

turned from Congress in midsummer, she wished to keep and board the students. The parents had assembled in council in her schoolroom and expressed their grief that they could not pay her themselves for their children's board.[22] Sarah hoped that Stanford would value Natchez's farm and her school so highly that he would demand money from the fund in the Indian Office appropriated for Indian education. Then they could board the children in the summer months. As it was, Natchez and his family were without bread or meat and living on pine nuts. They could not keep the students.

Elizabeth immediately began soliciting promissory notes for the "first school taught by an Indian." She was attempting to raise $100 a month, and within a week she had raised enough for April. She held high hopes of sustaining the boarders through August. In her solicitations Elizabeth wrote of Sarah, "I see that she knows, as I cannot, how the Indian mind is to be approached and set at work for that self-development which is the only real education."[23]

Natchez had demonstrated throughout his life his shrewdness in dealing with white men for the Numa's benefit, but Sarah had no confidence in his ability to handle money because of his generosity. As a consequence she handled the funds that were received. She wrote Elizabeth that Natchez never asked for money, though he sometimes looked very wistfully at it when he saw it in her hands. One day she gave him a silver dollar, which pleased him greatly, and he went out "gingling it" (as Sarah spelled the phrase). When he came home that night, Sarah asked him what he had done with it, and he replied, "Oh, I had a big time." Later an old uncle who had gone with Natchez told Sarah that her brother had bought tobacco for some of the old men with the money. Sarah reported to Elizabeth that Natchez would never be rich.[24]

Natchez's fencing proved to be inadequate. The neighbors' stock broke through and trampled on the young plants rising from the plowed ground. Sarah wrote Warren Delano, asking to borrow money for more fencing. He replied to her:

About loaning $200 to your brother on his Land, I must tell you I cannot do it—and more than that let me advise you and him not to borrow *any money*, of any body, on the farm! Just as sure as you borrow any money of *any white* man and mortgage your farm for its repayment, so *surely* will your farm be lost to your Brother and his family. Until you can get the money out of your crops, or from your kind friends, you must do the best you can without fences. Let the *children* when not in school or asleep, watch the boundarys of the farm and keep the cattle off, and when night comes the men must take turns and keep the necessary watch. But do *every* thing *possible* to take care of your farm and to avoid making any debts that will cause you to lose it. Remember the success of your school and your life depend upon your maintaining your hold and cultivating your farm. For your Brother to fail in this and lose his farm would enable your adversaries to scoff at you and say it is of no use to try to help the Indians. I know the case is a hard one but your brother must try to work it out.[25]

Mr. Delano's advice was followed, as there was no other choice.

The Peabody Indian School, as Sarah called it continually interested local whites, who visited it and commended Sarah's work.[26] She took her pupils to Winnemucca, where observers, impressed with their knowledge, said that her school should be assisted by the Indian Bureau.[27] Yet, as far as the United States government was concerned, Sarah's school did not exist. The schools at Hampton, Virginia, and Carlisle, Pennsylvania, in the

East were run entirely by whites, and the Indian students could not use their own languages from the time they arrived. They were separated, often by thousands of miles, from their families and heritage. General Samuel Chapman Armstrong, the head of the Hampton Institute, believed that the sooner Indian children were taken from their parents, their languages, and their cultures the sooner they would be "Americanized." He refused to listen to Elizabeth's vindication of Sarah's character, nor would he concede a trace of merit to her program for teaching the children.[28] However, a western journalist wrote: "We believe that the Indian Department should found an Indian school in Nevada and put Sarah at the head of it. . . . She has ample culture, and she knows the Indian character thoroughly, while it is easy to believe that her example will be of great value in encouraging her pupils. When Indians have a white teacher there must naturally seem a great gulf between them."[29]

Sarah realized herself that her fluency in three Indian languages was of vital importance to the quality of education of her students. She wrote to the *Winnemucca Silver State*:

> It seems strange to me that the Government has not found out years ago that education is the key to the Indian problem. Much money and many precious lives would have been saved if the American people had fought my people with Books instead of Powder and lead. Education civilized your race and there is no reason why it cannot civilize mine. Indian schools are failures at many agencies, but it is not the fault of the children, but of the teacher and interpreter. Most of teachers have but one object, viz. to draw their salary. I do not think that a teacher should have no salary. But I think they should earn it first and then think of it. The most necessary thing for the success of an Indian school is a good interpreter, a perfect interpreter, a true interpreter. . . . I attribute the success of my school not to my being a scholar and a good teacher but because I am my own Interpreter, and my heart is in my work.[30]

Sarah's hopes of supporting funds from the United States government were short-lived. During the summer of 1886 an official from Washington arrived at the ranch and told the Winnemuccas that they could not receive any aid from the Reserved Fund for Indian Education unless Sarah surrendered the directorship of her school and unless Natchez gave up the ownership of his land.[31] Of course, Sarah refused to abandon her work and the original purpose of her school. Her brother certainly had strived too long for his small amount of acreage to let it go to the Indian Department.

Sarah and Natchez were in sore need of encouragement when Alice Chapin, the hoped-for teacher from the East, arrived in mid-July. She began working with Sarah, giving her moral and physical support. She had not fathomed the difficulties facing the Indian woman until she came to Nevada and saw for herself. Sarah's health particularly concerned her. Alice administered quinine for the malarial bouts of chills and fever and saw immediate improvement in her patient.[32] As she observed Sarah's school and her teaching methods, she kept up a steady stream of correspondence with Elizabeth, giving her details of the school's progress.

Miss Chapin, a normal school teacher with years of experience, was favorably impressed with Sarah's work. Though Sarah's students had only benches without backs, which they used as tables while kneeling on the floor, they were interested in learning. They produced superior work compared with the public-school students with whom Miss Chapin was familiar. She was pleased to find that they were in the second reader. Sarah read every lesson in English and in Paiute and used both languages in discussions of the subject matter.[33] Alice sent Elizabeth specimens of the students' writing and drawing. The old woman enthusiastically showed her friends the results of their contributions.

Each day, after a morning of academic subjects, Sarah taught the children to work about the ranch. The boys tended the garden and cared for the stock, and the girls cooked and sewed. Elizabeth called this "a vanguard of the 'New Education' in which doing leads thinking, and gives definite meaning to every word used."[34] Sarah's foremost objective was to make her students teachers—to use the older ones as assistants and substitutes and to encourage them to undertake their own self-education as she had done.[35]

As far as the farm production was concerned, Alice Chapin found that the lack of adequate fences and water were still the worst difficulties. The hoped-for windmill and well had not materialized. Natchez contracted to furnish thirteen men (including himself) for one month's work on a dam and ditches, in return for water from the irrigation canal that flowed through his land. Unfortunately, he did not receive a written agreement to this

orthern Paiute Indians near Bishop, California. (Courtesy of Nevada Historical ociety.)

arrangement. While Natchez's sixty-eight acres of wheat were maturing, representatives of the water company told him that he must keep his gates open, so that they could get to their ditches (some of which they had built on Natchez's land without his permission). Miss Chapin noticed that the white neighbors kept their gates shut, and, since Natchez's gates were open, the neighbors' cattle came on the land. An old uncle had to sit by the gates and drive them away—the remedy that Warren Delano had recommended.[36] Alice sought out the managers of the water company in Lovelock and discovered that Natchez did not have to leave the gates open. Thus the old man was freed for other work.

Meanwhile Natchez was accused of stealing and killing some cattle belonging to a neighboring farmer. These unfounded accusations, of course, angered Sarah, who wrote a letter to a local newspaper:

Lovelock, Nev. July 28. People without giving any proof have insinuated that Naches Winnemucca, of Lovelock, has killed beef not his own on his farm or up in the mountains, no where in particular. If any one knows anything about it let him come forward and tell it face to face like a man. If he has seen him kill or can prove anything, let him prove it in court. But if there is no proof, except that he is an Indian, and it is safe to slander him, then those who value their words will not say what they have no proof of.[37]

The coming harvest was looking promising when the water company turned off Natchez's water. Miss Chapin investigated why they had done so. The company claimed that the Paiutes had not worked enough on the irrigation ditches. "Indians are so lazy, we don't want them around," they said, and for illustration they used the old man who had sat all day by the open gate, protecting Natchez's fields. Miss Chapin's explanations did no good, and she realized that this maneuver had been planned all along to discredit the enterprise.[38]

Natchez still had no mower to cut the wheat. Fifteen Paiute men and women were hired, to be paid in grain. Some of the crop would also be needed to pay the men who had worked on the irrigation dam. Sarah notified Elizabeth that the literary exercises of the school would be suspended for a month while the

Wheat harvesting at Lovelock, Nevada. The women are using the traditional baskets for seed gathering. (Courtesy of Nevada Historical Society.)

children helped with the harvest. At the same time Alice Chapin had to return to the East, and Sarah took a needed rest.

When Elizabeth received a letter from Sarah some days later, she was shocked to read her message: to send no more money, "not one cent." A mutual friend had written Sarah that Elizabeth was giving away the provision for her old age in order to keep the boarding school going. Elizabeth wrote back immediately that this was not the case, saying, "the work I was doing for her was the greatest pleasure I had ever enjoyed in my life!"[39]

Sarah in the meantime wrote again, saying that "on account of our ill luck" she and Natchez were going away to earn some money. Elizabeth should not write again until she received a new address. The old woman was heartsick waiting for further word, wondering about the unexplained ill luck and concerned for the welfare of her Paiutes and the Peabody School.[40]

On September 25, Elizabeth was surprised by a telegram from Sarah asking for $200. Miss Peabody could not meet this need, and she sent the request on to Warren Delano, who had often helped in the past.

I was almost willing to say I would advance the money, . . . but a few hours thought have led me [to think] that *it is well,* not only for you, but possibly for Sarah herself, that you cannot meet her call. If Sarah had kept you advised of her doings and her doings had been such as to lead up to some need of money, the surprise would have been avoided and a reasonable ground for an answer yea or nay would have been presented—but the call for an immediate $200 to be placed at a point remote from her house [Elko, Nevada] and from her legitimate work, justifies a fear, a suspicion that there is some thing not quite right, if not wrong. It leads me to conjecturing various things: has she met her vagabond husband, Hopkins? or is it *possible* that there is truth in some of the scandalous reports of vicious habits: of drinking and gambling etc. etc. which have been so positively urged?

If I *knew* all about Sarah and her affairs and could be entirely satisfied that she is all you and I would like to know her to be, I might perhaps strain a point and lend her the $200—but as the matter stands I harden my heart against the application.[41]

23

Hopkins Again

Sarah stood before her people at a fandango near Lovelock and spoke. Except for a whimpering baby the Numa listened attentively. The September wind blew small whirlwinds of dust across the cleared dance place behind the crowd, but Sarah's strong voice carried well across the wide space. "These are the days of civilization," she told them. "We must all be good, sober and industrious and follow the example of our white brothers. We must become educated and give our children an education so that they may become farmers, mechanics and business men. We must build houses and earn an honest living."[1]

She told them that the Apaches had been fighting the soldiers in the mountains in the Southwest, on the borders of Mexico, but now their fighting was done. Their old ways were no more, and they would have to become farmers. Their leaders, Naiche and Geronimo, were in jail and would doubtless be hanged. She concluded, "Now we Paiutes know the white people are our friends and will help us if we help ourselves."[2]

After the fandango Sarah and Natchez set out with the wagon team. They headed northeast for the settlement of Rye Patch, where Natchez would work as a vaquero and Sarah had work as a housekeeper for a Mrs. Mary Wash. They now had only one dollar between them.[3]

Sarah remembered how, a few weeks before, the Paiute men and women workers on Natchez's ranch had come from harvesting the fields and demanded to be paid in silver coins instead of grain. A white neighbor had told them that Sarah was receiving $100 a month from Elizabeth Peabody and had said that Sarah was cheating them, since the money had been sent to pay the workers. The money, of course, had been intended to run the boarding school and had been used for that purpose; there was no silver to pay the harvesters. Hence the telegramed appeal for money that Elizabeth had not been able to meet and that Warren Delano had refused.[4] The white farmers had succeeded in turning the Numa against the Winnemuccas. As it turned out, this resulted in a loss in the sale of the crop. After Sarah had worked at Rye Patch for a few weeks, she returned to Lovelock and at last wrote the anxious Miss Peabody:

> If we could have borrowed $200 for two months . . . we could have paid them in money, and then sold the rest of the crop for $30 a ton. But it was the game to force us to sell the crop to the storekeepers for $17 a ton, which (thanks to the Spirit Father for so much) paid all our debts, but left nothing over; and I could not feed on love, so could not renew the school; and I was perfectly discouraged and worn out.[5]

Natchez's little daughter Delia had been ill with consumption since her older brother Kit Carson had died of pneumonia. Now she too was dying. Sarah helped care for the child, who had been placed in a small *nobee*, as was the custom. At Delia's death, in early November, 1886, the strength that she had given the child abandoned Sarah, and she wrote Elizabeth that she was glad that Delia was "safe in heaven." She expressed the hope that the "Spirit Father may soon let me die": "So, darling, do not talk any more on my behalf, but let my name die out and be forgotten: Only, don't you forget me, but write to me sometimes, and I will write to you while I live.[6]

With her characteristic enthusiasm Elizabeth would not let Sarah's mood daunt her, and she immediately began canvassing friends for new funds. She felt:

> [It was] a natural but temporary reaction of Sarah's nerves, and I see that she is still her whole noble self in this energetic action for personal independence, which I shall make known at once to all her friends, sure that it will challenge them to help her through another year until another

harvest. Meantime I believe that the entire change of work will prove a recreative rest, and her people will plainly see by it that it is not true that she had been living irrespective of them on the $100 a month, and that her enthusiastic scholars will not fail to bring their parents back to their confidence and gratitude to her.[7]

Elizabeth had 200 more copies of *Life Among the Piutes* printed. She also published a 36-page pamphlet, entitled *Sarah Winnemucca's Practical Solution of the Indian Problem*. In it she described Sarah's philosophy of education for Indian children and pleaded for support of her cause.[8] This she mailed to congressmen and influential friends of the Indians.

Sarah repaired her winter clothing and found more housekeeping work. She did not return to the ranch until November. By then her health and courage had improved, bolstered by Elizabeth's zeal. The Peabody School was reopened as a day school.[9] Later, in the first part of 1887, it was again a boarding school, for by then Elizabeth had found half a dozen friends who each sent $12 weekly for its upkeep.[10] Soon Sarah had forty-five students, and her health and vital spirit seemed to have returned.[11] She found that the children had lost some of their newly acquired skills, but review and exercises soon brought them back. Elizabeth noted that some of the Paiute children attending Agent Gibson's school at Pyramid Lake wished to change to the Peabody Indian School. She felt that this was a real mark of success, considering that the government-sponsored school had so much more monetary backing and more facilities.[12]

An inadequate water supply and lack of fencing still plagued Natchez. Sarah complained in a local paper that hogs and a lot of cattle had been running on their land since harvest: "We drive them out, but it does no good, as those who own them drive them in again. What shall I do? Will someone please advise me?"[13] This appeal in the *Winnemucca Daily Silver State* was a good maneuver on Sarah's part, as it gave notice to every one of her neighbors that she knew what was going on and that future trespassing would confirm her allegations.

From her new residence in Jamaica Plain, Massachusetts, Mary Mann wrote a friend that her sister was quite happy about "her" Indian, who was doing wonders.[14] Earlier Mary had written to the same woman, "She still rules the ascendant with E. and scarcely less with me though there is not so much of the fanatic in me as in E."[15] Mary had been feeble all winter. Although she enjoyed the visits of her grandson, it tired her extremely every time he spent the day with her.[16] In January a close friend of Mary's died and remembered her in her will. This set Mary to considering the provisions of her own will. As it turned out, the doctors' bitter medicines, which she took faithfully, though without much hope, did not save her. The widow of Horace Mann died on February 11, 1887. She left her own small legacy to Sarah, an Indian woman whom she may not have loved "fanatically," but whom she had supported in her quiet, steadfast way from the time when she had first met her.[17]

After her sister's death Elizabeth Peabody felt that she was not separated from her but nearer than ever, and she believed that Mary Mann hovered over Sarah Winnemucca as well. She told a friend that Sarah had become independent with her model school on her brother's farm, thanks to Mary's contributions. One hundred dollars had even unexpectedly come from Japan. She felt that surely the shade of Mary had brought all of this about.[18]

In February, 1887, Congress had passed the Dawes Act, which had long been supported by the Protestant churches engaged in missionary work among the Indians, the Indian Rights Association, and the liberal wing of the Republican Party. Humanitarian advocates of the lands-in-severalty act supported it because they believed that the Indians were capable of adapting to white civilization and that, if they did prove incapable, they would likely die out. White settlers in the West wanted the large parcels of land on the Indian Reservations that the Dawes Act would open to white settlement after the Indian heads of families were each allotted 160 acres. The Indian owners were not to be allowed to sell the lands allotted to them for a period of twenty-five years, but then they were to be given title to their farms and receive their citizenship. At the end of twenty-five years their tribal ties, which were believed to contribute to lack of industry and lack of individual responsibility, would supposedly be forgotten. It was expected that the Indians would then be assimilated into the great American "melting pot."

Sarah had had a great deal of influence on Senator Dawes at the time he wrote his bill. She and Natchez wanted the Numa to adapt to the white man's world and to succeed under the new system, which seemed to them a natural and hopeful alternative to the hated reservations. Aided by their well-meaning friends in the East, they could not foresee the problems of alienation, the loss of Indian lands to acquisitive whites, and the breakup of vital tribal support that the act would bring.

Sarah and Elizabeth were much upset by one facet of the Dawes Act that they never could condone: Indian children were required to be educated in white, English-speaking schools, whether their parents approved or not. Boarding schools were to be established far from the reservations, where children would be isolated from their parents and not allowed to go home for holidays. It was forbidden to speak their native languages. Anything relating to Indian religions and culture was to be disdained and discredited by the white teachers. Elizabeth and Sarah were in agreement that these schools would "repress creative self-respect and the conscious freedom to act" that was necessary for the well-being of Indian youth.[19]

A few months after the passage of the Dawes Act a gentleman, named Mr. Davis, came to the Peabody Indian School and asked Sarah to turn over her students to him. He proposed to transport them to Grand Junction, Colorado, where a boarding school for Indian children had been established. Sarah would have nothing to do with his plan, and she told Davis that she would never send the students without their parents' consent. As it turned out, a dozen Paiute children were taken from Pyramid Lake to the Colorado Industrial School, and three Paiute boys from the vicinity of Lovelock as well.[20] Lee Winnemucca was in San Francisco at the time and came home to find that one of his sons had been removed to Colorado.

Sarah and Natchez soon decided to promote their school as an industrial school for the Paiutes. Natchez proposed to give forty acres of his land for the purpose. Sarah would make another trip to the East in the hope that she could convince government officials to support their new plans. The school would prepare young Indians for specific jobs, such as carpentry, blacksmithing, and shoemaking. Some industrial-arts schools had already been established on reservations, but none had been set up in Humboldt County. It was Sarah's belief that the Indian students would learn rapidly at almost any school with proper treatment, but the right place to teach them was in their own communities, where the country was familiar and where they would be near their parents and tribal associations.

The *Winnemucca Daily Silver State* supported Sarah's ambitious project, saying, "Experience has taught her what her young people need and the Government should make an appropriation and place her at the head of an Indian industrial school—There are some 400 Indian children in the county to be educated and Sarah believes in educating them at home."[21] The newspaper gave a tribute to Elizabeth: "That grand old lady—Miss Peabody. England claims Gladstone, the grand old man in the Irish cause, and America can truly claim in her the grand old lady in the cause of education."[22]

Sarah made her pilgrimage to the East, but she did not gain the attention and recognition that had accompanied her former efforts. The Indian Association continued to promote the cause of the eastern Indian boarding schools, such as the Carlisle Indian School and Hampton Institute.[23] The nation had salved its conscience for the time being on the Indian question, and now it was felt to be time to get on with other national business. Sarah was defeated before she began. Her concept is a controversial ideal even a century later: that Indians should run their own local schools with nominal white help and should preserve and promote their own value systems.

The tangible result of the trip was that Sarah saw Lewis Hopkins, and they were reconciled. Perhaps this had been one of her intentions in returning east, to see Lewis and have the marriage settled one way or another. Her friends had been dismayed by the first trouble in Baltimore in 1884 and had been encouraging her to divorce Hopkins. Mrs. Delano, for example, had written to Elizabeth in June, 1884:

> I cannot but feel pity for him, he must suffer and dispise [*sic*] himself to have fallen so low. He evidently appreciated his wife's character and loved her. He must suffer to see how he has made her suffer who was so devotedly attached to him. I thought they were equally attached to each other. I fear her enemies will take advantage of his misconduct to prove that she is equally base and false. . . . When writing will you please convey to her my love and sympathy.[24]

In the same letter, however, she stated: "I hope he will receive the imprisonment that his crime deserves which will make it impossible for him to follow her. I own myself greatly disappointed in him, for I thought I understood his character as a talented, clever, and honorable man."[25] In January, 1885, she wrote Elizabeth, "So long as she is his wife he will rob her of all the money she earns."[26]

When the Hopkinses returned to Nevada and came to the ranch, the usually placid and friendly Natchez got his back up. He would not speak to Lewis, and the rest of the family also ignored his presence. Natchez was embittered toward his brother-in-law, who he felt was only exploiting Sarah and gaining her sympathy because of his wan smile and frail appearance.[27] It seems probable that Lewis's health required him to rest, while Sarah would have been busy teaching and also cooking, sewing, cleaning, and drudging about the ranch like Natchez's wives.

Elizabeth shared the concern of Sarah's other friends that Hopkins was a phony. In due course Sarah wrote her about the bad feeling between Lewis and Natchez and begged to borrow money from Warren Delano so that her husband might get some medical attention. This time, she promised, they were about to realize a fair price for their wheat, and she would borrow against that. Delano wrote Elizabeth, "I do not believe that Hopkins is really very sick! I have the same opinion of him that *Nachez* has and believe that his weakness, loss of voice, his cough &c &c are all assumed or exaggerated to frighten the poor woman, and when he has got her last dollar the fellow will be himself again and up to some mischief."[28]

When the harvest was completed, Natchez had raised 400 sacks of wheat. He was proud of this achievement and felt that his venture into the whites' capitalist economy had proved successful. Hopkins in the meantime had suddenly come to life. He paid some workers to load the wheat and took it to Winnemucca, where he sold it. He then offered a small amount of what he received to Natchez as his share. Sarah apparently went along with this action. Natchez angrily refused the money on the grounds that the wheat had been raised on his land by his and his wives' labor and therefore all of the money belonged to him—all or nothing.[29] Soon after Hopkins left for San Francisco, taking the proceeds of the harvest with him.

When an article sympathetic to Natchez's plight was published in the *Silver State*, a neighbor of Sarah's wrote an irate letter to the editor. The neighbor claimed that, when Sarah had left the farm in Natchez's charge to go east, he had promptly quit the premises himself, and, if it had not been for his white neighbors, there would not have been a harvest at all.[30] This assertion, while it upheld Sarah's conduct in the trouble with Natchez, was not fair to her brother. He had farmed and produced good harvests for many seasons before Sarah ever appeared on the scene.

The letter continued:

Sarah has fed and clothed Natchez for years, fenced the ranch, cleared the land, plowed and leveled it, furnished seed, made irrigating ditches, paid harvesting and threshing bills, furnished sacks and paid for hauling the grain to market. After all this expense she offered him [Natchez] $75, which he refused to take, saying he wanted it all or nothing.

It is true, Sarah sent her husband to Oakland to place him under a doctor's care, he having been very ill for 6 months past and his life dispared of, and did not go herself as she sent nearly every dollar she had to the physician. This was a humane act on her part and should be placed on record on behalf of her race. Natches cannot get treated in Lovelock today for a sack of flour, while Sarah has unlimited credit.

Pale Face.[31]

Lewis Hopkins had not only caused dissension between Sarah and Natchez and taken the profits so zealously hoped for by generous friends but also caused the collapse of Sarah's Peabody Indian School. Sarah must have been torn making such a choice, fully knowing the consequences. She saved only enough from Lewis to pay back the debt to Warren Delano.[32] News of the rupture between brother and sister soon reached the East, and Mr. Delano complained of sadly shattered nerves over the whole affair. He wrote Elizabeth:

Poor Woman, she is in sad straits, not to be blamed, but greatly to be pitied and helped—but how to help her is the problem . . . . Sarah must try to suppress her feelings and resume her good work, but to do this she must be reconciled to her Brother and we must use any influence we have to bring Natchez around to a better mood and from all I have heard of him I think he may not be found unreasonable. He owes his improved condition and circumstances very largely to Sarah and her friends whose continued good offices will doubtless be for his future benefit.[33]

Lewis Hopkins returned to the ranch in a few weeks. He had run through the Winnemuccas' money, and the doctors in Oakland had been unable to arrest his tuberculosis. He died on

A memorial card ordered by Sarah for her late husband, an indication of her continued regard for him. (Courtesy of Nevada Historical Society.)

October 18, 1887, and was buried in the Lone Mountain Cemetery at Lovelock.[34] Sarah had a special card printed for her family and friends, as was the custom of the day, containing a sentimental poem in her husband's memory. In March, Elizabeth had been confident that her Indian work was successfully finished, since Sarah had received several sums from Mary's estate and other sources.[35] Now, six months later, the status of the Indian project that had occupied Elizabeth's later years was once more precarious.

24
Henry's Lake

The winter of 1887–88 was a time of looking back for Sarah, even though she was only forty-three years old. She was bitterly disappointed that the model farm and school, for which she and Natchez had worked so hard, had received no official attention and no commendation from officials such as Senator Stanford. The Peabody Indian School now obtained little money from eastern sympathizers. Sarah had given up the idea of an industrial school, since she had not received the necessary support from the government.

According to Elizabeth "the surplus of the money donated without solicitation to enable Sarah to carry on the boarding school, she has appropriated to make Natchez a partner in the water company, and so permanently secure irrigation."[1] Elizabeth knew this was a wise decision, for water would always be a problem in the Nevada desert. As it was, Elizabeth felt that there was a fair chance for the Paiute enterprise to become self-supporting. It was Sarah's plan to go on by herself and continue the day school, "which costs her nothing but her time and the strength of her heart and mind."[2] Twenty-four students remained.[3]

Elizabeth did feel that Sarah had made some mistaken judgments of character, undoubtedly referring to her attachment to Hopkins.[4] Still Elizabeth was not disappointed in her protégé.

With her usual vivacity Miss Peabody published another pamphlet on the Peabody Indian School[5] and sent it to Senators Stanford, Long, Dawes, and William S. Holman and to other congressmen, to induce them to write an amendment, in favor of the school, to an appropriation that was to be made for Indian education.[6] Elizabeth's plea was:

> Will not somebody propose in Congress, this coming session, that appropriation be made to enable Sarah to put up some lodging houses and take to board these four hundred children? (Those Paiutes of school age in Nevada.) It would not cost so much as any of the government or denominational schools do, and would have none of their disadvantages, being wholly Indian work.[7]

Elizabeth's effort stirred some interest on the part of Congressman Holman,[8] but nothing came of it. Sarah made up her mind that she would not expect or ask for help from the East again. Congress was not receptive, and Elizabeth had worked too hard and too long for the cause. Nonetheless, it seemed ironic that Sarah's approach to Indian education had been spurned by Washington when there were so many Indian parents begging Sarah to take their children.

In the spring of 1888, Major General Howard made a visit to the Peabody Indian School.[9] When he spoke to Natchez, he learned that the Paiute farmer still supported the continuance of his sister's enterprise.[10] Howard could not promise them that he could influence the government to support the school. It is possible that he was able to tell them at that time that the army was intending to abandon Fort McDermit and that the military reservation would soon be turned over to the Paiutes. The Interior Department was to take possession of Fort McDermit on July 24, 1889, and some of its buildings served as headquarters for the new McDermit Indian Reservation. Part of the land that Old Winnemucca had always desired was at last to be officially possessed by some of his people.

Summer came, and the children left school with their parents for their seasonal wanderings to gather food. There was little correspondence now between Sarah and Elizabeth; the old woman had her kindergarten interests and lectured at the Concord School of Philosophy.[11] Sarah knew that her dream had ended, and she regretfully realized too that Natchez would have difficulty sustaining himself independently on the ranch. She must have felt some pride that despite all the hardships and difficulties she had kept the Peabody School going for almost four years.

Several small newspaper items give us the only clues concerning Sarah's activities from the time when she closed her school until she again joined her sister, Elma Smith. In late February, 1888, she was located in Lovelock, where she was bested in a game of casino.[12] On September 18, 1889, she and Natchez accompanied some other members of the tribe, who took a handout breakfast from a hotel kitchen. The "princess" had been attending a fandango in Elko, and she excused herself, saying that "when among the Indians she had to conform to their maners and customs."[13] A week later a notice appeared in the *Elko Independent* that no one could purchase Natchez's farm without notifying Sarah, as she owned a part interest in it.[14]

Sarah may have made several trips to visit her sister Elma, probably wintering in Nevada and returning to Idaho in the summer. She would have taken the Central Pacific to Salt Lake City and then entrained northward to Monida, Montana, the closest station to Henry's Lake, Idaho.[15] The first night's stopover, after a ride by sleigh or wagon over the rutted roads, was in a primitive hostel at Lakeview. On the second day the trail passed the northern shore of Henry's Lake and then wound by the Sherwood General Store, which also served as a hotel for the sparsely inhabited countryside.

This was Bannock Indian country. If Sarah was present at the death of Elma's husband, John B. Smith, on January 19, 1889,[16] she would have seen the painted Bannocks, who came to bury their friend in their bright regalia, their ponies decorated with bells and beadwork. Joseph Sherwood, the store owner, who acted as the local postmaster and coroner, had laid Smith out and built a wooden casket. On the next day more Bannocks arrived on their ponies, and the Indians collected on a hillside, wailing and lamenting the sudden passing of Smith. After the burial Elma would have returned to her cabin, which was about two miles down the road and closer to the shores of the lake.[17]

Elma was well situated, compared to other pioneer women. Her husband John had worked hard during his life, and he left her his savings and the home. Elma had taken in two white teenagers, Will and Ed Staley, who were orphans.[18] When spring came, at least on days when Sarah felt well, we can imagine her wandering with the two boys through the flower-strewn meadows, watching the moods of the mountains about the lake and the glorious sunsets across the water. Occasionally Elma was called away for midwife duties. Then Sarah may have taken charge of the boys. She may have taught them their lessons or accompanied them down the road to the Dick Rock Ranch, where the owner kept some tame buffalo that he had raised and was training to pull a buggy. The boys would have enjoyed the shenanigans of the cowboys working on the ranch, who took hunting parties of city people into the mountains of the Yellowstone country.[19]

Food was plentiful at Henry's Lake, even in the winter months when snow lay heavily on the ground. Friends might bring fish, caught through holes in the lake ice, or meat from the hunt. In summer the two sisters picked wild berries for preserves and wine making.

Mary Ann Garner, who would later become Joseph Sherwood's second wife, moved with her family to Henry's Lake in 1890. As a girl of nineteen she enjoyed the companionship of the two Paiute sisters. She accompanied Sarah and Elma on their excursions through the woods, picking huckleberries and other fruits, and she visited in their home. Mary Ann's father, who was an excellent shot, was out hunting one day in the woods. He sighted an antelope and brought it down. Then his heart sank because he recognized it as one of Elma's pets by the red ribbon that was tied about its neck.[20]

When young Will Staley disappeared mysteriously, and not even the body was found, the neighbors were suspicious of the Indian women. Whispers grew loud that perhaps Will had been poisoned—after all, they said, the Indians knew about poisonous plants. Mary Ann did not share the neighbors' suspicions, and she reminded them that they were perfectly willing to call in Elma when a new baby was expected.[21]

One evening in the fall of 1891, Joseph Sherwood was disturbed by rapid hoofbeats on the road and a sudden pounding on his door. He had already closed the store and was in his family quarters, sitting down to a late dinner. It was postponed, however, when a neighbor appeared and told him that there had been another death at Elma's place. The date was October 17,

1891.[22] Joseph hurried into his coat and came along in his buggy as soon as he could hitch the horse.

Sarah was laid out on the bed, her eyes already closed. Sherwood, in his position as the local coroner, learned from Elma that they had eaten a large dinner and had had some chokecherry wine. Sarah had gasped and suddenly collapsed, and that was all. The storekeeper-druggist-undertaker decided that Sarah had died of too much wine, the same cause of death that he had determined for John Smith.[23] Natchez arrived too late for the Bannock ceremonies. He found Sarah's grave near that of John Smith, with the dirt piled high in a sharp-edged wedge. There was no marker, and there is none today. Only two months after Sarah's death Natchez sold his 160 acres in the Big Meadows[24] and moved with his family to the Pyramid Lake Reservation. There he died in 1907, five days after the death of his last wife.[25] In 1905 the buyer of his land sold in turn to a conglomerate. The lost Paiute dream thus became a part of a large ranch with quantities of dairy and stock cattle. The corrals were equipped with modern machinery, and irrigating and drainage systems brought water to the buildings and land at the turn of a faucet.[26]

Elma Smith loaned money to Ed Staley to buy a place at Henry's Lake, and she lived with him there for a while on the Staley Ranch. At the time of her death in 1920 there were no longer any Indians left in the vicinity to mourn her as they had her sister Sarah in 1891.[27]

The New York Times carried Sarah's death notice and printed a review of her zealous, adventurous life of forty-seven years.[28] Colonel Frank Parker wrote how she had saved him and others during the Bannock War. He observed, "She was the only Indian on this coast who ever took any prominent part in settling the Indian question, and as such her memory should be respected."[29]

General Howard, in writing a short biography of Sarah, emphasized, "She did our government great service, and if I could tell you but a tenth part of all she willingly did to help the white settlers and her own people to live peaceably together I am sure you would think, as I do, that the name of Toc-me-to-ne [or Shell-flower] should have a place beside the name of Pocahontas in the history of our country."[30]

Ironically, Sarah's life did not catch the attention of the public in the years to come as the stories of Sacajawea and Pocahontas

Elma Winnemucca Smith, Sarah's sister, in 1919, the year before her death. (Courtesy of Nevada Historical Society.)

had. She had not helped to find a new trail through the wilderness, nor did she save the life of an early colonist. Perhaps in the future, however, Sarah Winnemucca's leadership for brotherhood and human rights and her tremendous efforts for peace between races will be recognized and celebrated. In one of the last passages of her autobiography Sarah had written:

> Those who have maligned me have not known me. It is true that my people sometimes distrust me, but that is because words have been put into my mouth which have turned out to be nothing but idle wind. Promises have been made to me in high places that have not been kept, and I have had to suffer for this in the loss of my people's confidence. I have not spoken ill of others behind their backs and said fair words to their faces. I have been sincere with my own people when they have done wrong, as well as with my white brothers. Alas, how truly our women prophesied when they told my dear old grandfather that his white brothers, whom he loved so much, had brought sorrow to his people. Their hearts told them the truth. My people are ignorant of worldly knowledge, but they know what love means and what truth means. They have seen their dear ones perish around them because their white brothers have given them neither love nor truth. Are not love and truth better than learning? My people have no learning. They do not know anything about the history of the world, but they can see the Spirit-Father in everything. The beautiful world talks to them of their Spirit-Father. They are innocent and simple, but they are brave and will not be imposed upon. They are patient, but they know black is not white.[31]

Notes

Chapter I. **Early Years**

1. Julian H. Steward and Erminie Wheeler-Voegelin, *Paiute Indians,* vol. 3, *The Northern Paiute Indians.* Two main premises of that study are that the Paiutes had no single great chief, but instead had small-band leaders, and that they had no sense of being a large separate tribe in aboriginal times.

2. *Reese River Reveille* (Austin, Nev.), September 2, 1884, p. 1, col. 1.

3. Old Winnemucca was also called Poito or Mubetawaka ("man with hole in his nose") for the bone that he wore through the septum of his nose. Young Winnemucca was also called Numaga. Robert F. Heizer, *Notes on Some Paviotso Personalities,* p. 2.

4. *Nevada State Journal* (Reno), February 12, 1873, p. 1, col. 2.

5. Moses Schallenberger, *The Opening of the California Trail: The Story of the Stevens Party from the Reminiscences of Joseph Schallenberger,* ed. George R. Stewart (Berkeley: University of California Press, 1953), pp. 19–21, 64–66.

6. Joseph Aram, "The Reminiscences of Captain Aram," in Colonel James Thompkins Watson, "Across the Continent in a Caravan," *Journal of American History* 1 (1907):627–29.

7. Sarah Winnemucca Hopkins, *Life Among the Piutes: Their Wrongs and Claims,* ed. Mrs. Horace Mann, p. 20.

8. Robert J. Heizer and Thomas R. Hester, eds., *Notes on Northern Paiute Ethnography: Kroeber and Marsden Records,* p. 32. Also Hopkins, *Life Among the Piutes,* pp. 25, 29.

9. Hopkins, *Life Among the Piutes,* p. 12.

10. Ibid., p. 18.

11. Ibid.

12. Hopkins, *Life Among the Piutes,* p. 21.

13. Also spelled *pe-har-ve.* The clumps of sugar that formed naturally on the outside of the cane were shaken off and rolled into balls that often included

the wasps and other insects that were attracted to the sugar. Early settlers found the sugar delicious until they discovered that fact.

14. Hopkins, *Life Among the Piutes,* p. 23.

15. Ibid., pp. 27–33.

16. California Historical Landmark 437 is on the site of the ferry, which was established by John Doak and Jacob Bonsall in 1848 and was the first ferry on the San Joaquin River. After passing through Stockton, Doak had crossed the San Joaquin River at the present Mossdale Fork, following an Indian trail to San Jose. Hiram Scott bought out Doak in 1849. V. Covert Martin, *Stockton Album Through the Years,* pp. 77–78.

17. Hopkins, *Life Among the Piutes,* pp. 34–35.

18. V. Covert Martin, *Stockton Album Through the Years,* pp. 77–78.

19. Hopkins, *Life Among the Piutes,* pp. 41–43.

20. John Reese, unpublished manuscript, Bancroft Library, University of California, Berkeley.

21. James F. Downs, *The Two Worlds of the Washo: An Indian Tribe of California and Nevada,* pp. 73–76.

22. Hopkins, *Life Among the Piutes,* p. 42.

23. William Wright [Dan DeQuille], *The Big Bonanza,* p. 10.

24. Frederick Dodge to Jacob Forney, January 4, 1859, Letters Received, Office of Indian Affairs, Utah Superintendency, 1859–1880, Record Group 75, M234, National Archives, Washington, D.C.

25. Wright, *The Big Bonanza,* p. 192, and the account of Captain Juan in California on p. 204.

26. *Nevada State Journal,* February 12, 1873. See also *San Francisco Chronicle,* November 14, 1879: "My brothers Tom and Naches here went to work for four years on a ferryboat."

27. *Nevada State Journal,* February 12, 1873: "I went to California, and in Stockton met Mrs. Roach and was adopted into her family."

28. Sarah is mistaken in dating her residence with Major Ormsby in Genoa to 1858. By that time the major and his family had moved to Carson City, Nevada. The Williams-McMarlin affair, which she observed while she was with the Ormsbys, is also dated by Angel to 1857. Myron Angel, ed., *History of Nevada,* p. 551.

29. Hopkins, *Life Among the Piutes,* pp. 58–59.

30. "The most of these Indians have evidently once lived in California, which accounts for their knowledge of the English language, many of them have become domesticated, and are employed by the settlers of the Carson Valley as herdsmen and laborers on their farms." Garland Hurt, "Report to His Excellency Brigham Young Gov. and Ex-officio Supt. of Indian Affairs, Territory of Utah," in James H. Simpson, *Report of Explorations Across the Great Basin of the Territory of Utah for a Direct Wagon Route from Camp Floyd to Genoa in Carson Valley in 1859,* p. 228.

31. Hopkins, *Life Among the Piutes,* p. 59. For another account see Myron T. Angel, ed., *History of Nevada,* p. 551.

32. Hopkins, *Life Among the Piutes,* p. 60.

33. Ibid., p. 61.

34. Ibid., p. 63.

35. Ibid.
36. Ibid., pp. 64, 66.

Chapter 2. **The Pyramid Lake War**

1. William Wright, *The Big Bonanza,* p. 11.
2. Ibid., p. 9.
3. Angel, ed., *History of Nevada,* p. 551.
4. U.S. Office of Indian Affairs, *Report of the Joint Special Committee: Condition of the Indian Tribes,* p. 517.
5. Frederick Dodge to Jacob Forney, January 4, 1859, Letters Received, Office of Indian Affairs, Utah Superintendency.
6. Robert F. Heizer, *Notes on Some Paviotso Personalities,* p. 6; Omer C. Stewart, "The Northern Paiute Bands," *Anthropological Records* 2, no. 3:129, 130.
7. Statement of William Weatherlow to William Willson Lawton, Notary Public, October 27, 1860, RG 75, M234, National Archives.
8. Wright, *The Big Bonanza,* pp. 7 and 9.
9. Frederick Dodge to Jacob Forney, January 4, 1859, Letters Received, Office of Indian Affairs, Utah Superintendency.
10. Frederick Dodge to Commissioner Greenwood, February 18, 1859, Letters Received, Office of Indian Affairs, Utah Superintendency.
11. James H. Simpson, *Report of Explorations Across the Great Basin of the Territory of Utah,* p. 9.
12. Wright, ed., *The Big Bonanza,* p. 33.
13. Angel, ed., *History of Nevada,* p. 554.
14. Sarah Winnemucca Hopkins, *Life Among the Piutes: Their Wrongs and Claims,* ed. Mrs. Horace Mann, p. 64.
15. Frederick Dodge to A. B. Greenwood, Commissioner of Indian Affairs, November 25, 1859, Letters Received, Office of Indian Affairs, Utah Superintendency.
16. William T. Whitney manuscript, California Historical Society, San Francisco, pp. 18–19.
17. Angel, ed., *History of Nevada,* p. 148.
18. Statement of Weatherlow to Lawton, October 27, 1860, RG 75, M234, National Archives.
19. Ibid.
20. Statement of Ira A. Eaton to F. W. Lander, superintendent of U.S. Wagon Road Expedition, October 23, 1860, Selected Correspondence and Papers from the Utah Superintendency File, 1860–1870, RG 75, M234, National Archives.
21. Angel, ed., *History of Nevada,* p. 151.
22. Ibid.
23. Hopkins, *Life Among the Piutes,* p. 16.
24. Angel, ed., *History of Nevàda,* p. 151.
25. Ibid., p. 153.
26. Ibid., pp. 155, 156.
27. Hopkins, *Life Among the Piutes,* p. 72; Sessions S. Wheeler, *The Desert*

Lake: The Story of Nevada's Pyramid Lake, p. 61, 64.

28. Angel, ed., *History of Nevada,* p. 158.

29. Ibid., p. 163.

30. Statement of Weatherlow to Lawton, October 27, 1860, RG 75, M234, National Archives.

31. Ibid.

32. Frederick Lander, superintendent of U.S. Wagon Road, to the Honorable A. B. Greenwood, commissioner of Indian affairs, October 31, 1860, with enclosures, Selected Correspondence and Papers from Utah Superintendency File, 1860–1870, RG 75, M234, National Archives.

33. Ibid.

34. Ibid.

35. U.S. Office of Indian Affairs, *Report of the Joint Special Committee* (1867), p. 518.

36. *Sierra Democrat* (Sacramento, Calif.), 1860, Bancroft Scraps, vol. 93, pp. 17–18, Bancroft Library, University of California, Berkeley.

37. U.S. Office of Indian Affairs, *Report of the Joint Special Committee* (1867), p. 519.

Chapter 3. **Growing Up Proud**

1. This account of the death of Truckee is based on Hopkins, *Life Among the Piutes: Their Wrongs and Claims.* The date that Sarah gives would indicate that Truckee died before the Pyramid Lake War. It does not agree with other sources, which show October, 1860. See C. D. Irons, *Edwards Tourists' Guide and Directory of the Truckee Basin* (1883), pp. 98–99; Wright, *The Big Bonanza,* p. 269; *Gold Hill* (Nev.) *News,* May 6, 1876.

2. Hopkins, *Life Among the Piutes,* p. 67.

3. Ibid.

4. Ibid.

5. Hopkins, *Life Among the Piutes,* p. 69.

6. Bancroft Scraps, vol. 93, p. 10, Berkeley. This article describes the honesty and the virtuous manner of the Paiutes in dealing with their white neighbors.

7. Hopkins, *Life Among the Piutes,* p. 70.

8. *Nevada State Journal,* February 12, 1873, p. 1, col. 2.

9. *San Francisco Morning Call,* November 22, 1879, p. 4, col. 1.

10. *Notre Dame Quarterly,* issues for 1914 and 1915.

11. *Notre Dame Quarterly,* June, 1936, p. 32.

12. On June 4, 1977, I interviewed and corresponded with Sister Mary Dominica McNamee, historian of the College of Notre Dame, Belmont, California. She wrote:

> There is no entry for her [Sarah Winnemucca] in our archives, school lists, and no photo. We have looked closely into this matter. If the story is true, she must have been in the boarding school at that early date, but the absence of her name even in the accounts would indicate that the Sisters doubted whether they could keep her. The complaint of the wealthy lady

would be no surprise to them. If there was one point of agreement between the Spanish and American girls at the time it was unwillingness to live under the same roof with an Indian. . . . Though the Sisters were strong for the native, they had no funds; in order to support schools for natives, they had first to open a boarding school for the elite. Then they opened three "poor schools" in San Jose, but that was after Sarah's time.

13. James W. Nye to the Honorable Caleb B. Smith, Secretary of the Interior, August 14, 1861, Letters Received, Office of Indian Affairs, Utah Superintendency.

14. "Governor Nye and the Indians," *Carson City* (Nev.) *Silver Age,* May 27, Bancroft Scraps, vol. 93, p. 16.

15. Jacob T. Lockhart to the Honorable W. P. Dole, Commissioner of Indian Affairs, June 25, 1863, Letters Received, Office of Indian Affairs, Utah Superintendency.

16. Angel, ed., *History of Nevada,* p. 169.

17. *Humboldt Register* (Winnemucca, Nev.), June 13, 1863.

18. John C. Burche to Governor James W. Nye, August 1, 1864, Letters Received, Office of Indian Affairs, Utah Superintendency.

Chapter 4. **On Stage**

1. Sarah Winnemucca, "The Pah-Utes," *The Californian,* September, 1882, p. 256. Norton I, "Emperor of the United States," was an eccentric gentleman of wide reputation who strode the streets of San Francisco during this period, wearing gold braid and a sword. He used his own imperial currency and was often accompanied by two dogs, Bummer and Lazarus.

2. Margaret G. Watson, *Silver Theatre,* pp. 323, 324.

3. Bancroft Scraps, vol. 93, p. 10.

4. Ibid.

5. Ibid.

6. *San Francisco Daily Alta California,* October 22, 1864.

7. Ibid., p. 1, col. 1, "City Items."

8. *Daily Alta California,* October 23, 1864, p. 1, col. 1, "City Items."

9. Bancroft Scraps, vol. 93, p. 27.

10. Ibid., p. 10.

Chapter 5. **Pyramid Lake Reservation**

1. Hopkins, *Life Among the Piutes,* p. 77.

2. Bancroft Scraps, vol. 93, p. 11; Angel, ed., *History of Nevada,* p. 170.

3. Hopkins, *Life Among the Piutes,* p. 78.

4. *Virginia Union* (Virginia City, Nev.), March 17, 1865, Bancroft Scraps, vol. 93, p. 12.

5. *Virginia Union,* March 15, 1865, Bancroft Scraps, vol. 93, p. 28.

6. Bancroft Scraps, vol. 93, p. 11.
7. Angel, ed., *History of Nevada,* p. 172.
8. Ibid., p. 173.
9. Ibid.
10. *Humboldt Register,* January 3, 1866.
11. For more information on Black Rock Tom and the Nevada Indian wars of 1865 and 1866, see Sessions S. Wheeler, *The Nevada Desert,* chapter 3, "The Black Rock Desert—Indian Stronghold," pp. 56-92, and appendix B, pp. 163-68.
12. Hopkins, *Life Among the Piutes,* p. 79.
13. Ibid., p. 85.
14. *Humboldt Register,* January 20, 1866.
15. *Humboldt Register,* March 17, 1866.
16. Angel, ed., *History of Nevada,* p. 174.
17. *Humboldt Register,* May 5, 1866.
18. *Humboldt Register,* February 10, 1866.
19. *Humboldt Register,* March 31, 1866.
20. George F. Brimlow, "The Life of Sarah Winnemucca: The Formative Years," *Oregon Historical Society Quarterly,* June, 1952, p. 118.
21. Hopkins, *Life Among the Piutes,* p. 79.
22. *Humboldt Register,* February 3, 1866.
23. Agreement with H. G. Parker, superintendent of Indian affairs, State of Nevada, November 20, 1866, Letters Received, Office of Indian Affairs, Nevada Superintendency, 1861-1880, RG 75, M234, National Archives.
24. Contract between Clark W. Thompson, Superintendent of Indian Affairs and Undersecretary of the Interior, and William N. Leet, Gold Hill, Nevada, May 27, 1867, Letters Received, Office of Indian Affairs, Nevada Superintendency.
25. Hopkins, *Life Among the Piutes,* pp. 76-77.
26. Resolution of the Nevada state legislature passed March 6, 1867, Letters Received, Office of Indian Affairs, Nevada Superintendency.
27. U.S. Office of Indian Affairs, *Report of the Joint Special Committee: Condition of the Indian Tribes* (1867), p. 521.
28. Hopkins, *Life Among the Piutes,* pp. 79-80.
29. Ibid., p. 81.
30. Ibid., p. 82.
31. Ibid.
32. Hopkins, *Life Among the Piutes,* p. 83.
33. Ibid., p. 84.
34. Ibid.
35. Ibid.
36. Ibid., p. 85.
37. Ibid.
38. *Reese River Reveille,* July 8, 1867; A. J. Liebling, "Lake of the Cui-ui Eaters," part 3, *The New Yorker,* January 15, 1955, p. 35; Lieutenant J. M. Lee to H. Douglass, December 20, 1869, Letters Received, Office of Indian Affairs, Nevada Superintendency. Angel names James Flemming as having died near Williams Station (*History of Nevada,* p. 160).
39. *Annual Report of the Commissioner of Indian Affairs to the Secretary of the Interior for the year 1868,* p. 145.

40. Quoted from the *Susanville Sagebrush,* August 17, 1867, in the *Reese River Reveille,* September 2, 1867.

Chapter 6. **Camp McDermit**

1. Hopkins, *Life Among the Piutes,* p. 99. In *Life Among the Piutes,* Seward is called "Major" Seward, but the *Official Army Register* shows him as a captain.
2. W. V. Rinehart, unpublished manuscript, Bancroft Library.
3. Hopkins, *Life Among the Piutes,* p. 100.
4. Ibid., pp. 100-103.
5. Ibid., p. 103.
6. Ibid., p. 92.
7. Ibid.
8. Lalla Scott, *Karnee: A Paiute Narrative,* pp. 32-33.
9. Hopkins, *Life Among the Piutes,* pp. 90-91.
10. Steward and Wheeler-Voegelin, *Paiute Indians,* vol. 3, *The Northern Paiute Indians,* p. 260.
11. Ibid., p. 163.
12. Ibid., p. 261.
13. Jacob T. Lockhart to N. G. Taylor, Commissioner of Indian Affairs, July 21, 1868, Letters Received, Office of Indian Affairs, Nevada Superintendency.
14. U.S. Office of Indian Affairs, *Annual Report of the Commissioner of Indian Affairs to the Secretary of the Interior for the Year 1868,* pp. 146-47.
15. H. G. Parker to Hon. N. G. Taylor, Commissioner of Indian Affairs, December 10, 1868, Letters Received, Office of Indian Affairs, Nevada Superintendency.
16. *Humboldt Register,* May 1, 1869.
17. Franklin Campbell to Commissioner of Indian Affairs, June 9, 1865, Letters Received, Office of Indian Affairs, Nevada Superintendency.
18. J. C. Kelton, Assistant Adjutant General, to Department of the Interior, Special Order 219, September 11, 1869, Letters Received, Office of Indian Affairs, Nevada Superintendency.
19. Sarah Winnemucca to Major H. Douglass, April 4, 1870, Letters Received, Office of Indian Affairs, Nevada Superintendency.
20. *Harper's Weekly,* May 7, 1870, p. 291, col. 3.
21. Helen Hunt Jackson, *A Century of Dishonor,* appendix, p. 395.
22. Major H. Douglass to Commissioner E. S. Parker, May 31, 1870, Letters Received, Office of Indian Affairs, Nevada Superintendency.
23. The *Humboldt Register,* May 14, 1870, reported Douglass's efforts as follows:

> Indians Pacified—Major Douglas and Lieut. Lee, Special Indian Agents for Nevada arrived in town on last Sunday and have so far been quite successful in pacifying the Chiefs and Warriors of the Piutes, that for the present at least, no fears of an outbreak by the savages are apprehended by our citizens. The agents left here a few days ago for the Big Meadows down the Humboldt, where they are now having a big talk with the natives. Natchez, who claims to be the Winnemucca or Big Chief of the tribe is at

the Meadows, and a shrewder specimen of redskin does not exist in Nevada.

24. Report by Major H. Douglass, United States Army, to Superintendent of Indian Affairs of conversation with Paiute Indians at Camp McDermit, Nevada, May 8, 1870, Letters Received, Office of Indian Affairs, Nevada Superintendency.

25. Major H. Douglass to the Honorable E. S. Parker, Commissioner of Indian Affairs, November 30, 1870.

Chapter 7. **Marriage and New Agents**

1. Sarah Winnemucca to Commissioner E. S. Parker, August 9, 1870, Letters Received, Office of Indian Affairs, Nevada Superintendency.

2. Ibid.

3. A correspondent of the *Sacramento Record* writing from Winnemucca, *Alta California* (San Francisco), August 29, 1870, Bancroft Scraps, vol. 93, p. 54.

4. Wright, *The Big Bonanza,* p. 202.

5. *San Francisco Morning Call,* January 22, 1885.

6. *Nevada State Journal,* February 12, 1873.

7. George Balcom to E. S. Parker, Commissioner of Indian Affairs, March 5, 1871, Letters Received, Office of Indian Affairs, Nevada Superintendency.

8. George Balcom to E. S. Parker, Commissioner of Indian Affairs, March 15, 1871, Letters Received, Office of Indian Affairs, Nevada Superintendency.

9. George Balcom to E. S. Parker, Commissioner of Indian Affairs, April 14, 1871, Letters Received, Office of Indian Affairs, Nevada Superintendency.

10. George Balcom, Telegram, March 27, 1871, Letters Received, Office of Indian Affairs, Nevada Superintendency.

11. George Balcom to E. S. Parker, Commissioner of Indian Affairs, April 8, 1871, Letters Received, Office of Indian Affairs, Nevada Superintendency.

12. George Balcom, Telegram to E. S. Parker, Commissioner of Indian Affairs, April 29, 1871, Letters Received, Office of Indian Affairs, Nevada Superintendency.

13. George Balcom to E. S. Parker, Commissioner of Indian Affairs, April 29, 1871, Letters Received, Office of Indian Affairs, Nevada Superintendency.

14. Sarah claimed that C. A. Bateman, the agent at Walker River, was the instigator of this "wild Indian" affair, but this could not have been the case, as Bateman's arrival at Carson City from the east was announced on April 29. Hopkins, *Life Among the Piutes,* p. 86.

15. C. A. Bateman to E. S. Parker, Commissioner of Indian Affairs, June 18, 1871, Letters Received, Office of Indian Affairs, Nevada Superintendency.

16. C. A. Bateman to E. S. Parker, Commissioner of Indian Affairs, July 8, 1871, Letters Received, Office of Indian Affairs, Nevada Superintendency.

17. Captain R. F. Bernard to Major Samuel Breck, Assistant Adjutant General, U.S.A., Headquarters, Department of California, June 23, 1871, Letters Received, Office of Indian Affairs, Nevada Superintendency.

18. E. O. C. Ord, Brigadier and Brev. Major General, endorsement to above letter, July 1, 1871, Letters Received, Office of Indian Affairs, Nevada Superintendency.

19. Hopkins, *Life Among the Piutes,* p. 90.
20. Ibid.
21. C. A. Bateman to H. R. Clum, Acting Commissioner of Indian Affairs, August 20, 1871, Letters Received, Office of Indian Affairs, Nevada Superintendency.
22. Sarah Winnemucca to General E. O. C. Ord, July 1, 1871, endorsed by Ord and included in transmissions to Adjutant General by Major General Schofield, July 5, 1871, Letters Received, Office of Indian Affairs, Nevada Superintendency.
23. George Balcom to H. R. Clum, Acting Commissioner of Indian Affairs, August 17, 1871, Letters Received, Office of Indian Affairs, Nevada Superintendency.
24. C. A. Bateman to H. R. Clum, Acting Commissioner of Indian Affairs, August 20, 1871, Letters Received, Office of Indian Affairs, Nevada Superintendency.
25. *Sacramento* (Calif.) *Union,* May 16, 1872.
26. C. A. Bateman to H. R. Clum, Acting Commissioner of Indian Affairs, November 10, 1871, Letters Received, Office of Indian Affairs, Nevada Superintendency.
27. Franklin Campbell, quoted in James Mooney, *The Ghost Dance Religion and the Sioux Outbreak of 1890,* p. 3.

Chapter 8. The Modoc War

1. Lt. Col. O. L. Hein, U.S. Army, Retd., *Memories of Long Ago* (New York: G. P. Putnam, 1925), p. 67.
2. *Humboldt Register,* March 1, 1873.
3. *Nevada State Journal,* February 12, 1873.
4. Hopkins, *Life Among the Piutes,* pp. 86–87.
5. C. A. Bateman to F. A. Walker, Commissioner, February 17, 1872, Letters Received, Office of Indian Affairs, Nevada Superintendency.
6. *Humboldt Register,* June 8, 1872.
7. Ibid., June 22, 1872.
8. *Nevada State Journal,* February 12, 1873.
9. *Humboldt Register,* July 27, 1872.
10. Ibid., August 3, 1872.
11. C. A. Bateman to F. A. Walker, October 26, 1872, Letters Received, Office of Indian Affairs, Nevada Superintendency.
12. Keith A. Murray, *The Modocs and Their War,* pp. 66–67, 71.
13. Ibid., p. 41.
14. *Humboldt Register,* April 19, 1873.
15. Wheaton to A. A. General, Department of the Columbia, May 6, 1873, Modoc War Official Correspondence, Bancroft Library.
16. Wheaton to Lt. James A. Rockwell, April 16, 1873, Modoc War Official Correspondence, Bancroft Library.
17. Steward and Wheeler-Voegelin, *Paiute Indians,* vol. 3, *The Northern Paiute*

Indians, p. 163; and Thomas S. Dunn from Camp Warner, May 23, 1873, Modoc War Official Correspondence, Bancroft Library.

18. *Portland Daily Bulletin*, April 23, 1873, Modoc War Official Correspondence, Bancroft Library.

19. Wheaton to A. A. General, Department of the Columbia, May 6, 1873, Modoc War Official Correspondence, Bancroft Library.

20. Smohalla was a prophet and teacher of the Sokulk, or Wanapum, tribe, who were related to the Nez Percés. He had been exposed to Catholic teaching in his boyhood. After a quarrel with a rival chief he had left his country on the Columbia River in eastern Washington, wandering as far as Mexico and returning to his home through Nevada. One wonders if he preached his new religion to the Paiutes on this journey, thus influencing Wodziwob, whose visions were similar. He maintained that he had been to the spirit world and returned with a message for all Indians, which was that the Native Americans must return to their primitive mode of life, refuse the teachings and claptrap of the white man, and in all their actions be guided by the will of the Indian god, as revealed to Smohalla and his priests. Chief Joseph of the Nez Percés was a devoted believer of Smohalla's teachings. Frederick Webb Hodge, ed., *Handbook of American Indians North of Mexico*, vol. 2, p. 602.

21. Wheaton to Assistant Adjutant General, Department of the Columbia, May 6, 1883, Modoc War Official Correspondence, Bancroft Library.

22. 2d Lt. J. P. Jocelyn to Maj. Thomas S. Dunn, May 26, 1873, Letter Book 3A, Modoc War Official Correspondence, Bancroft Library.

23. Telegram from Gen. W. T. Sherman to Gen. J. C. Davis, June 3, 1873, Modoc War Official Correspondence, Bancroft Library.

Chapter 9. **Law and Order**

1. *Carson Daily Appeal* (Carson City, Nev.), February 8, 1874.

2. Don D. Fowler and Catherine S. Fowler, eds., *Anthropology of the Numa: John Wesley Powell's Manuscripts on the Numic Peoples of Western North America, 1868–1880*, p. 16. There is a photograph of Natchez on p. 18 of this study. Vocabulary lists given by him at Salt Lake City in May, 1873, are on pp. 210–15. A collection of tales told by him is on pp. 215 and 218–20. See also *Carson Daily Appeal*, July 24, 1873, p. 3, col. 1.

3. *San Francisco Alta California*, November 18, 1873, Bancroft Scraps, vol. 93, pp. 54–55.

4. *Carson Daily Appeal*, February 1, 1874, reprinted from *Humboldt Register* (Winnemucca, Nev.).

5. *Daily Alta California*, January 30, 1874, p. 1, col. 2.

6. *Carson Daily Appeal*, February 3, 1874.

7. *Daily Alta California*, January 30, 1874, p. 1, col. 1.

8. Petition to the Honorable Edward P. Smith, February, 1874, Letters Received, Office of Indian Affairs, Nevada Superintendency.

9. Bancroft Scraps, vol. 93, p. 43.

10. *Virginia City* (Nev.) *Chronicle*, January 11, 1875, Bancroft Scraps, vol. 93, p. 55.
11. R. F. Bernard, 1st Cavalry Captain, Camp Bidwell, to Assistant Adjutant General, Department of California, May 17, 1874, Letters Received, Office of Indian Affairs, Nevada Superintendency.
12. *Virginia City* (Nev.) *Chronicle*, January 11, 1875, Bancroft Scraps, vol. 93, p. 55.
13. Ibid.
14. Ibid.
15. Ibid.
16. *Virginia City* (Nev.) *Territorial Enterprise*, January 14, 1875.
17. Ibid.
18. Vandever to Commissioner of Indian Affairs, June 11, 1875, Letters Received, Office of Indian Affairs, Nevada Superintendency.
19. Barstow to the Honorable E. P. Smith, October 15 and 19, 1875, Letters Received, Office of Indian Affairs, Nevada Superintendency.
20. Wagner to Assistant Adjutant General of the United States Army, Washington, D.C., February 16, 1875, Letters Received, Office of Indian Affairs, Nevada Superintendency.
21. Wagner to Breck, February 23, 1875, Letters Received, Office of Indian Affairs, Nevada Superintendency.
22. Breck to Commanding Officer, Camp McDermit, Nevada, February 27, 1875, Letters Received, Office of Indian Affairs, Nevada Superintendency.
23. *Winnemucca Silver State*, March 16, 1875, Bancroft Scraps, vol. 93, p. 34.
24. *Silver State*, March 27, 1875.
25. *Reese River Reveille*, April 1, 1875, p. 3, col. 2; *Silver State*, March 29, 1875.
26. Elmer R. Rusco, "The Status of Indians in Nevada Law," in Ruth M. Houghton, ed., *Native American Politics: Power Relationships in the Great Basin Today* (Reno: University of Nevada, Bureau of Governmental Research, 1973), p. 63.

Chapter 10. The Malheur Reservation

1. *Silver State*, April 28, 1875.
2. Hopkins, *Life Among the Piutes*, chapter 6, "The Malheur Agency."
3. George F. Brimlow, *The Bannock Indian War of 1878*, p. 31.
4. Hopkins, *Life Among the Piutes*, p. 105.
5. Ibid., p. 106.
6. Ibid., p. 107.
7. Ibid., p. 109.
8. Ibid., p. 110-11.
9. Ibid., p. 112.
10. "They all held to that peculiar religious creed called 'Dreamers' and practised all the peculiar rites of that strange belief—such as drumming and dancing, bowing and making strange signs, not unlike some of the Orthodox Christians." W. V. Rinehart to Mrs. F. F. Victor, March 6, 1874, Bancroft Library.

11. Hopkins, *Life Among the Piutes,* p. 113.
12. H. Linville to Major Elmer Otis, March 7, 1874, Letters Received, Office of Indian Affairs, Oregon Superintendency, RG 75, M274, National Archives.
13. Hopkins, *Life Among the Piutes,* pp. 112–15.
14. Oliver Otis Howard, *My Life and Personal Experiences Among Our Hostile Indians,* p. 377.
15. O. O. Howard, Department of Columbia, telegram to Adjutant General, October 12, 1875, Letters Received, Office of Indian Affairs, Oregon Superintendency.
16. Samuel B. Parrish to the Honorable E. P. Smith, Commissioner of Indian Affairs, April 26, 1875, Letters Received, Office of Indian Affairs, Oregon Superintendency; petition to the Honorable James K. Kelly from numerous citizens of Baker County, Oregon, November 11, 1875, Letters Received, Office of Indian Affairs, Oregon Superintendency.
17. Hopkins, *Life Among the Piutes,* p. 116.
18. Samuel B. Parrish to the Honorable E. P. Smith, Commissioner of Indian Affairs, April 4, 1876, Oregon Superintendency, Letters Received, Office of Indian Affairs.
19. Mattie later married Lee Winnemucca, and she and Sarah were close companions until Mattie's untimely death in 1879.
20. O. O. Howard, *Famous Indian Chiefs I Have Known,* pp. 255–58.
21. Samuel B. Parrish to Hon. E. P. Smith, April 4, 1876, Letters Received, Office of Indian Affairs, Oregon Superintendency.
22. Parrish to General O. O. Howard, April 27, 1876, Letters Received, Office of Indian Affairs, Oregon Superintendency.
23. Hopkins, *Life Among the Piutes,* pp. 117–18.
24. Ibid., pp. 119–20.
25. Hopkins, *Life Among the Piutes,* pp. 121–22.
26. Green to Assistant Adjutant General, Department of Columbia, May 26, 1876, endorsed by General O. O. Howard, Letters Received, Office of Indian Affairs, Oregon Superintendency.

Chapter 11. **Trouble at Malheur**

1. Documents of divorce proceedings of *Sarah Winnemucca* v. *Edward C. Bartlett,* September 21, 1876, Grant County Courthouse, Canyon City, Oregon.
2. W. V. Rinehart to Mrs. F. F. Victor, March 6, 1874, Bancroft Library, University of California, Berkeley.
3. W. V. Rinehart to Mrs. F. F. Victor, April 10, 1881, Bancroft Library.
4. Hopkins, *Life Among the Piutes,* p. 125. Most of the account of Rinehart's activities is taken from Sarah's book.
5. Hopkins, *Life Among the Piutes,* p. 124.
6. Ibid., p. 125.
7. Ibid., pp. 125–26.
8. Ibid., p. 133.

9. Ibid., pp. 133-34.
10. W. V. Rinehart to Commissioner of Indian Affairs, October 28, 1876, Letters Received, Office of Indian Affairs, Oregon Superintendency.
11. Marriage certificate of Sarah Winnemucca and Joseph Satwaller, November 3, 1876, Grant County, Oregon.
12. Major John Green to Assistant Adjutant General, Department of Columbia, November 16, 1876 (with endorsements by Adjutant General H. Clay Wood, Brigadier General O. O. Howard, and Major General Irwin McDowell), Letters Received, Office of Indian Affairs, Oregon Superintendency.
13. Ibid.
14. Ibid.
15. Ibid.; Major John Green to Assistant Adjutant General, December 20, 1876, Letters Received, Office of Indian Affairs, Oregon Superintendency.
16. W. V. Rinehart to General O. O. Howard, December 23, 1876, Letters Received, Office of Indian Affairs, Oregon Superintendency.
17. Ibid.
18. W. V. Rinehart to Commissioner of Indian Affairs, April 14, 1877, Special File no. 268 ("Sarah Winnemucca"), Bureau of Indian Affairs, M574, National Archives.
19. "The Indian Uprising," *Daily Silver State,* June 21, 1877.
20. *Daily Silver State,* June 23, 1877; telegram from Natchez Overton to General McDowell, June 23, 1877, Letters Received, Office of Indian Affairs, Oregon Superintendency.
21. *Daily Silver State,* June 23 and 29, 1877.
22. *Daily Silver State,* July 19, 1877.
23. O. C. Stewart, "The Northern Paiute Bands," *University of California Anthropological Record* 2 (1939), no. 3:132.
24. W. V. Rinehart to Commissioner of Indian Affairs, April 14, 1877, Special File no. 268, Bureau of Indian Affairs.
25. William M. Turner to the Honorable W. V. Rinehart, September 10, 1877, Letters Received, Office of Indian Affairs, Oregon Superintendency.
26. Ibid.
27. *San Francisco Chronicle,* November 29, 1877.
28. Ibid.
29. Ibid.
30. *Daily Silver State,* December 12, 1877.
31. W. V. Rinehart to Commissioner of Indian Affairs, March 23, 1878, Letters Received, Office of Indian Affairs, Oregon Superintendency.
32. Captain Henry Wagner, 1st Cavalry, to Assistant Adjutant General, February 8, 1878, Letters Received, Office of Indian Affairs, Oregon Superintendency.
33. Captain Henry Wagner, 1st Cavalry, to Assistant Adjutant General, March 11, 1878, Letters Received, Office of Indian Affairs, Oregon Superintendency.
34. Irvin McDowell to Adjutant General of U.S. Army, April 16, 1878, Letters Received, Office of Indian Affairs, Oregon Superintendency.
35. W. V. Rinehart to Commissioner of Indian Affairs, April 16, 1878, Letters Received, Office of Indian Affairs, Oregon Superintendency.
36. John J. Burke, Saddler, Company A, 1st Cavalry, to Congressman Newton

Booth, March 22, 1878, Letters Received, Office of Indian Affairs, Oregon Superintendency.

37. W. V. Rinehart to Major Danielson, March 25, 1878, and Rinehart to Commissioner of Indian Affairs, April 16, 1878, Letters Received, Office of Indian Affairs, Oregon Superintendency.

38. W. V. Rinehart to Commissioner of Indian Affairs, December 18, 1877, Letters Received, Office of Indian Affairs, Oregon Superintendency.

39. W. V. Rinehart to Commissioner of Indian Affairs, February 27, 1878, Letters Received, Office of Indian Affairs, Oregon Superintendency.

40. Petition to the President of the United States signed by approximately 70 settlers near or on Malheur Reservation; and Captain George M. Downey, 1st Infantry, April 20, 1878, endorsed by General O. O. Howard and General Irvin McDowell, Letters Received, Office of Indian Affairs, Oregon Superintendency.

41. W. V. Rinehart to Commissioner of Indian Affairs, May 18, 1878, Letters Received, Office of Indian Affairs, Oregon Superintendency.

42. W. V. Rinehart to Commissioner of Indian Affairs, May 20, 1878, Letters Received, Office of Indian Affairs, Oregon Superintendency.

43. W. V. Rinehart to Commissioner of Indian Affairs, May 21, 1878, Letters Received, Office of Indian Affairs, Oregon Superintendency.

Chapter 12. **The Beginning of Hostilities**

1. Thomas E. Cooley's memories in "I Always Wondered," by Jo Southworth, *Blue Mountain Eagle* (John Day, Ore.), January 4, 1973: "The scouts found Sally Winnemucca out in the mountains, after she had been deserted by her husband." Also, Hopkins, *Life Among the Piutes*, p. 137. Sarah says that she spent the winter at Mrs. Courley's.

2. Hopkins, *Life Among the Piutes*, pp. 140–41.

3. General O. O. Howard, *Famous Indian Chiefs I have Known*, p. 269.

4. Hopkins, *Life Among the Piutes*, p. 146.

5. W. V. Rinehart to Commissioner of Indian Affairs, June 7, 1878, Letters Received, Office of Indian Affairs, Oregon Superintendency.

6. General Irvin McDowell, telegram to General Sherman, June 4, 1878, Letters Received, Office of Indian Affairs, Oregon Superintendency.

7. Elizabeth P. Peabody, *Sarah Winnemucca's Practical Solution of the Indian Problem*, p. 30–31.

8. W. V. Rinehart to Commissioner of Indian Affairs, May 12, 1879, Special file no. 268, Bureau of Indian Affairs.

9. W. V. Rinehart, telegram to Commissioner Hoyt, June 10, 1878, *New York Times*, June 14, 1878.

10. Levi Gheen, telegram to Commissioner of Indian Affairs, June 7, 1878, Letters Received, Office of Indian Affairs, Nevada Superintendency.

11. Hopkins, *Life Among the Piutes*, pp. 148–49.

12. Ibid., p. 149.

13. Some newspapers carried a story that Sarah had been arrested in Jordan Valley while attempting to smuggle ammunition to the hostile Indians. *New York Times*, June 17, 1878, p. 1, col. 6.

14. Hopkins, *Life Among the Piutes*, p. 150.

15. General O. O. Howard, *My Life and Personal Experiences Among Our Hostile Indians*, p. 388.

16. Ibid.

17. Hopkins, *Life Among the Piutes*, p. 154.

18. Ibid., pp. 157–58.

19. Ibid., p. 159. Critics look upon Sarah's account of this adventure in her autobiography with skepticism, but the various Bannock bands were not organized as a single military unit, and, while they were occupied killing cattle in this safe refuge, they would not have been on their guard. Since the prisoners' guns and horses had been taken from them, there was no need to watch them closely unless there was an alarm.

20. Hopkins, *Life Among the Piutes*, p. 160.

21. An interesting aspect of Sarah's work as a scout with the army is the style of riding that she chose. One might assume that she rode astride, considering the number of miles that she traveled and the necessity for speed and hard work. Sarah insists that she rode sidesaddle, wearing a riding dress and a hat, throughout her work. That, in fact, was the style for ladies of the day, and Sarah was very eager to impress her ladylike qualities upon her public. Hopkins, *Life Among the Piutes*, p. 152, 158.

22. Ibid., p. 163.

23. Howard, *My Life and Personal Experiences Among Our Hostile Indians*, pp. 391.

24. W. V. Rinehart, telegram to Commissioner of Indian Affairs, July 7, 1878, Letters Received, Office of Indian Affairs, Oregon Superintendency.

25. Hopkins, *Life Among the Piutes*, p. 164. Also, Howard, *My Life and Personal Experiences*, p. 391.

26. The *New York Times* account of Sarah's experience was printed on June 17, 1878, p. 1, col. 6. It bore the headline "A BRAVE INDIAN SQUAW," and the lead sentence read, "Sarah, Daughter of the Piute Head Chief, Penetrates to the Hostiles' Camp and Rescues her Father and Brothers—Movements of the Indians." The report was very consistent with Sarah's autobiography, which was written four years later, but it had two very interesting additions. Sarah was quoted as saying that her brother George (whom she calls her cousin in her book) accused her of destroying her tribe by inducing some to escape, because he thought that those left behind would be doomed without a chance of getting away from Oytes and the Bannocks. Also, more information is given on Chief Egan: "She describes Eagle of Light, the Nez Perce renegade chief, whose son was with Joseph last year taunting Egan with cowardice. Egan, the brave war chief of the Piutes, sat on his horse and exhorted the hostiles to leave them and not draw soldiers upon them. He said: 'Why do you bring war upon my people? I will not fight.' The tears were streaming down his cheeks. 'You coward,' said Eagle of Light, striking at him with his knife."

Chapter 13. **The Bannock Indian War**

1. *New York Times*, June 23, 1878, p. 5, col. 6, reprinted from the *Omaha* (Neb.) *Herald*, June 18, 1878.

2. *New York Times*, June 25, 1878, p. 1, col. 1.

3. W. V. Rinehart to Commissioner of Indian Affairs, June 28, 1878, Letters Received, Office of Indian Affairs, Oregon Superintendency.
4. Ibid.
5. Ibid.
6. Ibid.
7. Hopkins, *Life Among the Piutes,* p. 165.
8. Ibid., p. 168.
9. Ibid., p. 169.
10. Ibid.
11. Howard, *My Life and Personal Experiences Among Our Hostile Indians,* pp. 399–400.
12. Howard to McDowell, October, 1878, House Executive Document 1, Ser. 1843, 45th Congress, 3rd Session, Part 2, p. 219, quoted in Brimlow, *The Bannock Indian War of 1878.*
13. Howard, *Life Among Our Hostile Indians,* p. 401; Hopkins, *Life Among the Piutes,* p. 170.
14. Howard, *Life Among Our Hostile Indians,* p. 400.
15. W. V. Rinehart to Commissioner of Indian Affairs, July 1, 1878, Letters Received, Office of Indian Affairs, Oregon Superintendency.
16. Ibid.
17. Ibid.
18. Ibid.
19. Ibid.
20. Ibid.
21. *New York Times,* July 6, 1878, p. 4, cols. 3 and 4.
22. W. V. Rinehart, telegram to Commissioner of Indian Affairs, July 7, 1878, Letters Received, Office of Indian Affairs, Oregon Superintendency.
23. Captain H. C. Hasbrouck to Assistant Adjutant General, Military Division of the Pacific, July 9, 1878, Letters Received, Office of Indian Affairs, Oregon Superintendency.
24. Ibid.
25. *New York Times,* July 9, 1878, p. 1, col. 3.
26. Ibid., July 10, 1878, p. 1, col. 3.
27. Hopkins, *Life Among the Piutes,* pp. 174–75.
28. Ibid., p. 175. Also Howard, *Life Among Our Hostile Indians,* pp. 404–405.
29. Hopkins, *Life Among the Piutes,* p. 176; Howard, *Life Among Our Hostile Indians,* pp. 404–405.
30. Hopkins, *Life Among the Piutes,* p. 175.
31. Howard, *Life Among Our Hostile Indians,* pp. 404–405.
32. Ibid., pp. 175–76.
33. Ibid., p. 177.
34. Ibid., p. 178. Also Brimlow, *Bannock Indian War,* p. 143.
35. Hopkins, *Life Among the Piutes,* p. 177.
36. Brimlow, *Bannock Indian War,* p. 146.
37. N. A. Cornoyer to Commissioner of Indian Affairs, July 19, 1898, Letters Received, Office of Indian Affairs, Oregon Superintendency.
38. Ibid.
39. Ibid.

40. Howard, *Famous Indian Chiefs I Have Known*, pp. 259-60.
41. Ibid., p. 277.
42. Brimlow, *Bannock Indian War*, pp. 150-54.
43. J. F. Santee, "Egan of the Piutes," *Washington Historical Society Quarterly*, January, 1935, pp. 22-24.
44. Ibid.
45. Howard, *Famous Indian Chiefs I Have Known*, p. 241.
46. Hopkins, *Life Among the Piutes*, pp. 178-79.
47. Ibid., pp. 180-81.
48. Ibid., p. 181.
49. Ibid., pp. 181-82.
50. Ibid., p. 182.
51. Ibid., p. 186.
52. Ibid., pp. 188-93.

Chapter 14. **Yakima**

1. Hopkins, *Life Among the Piutes*, p. 195.
2. Ibid., p. 196.
3. *New York Times*, August 14, 1878, p. 1, col. 6.
4. Hopkins, *Life Among the Piutes*, pp. 199-200.
5. Ibid., p. 200.
6. Ibid., pp. 200-201.
7. Commander Corliss of Fort McDermit, telegram to Adjutant General, October 4, 1878, Letters Received, Office of Indian Affairs, Oregon Superintendency.
8. Hopkins, *Life Among the Piutes*, p. 201.
9. Letters of Capain M. A. Cochran, November 18 and December 6, 1878, in *Annual Report of the Commissioner of Indian Affairs to the Secretary of the Interior for the Year 1879*, p. 129.
10. Hopkins, *Life Among the Piutes*, p. 203.
11. Ibid., p. 204.
12. Ibid., p. 205.
13. Letters of Captain M. A. Cochran, November 18 and December 6, 1878, *Annual Report of the Commissioner of Indian Affairs . . . 1879*, p. 129.
14. *Daily Silver State*, January 2, 1879.
15. Hopkins, *Life Among the Piutes*, pp. 206-207.
16. W. V. Rinehart, unpublished manuscript, Bancroft Library.
17. Hopkins, *Life Among the Piutes*, p. 207.
18. Ibid., pp. 207-208.
19. Ibid., p. 208.
20. W. V. Rinehart to Commissioner of Indian Affairs, March 3, 1879, Special File No. 268, Bureau of Indian Affairs.
21. James H. Wilbur to Commissioner of Indian Affairs, February 6, 1879, Letters Received, Office of Indian Affairs, Oregon Superintendency.
22. Hopkins, *Life Among the Piutes*, pp. 210-11.
23. Ibid., p. 211.

24. Ibid., pp. 211–12.
25. Ibid., p. 214.
26. Ibid., p. 212.
27. W. V. Rinehart to Commissioner of Indian Affairs, May 12, 1879, Special File no. 268, Bureau of Indian Affairs.
28. *Daily Silver State,* June 25, 1879.
29. Ibid., June 13, 1879.
30. Ibid., June 6, 1879.
31. Ibid., June 13, 1879.
32. Ibid., June 14, 1879.
33. *Daily Silver State,* July 15, 1879.
34. Hopkins, *Life Among the Piutes,* p. 216. Also, General O. O. Howard to General B. Whittlesey, November 7, 1879, Letters Received, Office of Indian Affairs, Oregon Superintendency.
35. Hopkins, *Life Among the Piutes,* p. 214.
36. Ibid.
37. Ibid., p. 216.
38. James Wilbur to Commissioner of Indian Affairs, July 21, 1879. Letters Received, Office of Indian Affairs, Oregon Superintendency, Special File no. 268, Bureau of Indian Affairs.
39. James Mooney, *The Ghost Dance Religion and the Sioux Outbreak of 1890,* p. 3.

Chapter 15. **The "Princess" Sarah**

1. *San Francisco Call,* November 22, 1879.
2. *San Francisco Chronicle,* November 23, 1879, p. 1, col. 5.
3. *San Francisco Chronicle,* November 14, 1879.
4. *San Francisco Chronicle,* November 23, 1879, p. 1, col. 5.
5. *San Francisco Chronicle,* November 14, 1879.
6. *San Francisco Call,* November 22, 1879.
7. W. V. Rinehart to Commissioner of Indian Affairs, February 6, 1879, Special File no. 268, Bureau of Indian Affairs.
8. *Daily Silver State,* November 28, 1879, reprinted from *San Francisco Chronicle.*
9. Ibid.
10. *Alta California,* November 26, 1879, p. 1, col. 3.
11. *Daily Silver State,* November 28, 1879.
12. *Daily Alta California,* November 26, 1879, p. 1, col. 3.
13. Hopkins, *Life Among the Piutes,* p. 217.
14. *Daily Silver State,* November 6, 1879.
15. *Daily Silver State,* December 16, 1879.
16. *Daily Alta California,* December 24, 1879, p. 1, col. 5.
17. Ibid.
18. *Daily Alta California,* December 4, 1879, p. 1, col. 3.
19. *Daily Silver State,* December 30, 1879.
20. Ibid. After legal action had forced the departure of Agent A. J. Barnes from the Pyramid and Walker River reservations, the American Baptist Home

Mission Society had difficulty filling the position. William Garvey held it for only five months before he was suspended. Then on September 17, 1879, James E. Spencer assumed the charge. Spencer was not only competent but also honest, and he treated the Paiutes with respect and kindness before his untimely death of pneumonia on November 26, 1880. He found trustworthy farmers and traders to work on the reservations, attempted the removal of white cattlemen and sheepherders, started the building of two school buildings (one each on the Walker River and Pyramid reservations), and built a working flume designed by a civil engineer. He worked alongside the Indians in digging ditches and in building the flume. Wading in the icy waters of the Truckee may have brought on his final illness. This information is derived from numerous letters that Spencer wrote to the commissioner of Indian affairs in 1879 (Letters Received, Office of Indian Affairs, Nevada Superintendency, RG 75, M234, National Archives).

21. *Daily Silver State,* August 23, 1879.
22. *Daily Silver State,* October 2, 1879.
23. *Daily Silver State,* December 30, 1879.
24. Ibid.
25. Ibid.
26. *Daily Silver State,* January 5, 1880.
27. *Daily Silver State,* January 14, 1880.

Chapter 16. **Washington City**

1. Hopkins, *Life Among the Piutes,* p. 219.
2. John Muldrick, Phil Mitschan, William Hall, Edwin Hall, J. W. Church, J. H. Wood, F. C. Sels, D. G. Overholdt, and William Luce to the Honorable T. H. Brents, January 14, 1880, Special File no. 268, Bureau of Indian Affairs.
3. W. V. Rinehart to the Honorable E. A. Hoyt, January 15, 1880, enclosing three affidavits by William Currey, Thomas O'Keefe, and W. W. Johnson (all dated, sworn, and subscribed to Rinehart, January 13, 1880), Special File no. 268, Bureau of Indian Affairs.
4. Ibid.
5. Ibid.
6. *Daily Silver State,* January 31, 1880, reprinted from *Washington National Republican.*
7. Hopkins, *Life Among the Piutes,* p. 221.
8. Ibid., pp. 223-24. The letter was also paraphrased in the *Silver State,* February 2, 1880.
9. Ibid., p. 222.
10. Ibid.
11. Ibid., p. 225.
12. Ibid., pp. 224-25.
13. John Howe to the Hon. R. E. Trowridge, Commissioner of Indian Affairs, May 1 and 6, 1880, Letters Received, Bureau of Indian Affairs.
14. *Silver State,* June 2, 1880.
15. *Daily Silver State,* May 5 and 6, 1880.
16. *Daily Silver State,* February 16, 1880.

17. *Daily Silver State,* February 17, 1880.

18. *Baker City* (Ore.) *Bedrock Democrat,* from *Esmeralda* (Nev.) *Herald,* in John Muldrick et al. to Hon. T. H. Brent, January 14, 1880, Special File no. 268, Bureau of Indian Affairs.

19. W. V. Rinehart to Commissioner of Indian Affairs, March 20, 1880, Special File no. 268, Bureau of Indian Affairs.

20. Ibid.

21. Sarah Winnemucca to W. V. Rinehart, April 4, 1880, Special File no. 268, Bureau of Indian Affairs.

22. W. V. Rinehart to Sarah Winnemucca, April 20, 1880, Special File no. 268, Bureau of Indian Affairs.

23. W. V. Rinehart to the Honorable R. E. Trowbridge, Commissioner of Indian Affairs, April 20, 1880, Special File no. 268, Bureau of Indian Affairs.

24. Hopkins, *Life Among the Piutes,* p. 226.

25. Ibid., p. 227.

26. Ibid., pp. 231–32.

27. Ibid., pp. 232–33.

28. Ibid., p. 236.

29. Ibid., p. 238.

30. *Daily Silver State,* July 10, 1880.

31. James H. Wilbur to Commissioner of Indian Affairs, July 9, 1879, in Katherine Turner, *Red Men Calling on the Great White Father,* p. 166.

32. Hopkins, *Life Among the Piutes,* p. 239.

33. Ibid.

34. Ibid., pp. 239–40.

35. Turner, *Red Men Calling,* p. 171.

36. Ibid., p. 172.

37. James H. Wilbur to Commissioner of Indian Affairs, June 29, 1880, quoted in Turner, *Red Men Calling,* p. 173.

38. United States Office of Indian Affairs, *Annual Report of the Commissioner of Indian Affairs to the Secretary of the Interior for the Year 1879,* p. 159.

39. Howard, *My Life and Personal Experiences Among Our Hostile Indians,* p. 420.

40. Brig. Gen. O. O. Howard to Assistant Adjutant General, Presidio, S.F., August 21, 1878, Letters Received, Office of Indian Affairs, Oregon Superintendency.

41. Brig. Gen. O. O. Howard to Adjutant General, Presidio, S.F., October 8, 1878, Letters Received, Office of Indian Affairs, Oregon Superintendency.

42. W. V. Rinehart to Commissioner of Indian Affairs, May 12, 1879, Special File no. 268, Bureau of Indian Affairs.

Chapter 17. **Mrs. Hopkins**

1. Sarah Winnemucca to the Honorable Secretary of the Interior, March 28, 1881, in Hopkins, *Life Among the Piutes,* p. 244.

2. O. O. Howard to Whom It May Concern, April 3, 1883, in Hopkins, *Life Among the Piutes,* p. 249.

3. *Silver State,* October 9, 1880.

4. *Portland Oregonian,* October 8, 1880.

5. Hopkins, *Life Among the Piutes*, p. 246.

6. W. V. Rinehart to Commissioner of Indian Affairs, July 10, 1881, Special File no. 268, Bureau of Indian Affairs. *Silver State*, July 14, 1881.

7. Ibid.; *Silver State*, July 23, 1881.

8. James H. Wilbur to Commissioner of Indian Affairs, May 31, 1880, Special File no. 268, Bureau of Indian Affairs.

9. Ibid., November 21, 1881.

10. Ibid., October 27, 1881.

11. Hopkins, *Life Among the Piutes*, p. 243. Wilbur tried to counter Chapman's observations to the military by writing himself to the Honorable H. Price, Commissioner of Indian Affairs, on February 28, 1882, Special File no. 268, Bureau of Indian Affairs.

12. *Silver State*, September 29, 1881.

13. *Daily Silver State*, November 30, 1881.

14. Sarah Winnemucca Hopkins, "The Pah-Utes," *The Californian* 6 (1882): 256.

15. *Silver State*, December 8, 1881. The *San Francisco Examiner* of December 8, 1881 (quoted in *New York Times*, December 18, 1881, p. 5, col. 2) states that Sarah was married on the Monday, which would indicate December 5, 1881. Records of marriages and divorces in San Francisco prior to July 1, 1904, were destroyed by the general conflagration on April 1, 1906. Consequently, it would be difficult to confirm whether Sarah divorced Joseph Satwaller before her marriage to Hopkins.

16. Patricia Stewart, "Sarah Winnemuca," *Nevada Historical Society Quarterly* 14 (1971): 31.

17. *New York Times*, December 18, 1881, p. 5, col. 2; *Silver State*, December 8, 1881.

18. *Silver State*, December 8, 1881.

19. *New York Times*, December 18, 1881, p. 5, col. 2.

20. *Daily Silver State*, January 9, 1882.

21. Hopkins, *Life Among the Piutes*, p. 94.

22. Ibid.

23. Ibid., p. 95.

24. Ibid., p. 99.

25. *Silver State*, February 20, 1882; *Reno* (Nev.) *Evening Gazette*, April 10, 1883.

26. W. V. Rinehart, unpublished manuscript, Bancroft Library. Probably Rinehart was held personally responsible for paying for the property.

27. *Daily Silver State*, August 1, 1882.

28. James H. Wilbur to Hon. H. Price, Commissioner of Indian Affairs, February 28, 1882, Special File no. 268, Bureau of Indian Affairs.

29. Brig. Gen. O. O. Howard to Adjutant General of Army, December 16, 1882, Special File no. 268, Bureau of Indian Affairs.

Chapter 18. **Old Winnemucca**

1. *Daily Silver State*, September 27, 1882.

2. *Daily Silver State*, October 8, 1882.

3. *Reno* (Nev.) *Evening Gazette*, October 25, 1882, p. 3, col. 1.

4. *Daily Silver State,* October 31, 1882.
5. Beatrice Blythe Whiting, *Piute Sorcery,* p. 69.
6. *Reno Evening Gazette,* October 27, 1882.
7. R. F. Heizer, *Executions by Stoning Among the Sierre Miwok and Northern Paiute* (Berkeley, Calif.: Kroeber Anthropological Society, 1955), pp. 44–48.
8. *Daily Silver State,* September 27, 1882.
9. *Reno Evening Gazette,* November 16, 1882.
10. Ibid.
11. Ibid.; *Silver State,* October 31, 1882.
12. Sarah Winnemucca Hopkins, "The Pah-Utes," *Californian* 6 (1882):252–55.
13. *Reno Evening Gazette,* April 10, 1883.

Chapter 19. **A Trip to the East**

1. Hopkins, *Life Among the Piutes,* editor's preface. Also, Elizabeth P. Peabody, *The Piutes: Second Report,* p. 7.
2. *Boston Evening Transcript,* May 3, 1883, p. 2, col. 6.
3. Elizabeth P. Peabody, *Sarah Winnemucca's Practical Solution of the Indian Problem,* p. 24.
4. Peabody, *The Piutes: Second Report,* p. 7.
5. Ibid., p. 5.
6. Peabody, *Sarah Winnemucca's Practical Solution,* pp. 8–9.
7. Hopkins, *Life Among the Piutes,* p. 53.
8. Mary Mann to Miss Eleanor Lewis, April 25, 1883, Olive Kettering Library, Antioch College, Yellow Springs, Ohio.
9. Ibid.
10. *Boston Evening Transcript,* May 3, 1883, p. 2, col. 6. Thomas Tibbles, a white writer married to a Ponca Indian woman (Susette La Flesche), had recently written of the "Hidden Power" by which Indians were kept as the helpless wards of the agents, their self-respect lost while the contractors on the reservation became affluent.
11. *Council Fire and Arbitrator* 6 (May, 1883): 69.
12. *Silver State,* June 19, 1883.
13. General O. O. Howard to Mrs. Mary Mann, September 13, 1883, Olive Kettering Library, Antioch College.
14. Hopkins, *Life Among the Piutes,* pp. 250–51.
15. Ibid., pp. 256–57.
16. Ibid, p. 258.
17. Elizabeth P. Peabody to the Honorable J. B. Long, January 11, 1884, Massachusetts Historical Society, Boston.
18. Elizabeth P. Peabody to Congressman Newton Booth [1883], Olive Kettering Library, Antioch College.
19. Hopkins, *Life Among the Piutes,* p. 76.
20. *Silver State,* November 7, 1883.
21. Elizabeth P. Peabody to the Honorable J. B. Long, March [27?], 1884,

Massachusetts Historical Society.

22. Elizabeth P. Peabody to Edwin Munroe Bacon [1883], Olive Kettering Library, Antioch College.

23. Mary Mann to Miss Eleanor Lewis, December 24, 1883, Olive Kettering Library, Antioch College.

24. *Silver State,* December 13, 1883.

25. Mary Mann to Miss Eleanor Lewis, December 24, 1883.

26. *Silver State,* December 5, 1883.

27. Peabody, *The Piutes: Second Report,* p. 8.

28. *Council Fire and Arbitrator* 6 (May, 1883):135.

29. Advertisements for Sarah's lectures appeared in the *Baltimore Sun* under "Special Notices" during the winter of 1884.

30. Peabody, *The Piutes: Second Report,* p. 7.

31. Lewis H. Hopkins to a subscriber for Sarah's book, May 10, 1884, Museum and Library of Maryland History, Maryland Historical Society, Baltimore.

32. *Daily Silver State,* September 7, 1883.

33. R. H. Milroy to the Honorable H. Price, Commissioner of Indian Affairs, August 11, 1883, Special File no. 268, Bureau of Indian Affairs.

34. Kate Douglas Wiggin raised $1,000 among advocates of the kindergarten movement for Elizabeth Peabody's eightieth birthday. Elizabeth eventually sent $800 of this money to help Sarah Winnemucca in her work for the Indians. Louise Hall Tharp, *The Peabody Sisters of Salem* (Boston: Little, Brown and Co., 1950), p. 168.

35. Elizabeth P. Peabody to the Honorable J. B. Long, January 11, 1884, Massachusetts Historical Society.

36. Elizabeth P. Peabody to the Honorable J. B. Long, March [27?], 1884, Massachusetts Historical Society.

37. Ibid.

38. M. Jarvis to Mrs. Mary Mann, April 17, 1884, Olive Kettering Library, Antioch College.

Chapter 20. **Disillusionment**

1. Peabody, *The Piutes: Second Report,* p. 8; Elizabeth P. Peabody to Hon. J. B. Long, January 11, 1884, Massachusetts Historical Society; *Silver State,* April 25 and 29, 1884.

2. Elizabeth P. Peabody to the Hon. John B. Long, May, 1884, Massachusetts Historical Society.

3. Ibid.

4. On July 3, 1880, Agent Spencer had written to Commissioner of Indian Affairs R. E. Trowbridge, "You are doubtless aware that after the lakes and the mountains, the deserts and the railroad subsidies are subtracted from these reserves, there remains hardly enough good grain or pastureland to give to each head of family desiring a ranch, ten acres" (Letters Received, Bureau of Indian Affairs, Nevada Superintendency).

5. Elizabeth P. Peabody to Hon. J. B. Long, January 21, 1885, Massachusetts

Historical Society.

6. Elizabeth P. Peabody to the Hon. John B. Long, January 21, 1885, Massachusetts Historical Society.

7. Peabody, *The Piutes: Second Report,* p. 18.

8. Ibid., p. 9.

9. Elizabeth P. Peabody to Hon. J. B. Long, January 21, 1885, Massachusetts Historical Society.

10. Ibid.

11. Ibid.

12. *Daily Silver State,* August 20, 1884.

13. Elizabeth P. Peabody to Hon. J. B. Long, January 21, 1885, Massachusetts Historical Society.

14. *Christian Register,* January 15, 1885, p. 38.

15. Elizabeth P. Peabody to Hon. J. B. Long, January 21, 1885, Massachusetts Historical Society.

16. Ibid.

17. Ibid.

18. Ibid.

19. Ibid.

20. Ibid.

21. Ibid.

22. *Silver State,* December 8, 1884.

23. *Territorial Enterprise,* December 12, 1884.

24. *Silver State,* July 14 and 21, 1884; *Territorial Enterprise,* December 12, 1884.

Chapter 21. **The Turning Point**

1. *Humboldt Register,* November 16, 1875.

2. *Silver State,* May 7, 1885.

3. *San Francisco Morning Call,* February 22, 1885, p. 1, col. 6.

4. Ibid., January 22, 1885.

5. Ibid.

6. Ibid.

7. *San Francisco Morning Call,* February 4, 1885, p. 3, col. 7.

8. *New York Times,* January 23, 1885, p. 2, col. 5.

9. *Daily Silver State,* February 9, 1885.

10. *San Francisco Morning Call,* February 4, 1885, p. 3, col. 7.

11. Ibid., February 22, 1885, p. 1, col. 6.

12. Ibid., February 11, 1885, p. 3, col. 8; Elizabeth P. Peabody, *The Piutes: Second Report,* pp. 11–12.

13. Elizabeth P. Peabody, *The Piutes: Second Report,* p. 3.

14. *Silver State,* March 12, 1885.

15. Elizabeth P. Peabody to Miss Eleanor Lewis, March 20, [1885], Olive Kettering Library, Antioch College, Yellow Springs, Ohio.

16. Mary Mann to Miss Eleanor Lewis, March 29, 1885, Olive Kettering Library, Antioch College.

17. Ibid.
18. D. Allen, Attorney at Law, to Elizabeth Peabody, May 5, 1885, Olive Kettering Library, Antioch College.
19. *Reese River Reveille,* September 17, 1884.
20. *Reese River Reveille,* November 20, 1884.
21. *Reese River Reveille,* January 6, 1886.
22. *Christian Register,* January 15, 1885, p. 38.
23. *Daily Silver State,* June 23, 1885; *Reno Evening Gazette,* June 26, 1885.
24. *San Francisco Call,* May 24, 1885.
25. *Daily Silver State,* June 23, 1885.
26. *Reno Evening Gazette,* June 26, 1884.

Chapter 22. **The Peabody Indian School**

1. Elizabeth P. Peabody, *The Piutes: Second Report,* p. 13.
2. Elizabeth P. Peabody to Commissioner of Indian Affairs, October 12, 1885, Special File no. 268, Bureau of Indian Affairs.
3. M. S. Bonnifield to Elizabeth P. Peabody, July 1, 1885, Special File no. 268, Bureau of Indian Affairs.
4. M. S. Bonnifield to Elizabeth P. Peabody, July 1, 1885, Special File no. 268, Bureau of Indian Affairs. Attorney Bonnifield wrote Elizabeth that Natchez had inherited a fine span of work horses from his brother Tom. Elizabeth knew better, as she and her friends had contributed the money for them. She wrote a note in the margin of the letter correcting the error.
5. Ibid.
6. Elizabeth P. Peabody to Commissioner of Indian Affairs, October 12, 1885, Special File no. 268, Bureau of Indian Affairs.
7. Peabody, *The Piutes: Second Report,* pp. 13–14.
8. Ibid.
9. *Daily Silver State,* July 14, 1885.
10. *Daily Silver State,* December 17, 1885.
11. Elizabeth P. Peabody to Commissioner of Indian Affairs, October 12, 1885, Special File no. 268, Bureau of Indian Affairs.
12. *Daily Silver State,* October 22, 1885.
13. Alice Chapin to Elizabeth P. Peabody, [July, 1885], and August 15, 1885, Olive Kettering Library, Antioch College.
14. Elizabeth Powell Bond to Elizabeth P. Peabody, December 9, 1885, Olive Kettering Library, Antioch College.
15. Elizabeth Powell Bond to Elizabeth P. Peabody, December 19, 1885, Olive Kettering Library, Antioch College.
16. Amelia B. James to Elizabeth P. Peabody, December 15, 1885, Olive Kettering Library, Antioch College.
17. Mary Y. Bean to Elizabeth P. Peabody, December 29, 1885, Olive Kettering Library, Antioch College.
18. Elizabeth P. Peabody, *Sarah Winnemucca's Practical Solution,* pp. 10–11.
19. Warren Delano to Elizabeth P. Peabody, March 24, 1886, Olive Kettering

Library, Antioch College.

20. Warren Delano to Sarah Winnemucca Hopkins, April 8, 1886, Olive Kettering Library, Antioch College (copy to Elizabeth P. Peabody).

21. Warren Delano to Elizabeth P. Peabody, April 9, 1886, Olive Kettering Library, Antioch College.

22. Peabody, *Sarah Winnemucca's Practical Solution,* p. 14.

23. Ibid., p. 12.

24. Mary Mann to Eleanor Lewis, May 23, 1886, Olive Kettering Library, Antioch College.

25. Warren Delano to Sarah Winnemucca Hopkins, May 6, 1886, Olive Kettering Library, Antioch College (copy to Elizabeth P. Peabody).

26. *Reese River Reveille,* June 9, 1886.

27. *Reese River Reveille,* July 10, 1886.

28. Warren Delano to Elizabeth P. Peabody, May 24, 1886, Olive Kettering Library, Antioch College.

29. Peabody, *Sarah Winnemucca's Practical Solution,* p. 22.

30. Sarah Winnemucca to *Silver State,* July 9, 1886.

31. Peabody, *Sarah Winnemucca's Practical Solution,* p. 22.

32. Ibid., p. 17.

33. Ibid.

34. Ibid., p. 18.

35. Peabody, *The Piutes: Second Report,* p. 15.

36. Peabody, *Sarah Winnemucca's Practical Solution,* p. 21.

37. *Reese River Reveille,* August 2, 1886.

38. Peabody, *Sarah Winnemucca's Practical Solution,* p. 21.

39. Ibid., p. 33.

40. Ibid.

41. Warren Delano to Elizabeth P. Peabody, September 27, 1886, Olive Kettering Library, Antioch College.

Chapter 23. **Hopkins Again**

1. *Reese River Reveille,* September 24, 1886.

2. Ibid.

3. Peabody, *Sarah Winnemucca's Practical Solution,* p. 34.

4. Ibid.

5. Ibid.

6. Ibid.; *Reese River Reveille,* November 15, 1886, p. 1, col. 3.

7. Peabody, *Sarah Winnemucca's Practical Solution,* p. 35.

8. Ibid.

9. *Reese River Reveille,* November 15, 1886.

10. Elizabeth P. Peabody to Miss Eleanor Lewis, January 18, 1887, Olive Kettering Library, Antioch College.

11. Mary Mann to Miss Eleanor Lewis, January 26, 1887, Olive Kettering Library, Antioch College.

12. Elizabeth P. Peabody, *The Piutes: Second Report,* p. 16.

13. *Silver State,* December 1, 1886.

14. Mary Mann to Miss Eleanor Lewis, January 26, 1887, Olive Kettering Library, Antioch College.

15. Mary Mann to Eleanor Lewis, November, 1886, Olive Kettering Library, Antioch College.

16. Ibid.

17. Elizabeth P. Peabody to Miss Eleanor Lewis, March 27, [1887], Olive Kettering Library, Antioch College.

18. Ibid.

19. Peabody, *Sarah Winnemucca's Practical Solution,* p. 8.

20. *Daily Silver State,* April 25 and 27, 1887; Peabody, *The Piutes: Second Report,* p. 16. On the copy of her pamphlet now owned by Yale University Library, New Haven, Connecticut, Miss Peabody wrote on page 18: "Which their parents are pressing on her to take, having been frightened because the despotic agent of Pyramid Lake Reservation has forced 10 or 12 children to go against shrieking protests of their mothers to a Colorado Industrial School to learn of teachers who do not know Indian languages which disheartened and demoralized the children besides breaking the parent's hearts."

21. *Silver State,* June 3, 1887.

22. Ibid.

23. *Christian Union,* October 6, 1887. The "Special Supplement on American Indians" in that issue is a sampling of the leading ideas and institutions of the period dealing with the subject.

24. Sylvia H. Delano to Miss Elizabeth P. Peabody, June 21, 1884, Olive Kettering Library, Antioch College.

25. Ibid.

26. Sylvia H. Delano to Miss Elizabeth P. Peabody, January 29, 1885, Olive Kettering Library, Antioch College.

27. Warren Delano to Miss Elizabeth P. Peabody, October 12, 1887, Olive Kettering Library, Antioch College.

28. Ibid.

29. *Daily Silver State,* September 21, 1887.

30. Letter to the Editor of the *Daily Silver State,* September 23, 1887.

31. Ibid.

32. Warren Delano to Elizabeth P. Peabody, October 12, 1887, Olive Kettering Library, Antioch College.

33. Ibid.

34. *Silver State,* October 20, 1887, p. 3, cols. 1 and 3.

35. Elizabeth P. Peabody to Miss Eleanor C. Lewis, March 27, 1887, Olive Kettering Library, Antioch College.

Chapter 24. **Henry's Lake**

1. Peabody, *The Piutes: Second Report,* p. 15.

2. Ibid., p. 16.

3. Ibid., p. 15.

4. Ibid., p. 18.

5. Elizabeth P. Peabody, *The Paiutes: The Second Report of the Model School of Sarah Winnemucca* (Cambridge: John Wilcox and Son, 1887), 18 pages.

6. Elizabeth P. Peabody to Senator John B. Long, December 4, 1887, Massachusetts Historical Society.

7. Peabody, *The Piutes: Second Report,* p. 18.

8. Ibid.

9. *Elko* (Nev.) *Daily Independent,* March 26, 1888.

10. Ibid.

11. Robert L. Straker's Horace Mann bibliography, Olive Kettering Library, Antioch College.

12. *Carson Morning Appeal* (Carson City, Nev.), February 29, 1888, p. 3, col. 2.

13. *Elko Independent,* September 30, 1889, p. 3, col. 1.

14. *Elko Independent,* November 8, 1889.

15. Conversations with Samuel Eagle of El Cerrito, California, historian of the West Yellowstone area, on July 30, 1976, and February 10 and 28 and March 13 and 19, 1977.

16. Interview and correspondence with Mrs. R. W. Talbot of Henry's Lake, Idaho, daughter of Joseph and Mary Ann Garner Sherwood; letters from Mrs. Talbot to author, dated September 10 and December 17, 1974, and June 6, 1976, in the author's possession.

17. Interview and correspondence with Mrs. R. W. Talbot, Henry's Lake.

18. Conversations with Samuel Eagle, El Cerrito, California.

19. Interview and correspondence with Mrs. R. W. Talbot, Henry's Lake.

20. Interview and correspondence with Mrs. R. W. Talbot, Henry's Lake.

21. Conversations with Samuel Eagle, El Cerrito, California.

22. Conversations with Samuel Eagle, El Cerrito, California; *Bozeman* (Mont.) *Chronicle,* October 28, 1891, p. 1.

23. Correspondence with Mrs. R. W. Talbot, Henry's Lake, Idaho.

24. Letters to the author from Ruth Tipton, clerk for Gladys Aul, recorder and auditor of Humboldt County (Book 30, Deeds, p. 254), April 28, 1976, and November 28, 1978, in the author's possession.

25. Gilbert Natchez, a son of Natchez born about 1880, came to the University of California at Berkeley in 1914 to assist in editing Dr. W. L. Marsden's Northern Paiute texts (see Bibliography under T. T. Waterman and W. L. Marsden) and left a Paiute vocabulary. He was a landscape painter of some note.

26. Allen C. Bragg, *Humboldt County 1905,* pp. 93–94.

27. Interview and correspondence with Mrs. R. W. Talbot, Henry's Lake, Idaho.

28. *New York Times,* October 27, 1891, p. 1, col. 4.

29. Frank J. Parker, editor of the *Walla Walla Statesman,* quotes in *Reno Weekly Gazette and Stockman,* November 26, 1891.

30. Oliver Otis Howard, *Famous Indian Chiefs I Have Known,* p. 237.

31. Hopkins, *Life Among the Piutes,* pp. 258–59.

Bibliography

BOOKS AND ARTICLES

Angel, Myron T., ed. *History of Nevada.* Oakland, Calif.: Thompson and West, 1881.

Aram, Joseph. "The Reminiscences of Captain Aram," in Col. James Thompkins Watson, "Across the Continent in a Caravan." *Journal of American History* 1 (1907):627–29.

Bidwell, John. *A Journey to California, 1841: First Emigrant Party to California.* Berkeley: Friends of the Bancroft Library, 1964.

Bragg, Allen C. *Humboldt County 1905.* Winnemucca, Nev.: North Central Nevada Historical Society, 1976.

Brimlow, George F. *The Bannock Indian War of 1878.* Caldwell, Idaho: Caxton Printers, 1938.

———. *Harney County, Oregon, and Its Range Land.* Portland, Ore.: Binfords and Mort, 1951.

———. "The Life of Sarah Winnemucca: The Formative Years." *Oregon Historical Society Quarterly,* June, 1952.

Council Fire 6 (May, 1883):69.

Council Fire 6 (September, 1883):134.

Dana, Julian. *The Sacramento, River of Gold.* New York: Farrar and Rinehart, 1939.

Dangberg, Grace. "Wovoka." *Nevada Historical Society Quarterly* 11, no. 2 (Summer, 1968).

Downs, James F. *The Two Worlds of the Washo: An Indian Tribe of California and Nevada.* New York: Holt, Rinehart and Winston, 1966.

Egan, Ferol. *Sand in a Whirlwind: The Paiute Indian War of 1860.* Garden

City: Doubleday and Company, 1972.
Forbes, Jack D. *Native Americans of California and Nevada, A Handbook.* Healdsburg, Calif.: Naturegraph Publishers, 1969.
Fowler, Don D., and Catherine S. Fowler, eds. *Anthropology of the Numa: John Wesley Powell's Manuscripts of the Numic Peoples of Western North America, 1868–1880.* Washington, D.C.: Smithsonian Institution Press, 1971.
Harnar, Nellie Shaw. *Indians of Coo-yu-ee Pah (Pyramid Lake).* Sparks, Nev.: Dave's Printing and Publishing, 1974.
Heizer, Robert F. *Notes on Some Paviotso Personalities.* Anthropological Papers, no. 2. Carson City: Nevada State Museum, 1960.
——— and Thomas R. Hester, eds. *Notes on Northern Paiute Ethnography: Kroeber and Marsden Records.* Berkeley: University of California, Department of Anthropology, Archaeological Research Facility, 1972.
Hermann, Ruth. *The Paiutes of Pyramid Lake: A Narrative Concerning a Western Nevada Indian Tribe.* San Jose: Harlan-Young, 1972.
Hodge, Frederick Webb, ed. *Handbook of American Indians North of Mexico.* 2 vols. Bureau of American Ethnology Bulletin no. 30. Washington, D.C.: Government Printing Office, 1912.
Hopkins, Sarah Winnemucca. *Life Among the Piutes: Their Wrongs and Claims.* Edited by Mrs. Horace Mann. Boston and New York: privately printed, 1883. Reprint. Bishop, Calif.: Chalfant Press, 1969.
Howard, Oliver Otis. *Famous Indian Chiefs I Have Known.* New York: Century Company, 1908.
———. *My Life and Personal Experiences Among Our Hostile Indians.* Hartford, Conn.: A. D. Worthington Co., 1907.
———. "Toc-me-to-ne, American Indian Princess." Part 2. *St. Nicholas Magazine* 25 (May–Oct. 1908).
Intertribal Council of Nevada. *Life Stories of Our Native People, Shoshone, Paiute, Washo.* 1974.
———. *Personal Reflections of Shoshone, Paiute, Washo.* 1974.
Jackson, Helen Hunt. *A Century of Dishonor.* New York: Harper, 1881.
James, Edward J. and Janet W. James, eds. *Notable American Women, 1607–1950: A Biographical Dictionary.* 3 vols. Cambridge, Mass.: Harvard University Press, 1971.
Johnson, Edward C. *Walker River Paiutes: A Tribal History.* Salt Lake City: University of Utah Printing Service, 1975.
Kelly, Isabel T. "Ethnography of the Surprise Valley Paiute." *American Archaeology and Ethnology.* Berkeley: University of California, 1932.
Liebling, A. J. "The Lake of the Cui-ui-Eaters," in "The Reporter at Large." *New Yorker.* Parts 1–4. January 1, 8, 15, and 22, 1955.
Lowie, Robert H. "Shoshonean Ethnography." *American Museum of Natural History Anthropological Papers* 20, Part 3 (1924).

Madsen, Brigham D. *The Bannock of Idaho*. Caldwell, Idaho: Caxton Press, 1958.
Martin, V. Covert. *Stockton Album Through the Years*. Stockton, Calif., 1959.
Miller, William C., ed. "The Pyramid Lake Indian War of 1860." *Nevada Historical Society Quarterly* 1, nos. 1-2 (1957).
Mooney, James. *The Ghost Dance Religion and the Sioux Outbreak of 1890*. Chicago: University of Chicago Press, 1965.
Murray, Keith A. *The Modocs and Their War*. Norman: University of Oklahoma Press, 1959.
Natches, Gilbert. "Northern Paiute Verbs." *American Archaeology and Ethnology* 20 (December 1, 1923).
Park, Willard Z. "Paviotso Shamanism." *American Anthropologist* 36 (January-March, 1934).
Peabody, Elizabeth P. *The Piutes: Second Report of the Model School of Sarah Winnemucca*. Cambridge, Mass.: John Wilcox and Son, 1887.
———. *Sarah Winnemucca's Practical Solution of the Indian Problem*. Cambridge, Mass.: John Wilcox and Son, 1886.
Scott, Lalla. *Karnee: A Paiute Narrative*. Reno: University of Nevada Press, 1966.
Simpson, James H. *Report of Explorations Across the Great Basin of the Territory of Utah for a Direct Wagon Route from Camp Floyd to Genoa in Carson Valley in 1859*. Washington, D.C.: Government Printing Office, 1876.
Steward, Julian H. "Ethnography of Owens Valley Paiute." *Publications in American Archaeology and Ethnology* 33 (September 6, 1933).
———. "Myths of the Owens Valley Paiute." *American Archaeology and Ethnology* 34 (1937).
——— and Erminie Wheeler-Voegelin. *Paiute Indians*. New York: Garland Publishing, 1974. Vol. 3, *The Northern Paiute Indians*.
Stewart, Omer C. "The Northern Paiute Bands." *Anthropological Records* 2, no. 3. Berkeley: University of California, 1939.
Stewart, Patricia. "Sarah Winnemucca." *Nevada Historical Society Quarterly* 14, no. 4 (Winter, 1971).
Tharp, Louise Hall. *The Peabody Sisters of Salem*. Boston: Little, Brown and Co., 1950.
Tibbles, Thomas. *The Hidden Power*. New York: Carleton and Company, 1881.
Turner, Katherine C. *Red Men Calling on the Great White Father*. Norman: University of Oklahoma Press, 1951.
Underhill, Ruth. "The Northern Paiute Indians of California and Nevada." *United States Department of the Interior Bulletin*, 1941.
United States Department of the Interior, Bureau of Indian Affairs.

Bureau of Indian Affairs Planning Support Group. *The Burns-Paiute Colony: Its History, Population and Economy.* Report No. 227. Billings, Mont.: October, 1974.

———. *Fourth Annual Report of the Board of Indian Commissioners.* Washington, D.C.: Government Printing Office, 1872.

———. *Annual Report of the Commissioner of Indian Affairs to the Secretary of the Interior.* 1867–1893. Washington, D.C.: Government Printing Office.

———. *Report of the Joint Special Committee: Condition of the Indian Tribes.* Washington, D.C.: Government Printing Office.

Waterman, T. T., and W. L. Marsden. "Phonetic Elements of Northern Paiute Language." *American Archaeology and Ethnology* 10 (November 15, 1911).

Watson, Margaret G. *Silver Theatre.* Glendale, Calif.: Arthur Clarke Co., 1964.

Wheat, Margaret M. *Survival Arts of the Primitive Paiutes.* Reno: University of Nevada Press, 1967.

Wheeler, Sessions S. *The Desert Lake: The Story of Nevada's Pyramid Lake.* Caldwell, Idaho: Caxton Printers, 1967.

———. *The Nevada Desert.* Caldwell, Idaho: Caxton Printers, 1971.

Whiting, Beatrice Blyth. *Paiute Sorcery.* Viking Fund Publications in Anthropology, no. 15. New York: 1950.

Wright, William [Dan De Quille]. *The Big Bonanza.* New York: Alfred A. Knopf, 1947.

———. *Washoe Rambles.* Los Angeles: Westernlore Press, 1963.

PERIODICALS

Alta California (San Francisco)

Baltimore Sun

Bancroft Scraps, vol. 93, "Nevada Indians," Bancroft Library, University of California, Berkeley

Boston Evening Transcript

Carson Daily Appeal (Carson City, Nev.)

Daily Alta California (San Francisco)

Daily Bulletin (Portland, Ore.)

Daily Silver State (Winnemucca, Nev.)

Elko (Nev.) *Independent*

Gold Hill (Nev.) *News*

Humboldt Register (Winnemucca, Nev.)

Nevada State Journal (Reno)

New York Times

Notre Dame Quarterly (College of Notre Dame de Namur, San Jose,

Calif.), 1913 and 1914
Reese River Reveille (Austin, Nev.)
Reno Evening Gazette
Reno Weekly Gazette and Stockman
Sacramento (Calif.) *Daily Union*
Sacramento (Calif.) *Record Union*
Sacramento (Calif.) *Union*
San Francisco Bulletin
San Francisco Call
San Francisco Chronicle
San Francisco Morning Call
San Francisco Post
Sierra Democrat (Sacramento, Calif.)
Silver State (Winnemucca, Nev.)
Territorial Enterprise (Virginia City, Nev.)
Virginia Chronicle (Virginia City, Nev.)

MANUSCRIPT MATERIALS

Mann, Mary. Personal correspondence. Olive Kettering Library, Antioch College, Yellow Springs, Ohio.

Peabody, Elizabeth Palmer. Personal correspondence. Olive Kettering Library, Antioch College, Yellow Springs, Ohio; and Massachusetts Historical Society, Boston, Massachusetts.

Rinehart, W. V. Unpublished manuscript and correspondence. Bancroft Library, University of California, Berkeley.

United States Office of Indian Affairs. "The Case of Sarah Winnemucca." Special File no. 268. M 574. National Archives.

———. Nevada Superintendency. Letters Received, 1861–80. Record Group 75, M 234. Microfilm rolls 538–45. National Archives.

———. Oregon Superintendency. Letters Received, 1874–78. Record Group 75, M 234. Microfilm rolls 619–26. National Archives.

———. Utah Superintendency. Letters Received, 1859–80. Record Group 75, M 234. Microfilm rolls 899–906. National Archives.

United States War Department. Official Correspondence, Modoc Indian War. Bancroft Library, University of California, Berkeley.

Whitney, Wm. T. Unpublished manuscript. California Historical Society, San Francisco.

Index